SUPERWEAPON

LIFE WASN'T MEANT TO BE EASY:
A POLITICAL PROFILE OF MALCOLM FRASER

SUPERWEAPON
The Making of MX

BY JOHN EDWARDS

W·W· NORTON & COMPANY · NEW YORK · LONDON

The text of this book is composed in 10/12 Century Schoolbook, with
display type set in Egizio Medium Condensed.
Manufacturing by The Haddon Craftsmen, Inc.
Book design by Nancy Dale Muldoon

FIRST EDITION

Library of Congress Cataloging in Publication Data
Edwards, John, 1947–
Superweapon, the making of MX.
Includes index.
1. MX (Weapons system)   I. Title.
UG1312.I2E38   358'.174'0973   82–6376
                                          AACR2
ISBN 0-393-01523-8

W. W. Norton & Company, Inc., 500 Fifth Avenue, New York, N. Y.
10110
W. W. Norton & Company, Ltd., 37 GreatRussell Street, London WC1B
3NU
1 2 3 4 5 6 7 8 9 0

For PAMELA; and for ANDY and MONICA,
who welcomed us.

Facts do in the end prevail, whatever doctrine may assert.
—*Harold Brown*

Contents

Preface

WITHIN a few years the first of a planned minimum of two-hundred-and-twenty-six new intercontinental ballistic missiles will begin coming off the assembly lines at the Martin Marietta Aerospace Corporation's plant at Denver, Colorado. Each missile will be fitted with ten nuclear warheads, all independently targetable, and each warhead will be three times as accurate as the most accurate of existing land missiles. The three-hundred-and-fifty-kiloton hydrogen bomb, designated W78, nestling in each warhead, will be more than seventeen times as powerful as the bomb that decimated Hiroshima in 1945. Already the Department of Defense has let contracts for a still more powerful warhead. This missile, still denoted by the acronym MX for "missile experimental" that had been given it in 1973, will be the first missile deployed by the United States for the declared purpose of threatening missiles still in their concrete silos in the Soviet Union. Equivalent in size to the "light" Soviet SS19 missile, the MX will be militarily superior to the "heavy" Soviet SS18 missile. It will be the most lethal weapon ever developed.

11

Three successive presidents of the United States—Gerald Ford, Jimmy Carter, and Ronald Reagan—committed their administrations to the production and deployment of this new weapon, yet there is no agreement on where it should be deployed, or how it should be deployed. In more than a decade of controversy, the United States Air Force and hundreds of civilian defense analysts have devised, tested, and rejected more than thirty different ideas for the basing of the missiles, ranging from balloons, boats, and barges to deep silos, trucks, and tunnels. In December 1976 President Ford decided that the missile should be based in long underground tunnels, a proposal that was rejected by his successor, Jimmy Carter. In September 1979 President Carter decided that it should be based in two hundred roadways built in the valleys of Utah and Nevada. That idea was rejected by his successor, Ronald Reagan, in September 1981. President Reagan, in turn, decided to base the missile in rebuilt missile silos in Arkansas, an idea that was rejected by an overwhelming majority of the U.S. Senate.

Today, forty-five major contractors and hundreds of minor contractors are working on the MX program. More than twelve thousand people are employed by it. To October 1982 the program had cost the taxpayer $7 billion. By the end of 1984 it will have cost at least $17 billion. While the controversy over basing the missile has continued, the missile itself has moved through all the stages from initial examination to development, advanced development, and finally full-scale development, meeting and often beating the schedules set up by the air force's Ballistic Missile Office at the Norton Air Force Base, California. The forthcoming production of the missile, which because of its stupendous power is a lucrative target in itself for Soviet war planners, poses afresh the so far insoluble problem of finding a place to put it.

At the heart of the controversy over MX is the fact that the enormous expansion in the numbers and quality of nuclear weapons in both the Soviet Union and the United States has at last succeeded in achieving what arms controllers have warned against since the mid-fifties. The Soviet Union and the United States have succeeded in making each other's land missiles vulnerable to attack. By 1985, according to both Jimmy Carter's secretary of defense, Harold Brown, and his successor, Caspar Weinberger, the Soviet Union will be able to destroy nine-tenths of American land missiles in their silos in a surprise attack. The United States already has a formidable capacity to destroy Soviet missiles in their silos, an ability that will be greatly enhanced by the deployment of MX. Nuclear strategists have recognized since the mid-fifties that the vulnerability of a major share of either side's nuclear deterrent poses an equal threat to both sides. The vulnerable side has an incentive to strike first, and knowing that, the side posing the threat has an incentive to strike preemptively. Both sides are equally threatened by the vulnerability of one side.

For this reason, the problem of finding a place for the MX is not just a technical difficulty for the United States, but an expression of the central difficulty of a new and vastly more threatening twist in the nuclear arms race which has over-shadowed the world since 1945. The premise of the invulnerable deterrent, upon which the absence of nuclear war for the last four decades has rested, has been undermined by the development of new and more accurate weapons on both sides, and by the accompanying rise of strategies, targeting plans, and doctrines that justify and implement the new weapons. After four decades of relative stability, both the Soviet Union and the United States are entering a new era of nuclear peril, where each side possesses hundreds of thousands of times the destructive power they had in the chilliest days of the cold war, where each side threatens the other's deterrent, and where there are increasing incentives to strike first in a crisis.

Almost all the major nuclear weapons systems before MX have been stories of successes, of ideas devised in laboratories, sold to Congress and the executive, developed with a minimum of controversy by air force and navy engineers, and fielded to the satisfaction of American public opinion. The Polaris/Poseidon submarine-launched missiles, the brilliantly executed Minuteman land missile programs, the development of multiple independently targetable warheads— they were all stories of orderly engineering achievement. The story of MX is the story of a costly failure, of the production of a weapon that requires for its deployment great changes in the way Americans think about nuclear weapons on their soil, in arms control agreements with the Soviet Union, in the theories of deterrence that underlie nuclear war planning. It is the story of decisions earnestly made and unmade, of the failure of three successive presidents and four successive secretaries of defense to cut the tangles in the project, of the unavailing efforts of hundreds of civilian and uniformed defense specialists to find a way out of the insuperable dilemmas of the arms race.

Introduction

ON Monday, 4 June 1979, two weeks before he was to fly to Vienna and sign the second strategic nuclear weapons agreement with the Soviet Union, Jimmy Carter convened the National Security Council in the Cabinet Room of the White House. The Council was to choose America's nuclear arsenal for the next several decades. The decision had been long in the making, disputed at every level of its percolation upward from the weapons laboratories to the Cabinet Room. It was a problem over which Robert McNamara had fought with the Joint Chiefs of Staff, Henry Kissinger with James Schlesinger, Harold Brown with Jimmy Carter. It had been argued between the air force and the navy, the Joint Chiefs of Staff and the secretary of defense, the president and his cabinet, and between liberal and conservative senators and congressmen for more than a decade. It was a problem of choosing a new generation of nuclear weapons, and it had arisen almost as soon as the first generation of weapons—the "triad" of B52 bombers carrying thermonuclear bombs, nuclear missile-carrying submarines, and nuclear armed missiles in silos—had been decided upon by Dwight Eisenhower.

For twenty years what Eisenhower and his successor, John Kennedy, had decided remained the basis for America's nuclear defense. But if the forces remained the same as they had in the sixties, the arguments over whether they were sufficient and what must replace them had never ceased. There were arguments over strategy and arguments over weapons. Most people imagined a nuclear war as a sudden and massive exchange of bombs and missiles that would obliterate both their country and their enemy's. To the war gamers of the Joint Strategic Target Planning staff at Omaha, the calculation was more complicated. Just how many people could be killed, and how many ought to be killed? How great a proportion of dams and bridges and factories and ports—the means of economic recovery—ought to be destroyed, and to what degree? Should the United States first destroy only military targets, or should it attack military and civilian targets simultaneously? How many "hard" targets, like concrete missile silos should be attacked, and how many "soft" targets, like armies or cities or submarine bases? What weapons were needed to destroy this variety of targets? Some weapons were quick and accurate, like the silo-based missile. Some were less accurate but more abundant, like the submarine missile. How should they be targeted?

Carter was trained in nuclear engineering, the first president of the eight who had made decisions about nuclear weapons who actually knew a little about their technology. He was not, as he sometimes claimed, a nuclear physicist, but he had commanded one of the first nuclear-powered submarines of Admiral Rickover's fleet, and he had worked with nuclear reactors. If Carter had once been familiar with nuclear technology, he was more familiar now with the meaning of nuclear weapons. A military assistant remained close to the president, carrying the communications box, the "football," that would put him in touch, through a military command post, with 1,054 missiles in silos, one hundred B52 bombers on runways, and twenty patrolling submarines armed with nuclear missiles. He knew that as he took his chair between his defense secretary, Harold Brown, and his secretary of state, Cyrus Vance, in the Cabinet Room, a general of the Strategic Air Command was aloft in the "looking glass" airborne command post, that there had been a Strategic Air Command general aloft continuously for the last seventeen years—one general in one plane taking off as the other landed—waiting to execute the fire order if the president gave the command. Carter knew that he had all these forces at his command at that instant, and that, given a few hours warning—enough time to move to what the Pentagon briefers called advanced generation—he would have two and three times those forces, a total of ninety-two hundred nuclear warheads at sea, in the air, poised in concrete tubes, the smallest warhead four times more powerful than the bomb that was dropped on Hiroshima, and the biggest seven-hundred times more powerful. The president also knew that if an exchange of weapons should ever take place between his country and the Soviet Union, the computer war simulations predicted there would be from twenty-five million to one hundred million people killed in each country from the short-term effects of blast, radiation, and fire alone; that 70 percent of the industry of each country would be destroyed; and that 80 percent of all cities with twenty-five thousand or more people would be attacked by at least one nuclear weapon. No leader in human history had had such terrible power within reach of his extended arm, and no decision Jimmy Carter could make in his presidency was as awesome as the one he had to make that day.

Jimmy Carter, in the third year of his term, was beginning to understand just how fragile the balance of terror on which peace depended really was, and how difficult it was to restrain that "mad momentum" in the arms race that former defense secretary, Robert McNamara, had once spoken of. He had also become aware of how difficult it was to refute the logic of the "military-industrial complex" against which Dwight Eisenhower had warned.

At the beginning of the nuclear age, the United States had only a few hundred atomic weapons. Now it had more than nine-thousand, and more than eight-thousand smaller tactical nuclear warheads in Europe and aboard ships. The Soviet Union had more than six-thousand strategic nuclear warheads, and it was expected soon to have many more. What had happened? Neither side was more secure as a result of this immense increase in the power to destroy each other, yet there seemed no way in which the increase could be stopped. Even if the SALT agreement, which Carter was about to sign, was approved by the Senate, it would not prevent another vast increase in the number of weapons on either side; indeed, some people said that SALT was one reason the increase had occurred. Carter had pointed out that one single submarine at sea armed with nuclear missiles, one single submarine which could destroy one hundred sixty Soviet cities, would deter the Soviet Union from initiating a nuclear war. Yet Jimmy Carter now found himself presiding over a meeting at which he was to decide not on reductions to that huge arsenal of weapons, but on new ways in which America could add to it. He was being advised by those who had studied the question that America had too few nuclear weapons, not too many, and that the ones it had were not of the right type. He was being told that America needed a new, bigger, and more lethal land missile, called MX.

The president had ended his navy career as the nuclear age was beginning. The atom bomb had transformed the nature of war and the relationships between nations. It was the greatest single fact of his time, and the decision he had to make that day was quite as momentous as the decision Roosevelt made to begin work on an atom bomb, the decision Truman had made to use it, and the decision Eisenhower made in 1957 to give national priority to the building of a land-based missile that could reach the Soviet Union.

The land-based intercontinental ballistic missile (ICBM) had become the most vital weapon possessed by the superpowers. General Richard Ellis of the Strategic Air Command once said that "no single system has had a greater effect on the world balance of power over the last fifteen years than the ICBM." It was a weapon of wonderful characteristics. It was quick, easy to control, and always ready. But the ICBM had been shown to have one very serious weakness: it could be attacked by the enemy's ICBMs. As accuracies improved, as both the Soviet Union and the United States acquired more and bigger warheads, the ICBMs on both sides were becoming more vulnerable to a strike from the other. The implications of this fact were the cause of today's meeting. Should the U.S. increase its ability to strike at Soviet missiles? What should it do about the vulnerability of its own missiles? The air force said the answer was MX, deployed in thousands of shelters in Utah and Nevada.

Carter had not come to office expecting it to be quite like it had turned out to be, or that he would find himself, thirty months after he had walked down a wintry Pennsylvania Avenue after his inauguration, making the kind of decisions he was going to have to make that day. He had come to office a liberal on foreign policy, opposed to American intervention abroad, and deeply suspicious of the Pentagon's unending demands for new weapons. He had come to office promising to cut $5 to $7 billion off the defense budget.

He had found that in practice he couldn't cut defense spending, and he was less and less willing or capable of doing so the longer he remained in office. By the beginning of June 1979, candidate Carter was unrecognizable in the president with his National Security Council. He looked different— older and grayer and strained. His ideas had changed. It had not proved sensible to do battle with the Pentagon. He no longer had plenty of time to build up his popularity for the presidential primaries the following year. He was about to sign a SALT treaty that had only an even chance of winning a two-thirds majority in the Senate, and he needed the support of the Joint Chiefs of Staff and hawkish Democrats to get that even chance. He was unpopular in the electorate; rivals were watching. He needed all the allies he could get.

He also thought differently about the arms race. It was not controllable. McNamara had been right. Neither side would unilaterally abandon a technology or a weapons system. Each side was far enough ahead in some systems not to want to give the other time to catch up while it stood still, and far enough behind in other weapons to insist on catching up before the race stopped. The Soviet Union had caught up in some things, surpassed the United States in some things, remained well behind in others. The annual National Intelligence Estimate predicted that, within five years, the Soviet Union would be able to destroy nine-tenths of American land missiles with a first strike. Did this matter and, if it did, what should be done about it? Carter had begun his administration determined to get a grip on this whole puzzling question, but he had found himself the victim of changing technology, of decisions made long ago, of old hostilities with the Soviet Union, and of his own inability to understand the forces at work. Seven months before, he was reported to have told his staff that the MX proposition to be debated at the National Security Council was "the craziest idea I've ever heard." Today it looked not only rational and reasonable, but inevitable.

Inevitable, but stupendous. It was stupendous first in the size and cost of the program. Air Force General Guy Hecker called MX "man's largest project." On revised figures, it would cost $33.3 billion over ten years, it would require the construction of a minimum of forty-six hundred hardened concrete shelters (five times the number constructed for the existing land missile force), and thousands of miles of road between the shelters. At least ten-thousand square miles of public land would be occupied by the system. More than twenty-four thousand workers would be building the shelters over five years, with the number of workers peaking at one-hundred thousand toward the end of the project. It would be the biggest construction project in the history of the United States—bigger than the Panama Canal and three times as costly as the Alaskan pipeline. The magnitude of the project was awesome, so much so that more than one participant at the meeting privately doubted it would ever be built.

The MX was awesome, too, in the power and characteristics of the weapon. It would be three times as accurate as the most accurate of existing land-based missiles. It could carry at least ten warheads, each independently targetable, compared to three on the Minuteman III; and, to bear this added load, it would be nearly three times as heavy, one-third again in diameter, and one-fifth longer than Minuteman. Each of the ten warheads would carry three hundred and fifty kilotons of explosive power or about seventeen times the Hiroshima explosion. The MX was an engineering marvel, and, even in the dry testimony of air force officers before the Senate Armed Services Committee, their enthusiasm for its brilliance shone out. It would have a tiny ten-inch diameter advanced inertial reference sphere to guide it within three-hundred feet of its target after a journey of thousands of miles. Its internal computer would use chip technology, so that although its volume was only one cubic foot, it would operate at forty times the speed of the Minuteman III computer, with one-sixth of the parts and five times the resistance to nuclear shock. Its "physics package," the thermonuclear warhead, was a weapon designated W78—a very high yield, compact device.

The MX would be the first prompt-reaction hard target weapon the United States had ever developed and deployed. There was never any ambiguity, never any attempt to conceal the obvious: the two thousand warheads would be targeted at Soviet ground-based missiles. As air force general Lew Allen would tell the Senate in 1979, "It is a fact that the

MX program will have some first strike capability."

MX would be built and deployed as a silo buster, and this implied three things of significance to the future of the arms race. The first of these implications was that MX had to be invulnerable to Soviet attack. Otherwise there would be great advantage to the Soviet Union in striking MX first and saving its own missiles from attack by MX. This conflicted with another equally important implication of MX, which was that its numbers had to be verified by the Soviet Union. If the Soviet Union could not confidently count the number the U.S. deployed, it would not agree to keeping the numerical limits on missiles it had accepted in SALT II, and the United States could no longer be confident that the destruction of MX was too big a job for the Soviet missile forces.

Verifiability conflicted with concealment. This was compounded by a third implication: if America possessed missiles so accurate and numerous they could destroy the entire Soviet force in their silos, then the Soviet Union could no longer rely on the invulnerability of its nuclear deterrent. How would the Soviet Union protect its forces? For the United States the very worst possibility was the most likely —that the Soviet Union would not try to protect its forces. That was the most threatening response of all.

The decision contained elements of catastrophe, bringing back in a new and more intense form that pessimism about the future of humanity that had followed the Soviet hydrogen bomb test of 1952. Yet the decision would not be made by unreasonable men, or too rashly, or with too little information. There did not seem to be any alternative. It was lunacy to leave land missiles in concrete shelters; it was lunacy to move them. The former Pentagon director of defense research and engineering, John Foster, had described the vulnerability of land missiles as the most difficult problem he had to deal with. His predecessor, Herbert York, had written that there seemed to be no solution, or at least not on land. Both Robert McNamara and Werner von Braun had studied the problem, and neither could find a solution. As Senator McIntyre of the Senate Armed Services Committee remarked in 1977: "The dilemmas of ICBM survivability are devilish. Most proposed solutions to this problem have at their center seeds of new dilemmas." It was a very clear example of McNamara's "mad momentum," a momentum that McNamara and Harold Brown and Cyrus Vance had themselves increased when they decided to put multiple independently targetable warheads (MIRVs) on U.S. land missiles in the sixties. Ironically, one of the arguments for MIRVing U.S. missiles was that the Soviet Union might MIRV first and therefore have the ability to threaten U.S. land missiles. This had some wild logic, except that the Soviet Union did not actually test or deploy MIRVs until well after the American program had begun. The Soviet MIRV, in turn, was the justification for MX.

The decision to produce MX was not Jimmy Carter's fault, nor Harold Brown's fault, nor America's fault, nor the fault of the Soviet Union. Its roots lay in changing technology, in innovations adopted for other purposes which had as their inescapable consequences the need for yet more changes to keep the balance between the superpowers. The decision to put more than one independently targetable warhead on each missile had been one of these changes; the increasing accuracy of missiles was another. Yet it was not only those technical changes that brought Carter and his administration to their decision at the 5 June meeting. Another compelling reason was the strategy developed for fighting nuclear wars. The MX decision was as much a product of the way politicians thought about nuclear war as it was of technical developments. So long as leaders in the Soviet Union and the United States relied on their ability to destroy the other side's population to deter a nuclear war, the vulnerability of one part of the nuclear arsenal would not imperil deterrence. But this balance of terror was threatened as soon as the superpowers developed the means to target one another's weapons with greater sophistication and accuracy. From McNamara's war blueprint of June 1962 to James Schlesinger's nuclear weapons employment policy of 1974 and Harold Brown's "countervailing strategy," the United States had adopted a nuclear targeting policy that emphasized attacks on military targets. Because of their accuracy, speed, and control, land-based missiles were absolutely essential to that policy, and it was increasingly apparent that only a mobile land missile would be survivable in the eighties. The roots of the MX decision lay in two decades of technical changes, marching in lockstep with political changes, and the result was that, while most people assumed the nuclear balance was becoming more stable, it was actually becoming more unstable and dangerous with each passing year.

SUPERWEAPON

1

City Busters and Silo Busters

SENATOR JOHN GLENN: I get lost in what is credible or not credible. This whole thing is so incredible when you consider wiping out whole nations, it is difficult to establish credibility.

DEFENSE SECRETARY HAROLD BROWN: That is why we sound a little crazy when we talk about it.

ON the afternoon of 20 June, 1974, three months before his resignation as president of the United States, and five years before Jimmy Carter's meeting to decide on MX, Richard Nixon convened a meeting of his National Security Council. During it, his intelligence was insulted.

The meeting concerned nuclear weapons.

Bored by both the subject and the people, Nixon listened with increasing irritation as his secretary of state, Henry Kissinger, and his secretary of defense, James Schlesinger, argued out their rival strategies for the forthcoming summit meeting between the president and the Soviet Communist party general secretary, Leonid Brezhnev, in Moscow. Nixon could hardly say so, but he regarded these NSC meetings simply as occasions when people who weren't in on his decisions could feel that they were. Jim Schlesinger was one of those who wasn't. He seemed to be making up for it with what Nixon thought was a characteristically tumid exposition of the Pentagon's point of view.

Nixon didn't like Schlesinger and hadn't liked him from the first time he had met him. This was when Schlesinger was deputy director of the new Bureau of the Budget and he had come in to brief the president on some weapons proposals. The president found the briefing as idle and pompous as this one, and he had later told Haldeman: "I don't want that guy in my office ever again." But Nixon had had to have Schlesinger in his office many times since, because Schlesinger had become the most dangerous source of opposition to the detente policies being pursued by his secretary of state.

Nixon's chances of getting through to the other side of Watergate as president depended, he felt, on a spectacular and quick success in dealing with the Soviet Union. That in turn depended on his defense secretary and the Joint Chiefs agreeing with the negotiating proposal on nuclear weapons that Kissinger wanted him to take to Moscow. At this meeting, Schlesinger was making it plain that he didn't agree and wouldn't agree with Kissinger's proposal, and so Nixon would have no alternative but to cut the Pentagon out of the arms proposal altogether and risk the refusal of the Joint Chiefs to go along with it later.

The alternative proposed by Schlesinger seemed almost deliberately designed to be unacceptable to the Soviet Union, which to Nixon signaled that Schlesinger was following the line of his patron, Senator Henry Jackson of Washington State, in urging weapons limits that could never be successfully negotiated. The case Schlesinger was presenting, Nixon would write, "amounted to an unyielding hard line against any SALT agreement that did not ensure an overwhelming American advantage."

Instead of a reasonable bound on Soviet and American weapons, Schlesinger wanted to draw down the forces on both sides by actual cuts; he wanted the Soviets to stop putting multiple warheads on missiles and to refrain from deploying new missiles. The big problem, Schlesinger believed, was that American land missiles could be attacked by Soviet land rockets if their great lifting power was combined with the multiple warhead technology that America had already deployed and the Soviet Union was now testing. The U.S. had already announced that it was developing a new, large land missile, and the president should tell Brezhnev next month that America would go ahead with the production of this new weapon, and others as well, unless the Soviets would agree to deep cuts in their missile armory. He believed the U.S. must face the Soviets down on their evident intention to deploy four new missiles, or the U.S. must buckle down to a five-year all-out arms race. As for Secretary Kissinger's proposal to simply cap things as they were, he couldn't go along with it.

Nixon didn't like these National Security Council meetings at any time. He particularly didn't like disputes about nuclear weaponry. The president had already been sorely tried in recent weeks. He had returned from what he thought was a highly successful visit to the Middle East to find that it hadn't helped him, either in the polls or with the House Judiciary Committee which the following day finished hearing all the evidence on the charges against him —seven thousand pages of careful testimony that constituted the case for his impeachment. In the past week, he had had to file briefs in the tapes case before the Supreme Court, his office had had to prepare pretrial hearings in the Watergate cover-up case and respond to demands from the District Court which was hearing the Ellsberg break-in case. The Ervin Committee was demanding more documents, the House Judiciary Committee wanted more tapes, and Henry Kissinger was returning to testify on wiretaps before the Senate Foreign Relations Committee.

It had not been a good week, and Nixon thought it crass of Schlesinger to irritate him at so difficult a time. Nixon

loathed any sort of personal confrontation and usually re-
frained from arguing with opponents at these meetings, but
this time he crisply cut into Schlesinger's speech by remark-
ing, "I think we should try to use this time to frame a more
practical approach to this problem. We have to accept the
fact that Secretary Schlesinger's proposal simply has no
chance of being accepted by the Soviets, so we should try to
work out something consistent with our interests that will."

Schlesinger, sitting next to the president, pondered this
rebuke and replied, "But, Mr. President, everyone knows
how impressed Krushchev was with your forensic ability in
the kitchen debate. I'm sure if you applied your skills to it
you could get them to accept it."

In the silence that followed even the chairman of the Joint
Chiefs, General George Brown, who was so tactless he had
once made anti-Semitic remarks *in public,* was mute, and
the usually voluble Kissinger let Schlesinger's remark hang.
Only Vice-President Jerry Ford seemed to be unaware of the
embarrassment, though as minority leader on the House
Appropriations Committee he had often had reason to dis-
like Schlesinger, and he found the general pause a good
opening to deliver his speech on the need for more defense
spending, a speech he knew by heart from frequent repeti-
tion and which he had found suitable for almost all occasions.

Nixon was not sure whether Schlesinger was serious or
making a joke, or whether he thought Nixon really had been
smart with Krushchev or whether he really meant that the
kitchen debate was a trivial charade, but whatever Schlesinger really meant, Nixon thought it was patronizing and
stupid and that the secretary of defense might have a good
head for figures but he wasn't much as a politician.

That night, a still unhappy Nixon confided to his dicta-
phone that "the NSC meeting was a real shocker insofar as
the performance of the Chiefs and particularly of Schlesinger was concerned. His statement that he knew Krush-

chev had been very impressed by my 'forensic ability,' and that with forensic ability I could sell the idea that he presented, was really an insult to everybody's intelligence and particularly to mine. . . . Many of the defense people don't want any agreement because they want to go ahead willy-nilly with all the defense programs they possibly can and they do not want constraints."

The man who the president would later suspect of not wanting agreement with the Soviet Union was forty-three years old when Nixon appointed him secretary of defense in April 1973. Many people still thought he was Arthur. James Schlesinger was the first member of the hitherto obscure weapons community to be given the top defense job, the first to bring to the third-floor Pentagon office overlooking the Potomac, a huge white office with a walk-in safe as big as a bathroom, the skills and ways of thinking of the RAND Corporation. Nearly all his predecessors had been successful lawyers or businessmen. Schlesinger was the first to come in already familiar with the bizarre esoterica of nuclear war planning and the routine computation of megadeaths. He knew how to compute the yield and accuracy of a nuclear weapon to discover its lethality, how to calculate the hypothetical results of an exchange of nuclear tipped missiles, how to infer from wind patterns, census data, and medical studies, the fatalities from blast and fire and radiation if a bomb of a certain megatonnage was detonated at a certain height at a certain time of the day over, say, Chicago, and how to balance a force of submarines, bombers, and land rockets to optimize the strength of a nuclear attack. In the tiny community that had grown up around the theory of nuclear weapons, he knew everyone and was known to everyone, from Harold Brown and Edward Teller to Herbert York and Albert Latter—hawks and doves, young and old, nominal Republicans and nominal Democrats. It was a community that was uniquely a creation of the Manhattan Project, and in Jim Schlesinger the community saw its first member in the top civilian job in the national security apparatus.

It was not to be a long career as secretary of defense. Five years later, when he had been sacked from his second cabinet post by his third president, people would say that Jim Schlesinger was too arrogant and too narrow for the kind of highly technical yet highly political jobs for which he had seemed the ideal occupant. But in the twenty-seven months he was defense secretary, Schlesinger changed America's nuclear war plans and its nuclear weapons. Two months after he became defense secretary, the MX program crystallized, and one year later he signed out a new Nuclear Weapons Employment Policy—the guidelines for nuclear war. Six years after he reviewed his final Pentagon parade, the Reagan administration would be refining the nuclear war strategy he had laid down, and building the weapons he had begun to develop. One of these weapons was the MX.

By the time Schlesinger was sacked by Gerald Ford in November 1975, the meanly funded "Advanced Ballistic Missile Research Program" had become a generously funded MX program with dozens of contractors, a separate administering office, and a considerable investment of careers and prestige behind it. Its funds would be cut and restored, cut and restored in the next four years as proponents and opponents of the missile fought in the administration and Congress, until, at his June 1979 National Security Council meeting, Jimmy Carter ended one great phase of the controversy and began another by deciding to build and deploy the missile.

Schlesinger was first a protégé and then a rival and finally a victim of Henry Kissinger, and the principal issue in their cooperation and conflict was America's nuclear weaponry.

Their backgrounds were so similar and their personalities so different that it was inevitable that Kissinger and Schlesinger would clash if thrown together. "If Schlesinger and I fight, this town will blow apart," Kissinger once said. Both were New Yorkers, both were sons of European Jews, both went to Harvard College, and both graduated from there with distinction in 1950. Both went on to complete their doctorates at Harvard: Kissinger with a study of Castlereagh and Metternich, and Schlesinger with a treatise on the political economy of national security. Both were exceptionally bright and exceptionally arrogant, and both found patrons to bring them to Washington. For Kissinger, the patron was Nelson Rockefeller and then it was Richard Nixon. For Schlesinger, there was only one patron: Senator Henry (Scoop) Jackson of the state of Washington, principal hawk on the Senate Armed Services Committee, chairman of its Arms Control Subcommittee, and also chairman of the Senate Energy and Natural Resources Committee.

If their backgrounds were similar, their personalities were not. Kissinger was witty and charming, Schlesinger dry and abrupt. He refused dinner invitations, dressed shabbily, drove a 1964 Ford, and lived with his wife and eight children at the end of a tree-lined lane in suburban Arlington. He was then neither rich nor acquisitive. He liked playing military music on his stereo, and he was said to compose off-color songs.

Schlesinger's views were typical of his conservative school. He called himself a "Taft Republican" and was fond of saying that the modern age was too indulgent, that each generation had to relearn the need for vigilance and effort, that America's literate class was so long shielded by America's might it had forgotten the need for blood and treasure to protect its freedoms, that there was too much of a tendency these days to disregard old values, and that the world was a good deal more complicated than many people supposed. His mind was of a puzzling kind, not unlike that of his third president, Jimmy Carter. He was brilliant at Harvard and clever at his job. No one would deny that Jim Schlesinger was an intelligent fellow. Yet in what must have been the greatest intellectual wrench of his life, Schlesinger had

abandoned the complexities of Judaism after his barmitz-
vah, only to embrace the pallid pieties of a Virginia Pres-
byterianism, which was in turn exchanged for Lutheranism
in a compromise with his Methodist bride. He told interview-
ers he read Lutheran theology in his spare time, and his
speeches were speckled with quotations from a great number
of powerful thinkers—rather too great a number, actually,
to be convincingly his own harvest. In a 1968 paper on the
uses and abuses of analysis, written for Senator Jackson's
Armed Services Subcommittee, one of the first instances of
their growing intimacy, he had written that "in the search
for preferred policies, such encumbrances as social values
and goals, constraints, institutional requirements (both
broad and narrow) pertain. Truth becomes only one of a
number of conflicting objectives and, sad to relate, often-
times a secondary one." What theology supported this opposition between "social values" and "truth," and saw "social
values and goals" as encumbrances? That was the theology
of RAND, not Martin Luther.

Schlesinger won his doctorate in economics at Harvard in
1956, by which time he was already teaching at the University of Virginia. He found the atmosphere there more con-
genially conservative than Harvard. He wrote on national
security matters, lectured at the National War College, and
in the mid-sixties was recruited to work at RAND on national
security analysis. By 1968 he was head of National Security
Studies at RAND and he had formed his connection with
Jackson, who made it his business to bring the bright young
Republican to Washington.

Jackson was a Democrat, liberal on spending and labor
issues, deeply conservative on defense and foreign policy
issues. He was curious and knowledgeable about subjects
that other less far-sighted senators thought were tedious and
profitless, like arms and energy, and since these happened
also to be a considerable interest to the state of Washington,
Jackson's career had prospered. As chairman of the Arms

Control Subcommittee of the Senate Armed Services Committee, he was a major figure in the Senate's attitude to the nuclear weapons treaty with the Soviet Union. Nixon had so high an opinion of his abilities, and so fine an appreciation of his potential to make trouble where he was, that he offered to make him secretary of defense in 1968. Jackson refused, but was pleased when Nixon accepted his recommendation to make his protégé, James Schlesinger of RAND, deputy director of the Bureau of the Budget.

When Glenn T. Seaborg resigned as chairman of the Atomic Energy Commission, Nixon again obliged Jackson, who was as powerful in energy legislation as he was in defense, by moving Schlesinger into the vacated job. And when Richard Helms was sent to Iran as ambassador in 1972, Jackson and Kissinger, who had discovered that Schlesinger could be useful, both warmly recommended him to the president as the new director of the Central Intelligence Agency. Schlesinger went in and sacked one thousand employees— the first of the mass dismissals of covert agents from what had become a huge and ungoverned apparatus. As the Watergate crisis deepened and Nixon found he needed Defense Secretary Elliot Richardson, a reputable Bostonian, in the attorney general's job, Schlesinger was moved over to the Pentagon with Kissinger's backing and Jackson's vigorous support.

As an administrator, Schlesinger was surprisingly bad. He wasn't methodical, he couldn't be scheduled, and he didn't attend with sufficient care to the political duties of his job. He did not, like McNamara before him or like Kissinger in the National Security Office, recruit a group of bright young assistants to ride his fences. In office, he relied on the Chiefs of Staff or on old weapons community buddies. These omissions eventually showed up in the work of his department. His relationships with the principal Hill committees grew worse and worse. In the October 1973 Middle East war, he was unable to resupply Israel with anything like the alacrity

Nixon demanded, because he had accepted the Chiefs' way of doing things rather than imposing his own. And though he would later pronounce upon the failure of the Iran rescue mission, it was Schlesinger who was secretary of defense when American marines died attacking the wrong island in their search for the Mayaguez hostages.

But if Schlesinger was a poor administrator, he was a powerful thinker, and he brought to defense the strength and weaknesses of the RAND Corporation.

Founded by the air force to bring the knowledge of the physical and social sciences to bear on problems of weapons and war, the RAND Corporation had been in the forefront of work on missiles, satellites, bomber deployment, and national military strategy since the beginning of the fifties. Staff members at the Santa Monica think-tank had, since the mid-fifties, been discussing ways in which nuclear war might be limited, arguing that America ought to be prepared with weapons and strategy to fight less-than-massive nuclear wars and that, to be prepared for both, made both limited and total wars less likely. Jim Schlesinger belonged very firmly to this school as did Henry Kissinger, and together they brought to the Nixon administration a change in nuclear strategy which is still unfolding.

From the time the United States first began to build and deploy large numbers of nuclear weapons after World War II, strategists and policy-makers have been perplexed by the problem of how to use them. Because there has never been a nuclear war, there has never been any experience to guide strategy. The difference between a nuclear weapon and any of the weapons that preceded it is that a single nuclear weapon can do an enormous amount of damage to a city, and modern societies are city societies. Since so few weapons can cause so much destruction, it is extremely difficult to defend against them. If a defense succeeds in stopping ninety-eight of one hundred nuclear weapons aimed at New York City, the defense has failed. It was quickly recognized, in the first writings about nuclear weapons, that the major—if not the only—purpose of possessing them was to deter any other country from using them against the United States. Before nuclear weapons, a military force could actually plan to use its weapons in combat to achieve some useful goal like the destruction of an opponent's army and the taking of valuable territory. After nuclear weapons became part of the arsenal of the United States and the Soviet Union, and particularly after both had conquered the technology of making compact hydrogen bombs that would fit on top of intercontinental rockets, neither side could sensibly imagine circumstances in which they could be used against the other without inviting the destruction of their own societies. This was the "balance of terror" described by Winston Churchill in 1955, the dilemma of "absolute weapons" which the great American strategist, Bernard Brodie, had described at the dawn of the nuclear age.

In 1946 Brodie wrote: "Everything about the bomb is overshadowed by the twin facts that it exists and that its power is fantastically great." He saw that "no adequate defense against the bomb exists and the possibilities of its existence in the future are exceedingly remote." But so long as any country that proposes the use of its nuclear weapons fears retaliation, then the weapon cannot be used. As he wrote then: "If it must fear retaliation, the fact that it destroys its opponent's cities some hours or even days before its own are destroyed may avail it little." Accordingly, and this was the most important statement that would ever be made about nuclear weapons: "Thus far, the chief purpose of our military establishment has been to win wars. From now on its chief purpose must be to avert them."

One year after Hiroshima, Brodie had seen that the unprecedently great power of nuclear weapons created a new strategy of deterrence, and it would later be made explicit that deterrence depended on the invulnerability of the deterrent. Yet the weapons Brodie was describing were the first

primitive atom bombs produced from the Manhattan Project, weapons sufficiently powerful to cause a hundred thousand deaths in a Japanese city, but only a fraction of the
power of the hydrogen bomb, which would first be tested in
1949. The weapons used in Japan were equivalent to fourteen thousand to seventeen thousand tons of TNT. The hydrogen weapons would be equal to millions of tons of ns of TNT.
They could be produced in large numbers and to whatever
yield was required. The invention of the H-bomb strengthened Brodie's case. And after the invention of the H-bomb
came its production in smaller and smaller packages, until
it could fit on the tip of an intercontinental ballistic missile.
This development in the mid-fifties strengthened Brodie's
case even more—it was harder to defend against missiles
than bombers, and both sides could deploy them cheaply in
great numbers.

Recognition by policy-makers that nuclear weapons made
a fundamental difference did not come all at once, because,
for the first half of the decade of the fifties, the United States
was all but invulnerable to attacks from the Soviet Union's
primitive atomic forces. In the final year of the Truman
administration, 1952, the Soviet Union had no long-range
bombers and only a small stockpile of atomic bombs. Under
General Curtis E. LeMay, the United States Strategic Air
Command, equipped with more than a thousand medium-
and long-range bombers based in Europe and the United
States, planned to use its forces in World War III much as
General LeMay had used the 20th Air Force against Japan
in World War II. The plan was to drop all the atom bombs
in the U.S. arsenal on military and industrial targets in the
Soviet Union, Eastern Europe, and China, in what would be
a single, crippling blow at the ability of the Soviet Union and
its allies to fight war.

After the dismal experience of the protracted and incon-
clusive war in Korea, the incoming Eisenhower administration began to rely almost entirely on nuclear weapons to

fight future wars. Half of its military spending was on thermonuclear weapons. In 1954 Secretary of State John Foster Dulles announced that the United States would retaliate against any Soviet or Soviet-inspired attack, conventional or atomic, "by means and at places of our own choosing." That was taken to mean a nuclear response, and the policy became known as "massive retaliation." But, even as Dulles spoke, the Soviet development of hydrogen bombs and long-range rockets was undermining the policy's foundations. The Soviet Union first tested a hydrogen bomb in August 1953 and an intercontinental missile in 1957. As President Eisenhower acknowledged as early as 1953, "our former unique physical security has almost totally disappeared before the long-range bomber and the destructive power of a single bomb." If the Soviet Union could reply to an American attack with a devastating attack of its own, then there were obviously some provocations that the U.S. would accept rather than initiate the total destruction of both societies.

A fundamental strategic principle sprang from the growth of Soviet power. This was that the power to deter a Soviet strike depended not on the mass of forces that could be deployed against the Soviet Union in a first strike, but on the power of the forces that would be left, were the Soviet Union to strike first. This difficult but fundamental discovery, again made by Brodie, that deterrence depends on a secure retaliation, has remained the first principle of nuclear strategy in all administrations at all times. It arose from the realization that a powerful force that was vulnerable to attack was an invitation to war rather than a deterrent to war, and it was elaborated in a RAND study conducted by one of the most influential thinkers of the nuclear age, Albert Wohlstetter.

Asked at the beginning of the fifties to recommend how the Strategic Air Command should locate its bombers' bases, Wohlstetter began to realize that the then massive power of the command was actually vulnerable to attack from the

Soviet Union. It could cripple the Soviet Union in a first strike, but since it was itself vulnerable to a first strike, it had a much smaller retaliatory or second-strike ability. For Soviet planners, the SAC bomber squadron might therefore be a reason to attack rather than a reason not to. This distinction between first- and second-strike abilities, which Wohlstetter made in 1954 in a classified report to the air force, was very important—not only in subsequent decisions to bring SAC bombers back from Europe and to develop long-range bombers and aerial refueling, but also in later decisions which, in an unbroken sequence through increasingly sophisticated means of attack warning, concrete hardened missile silos, and concrete hardened command centers, led to the debate about a safe base for MX. And the warning that bomber bases might be vulnerable led, through the same process, to a sequence of national security crises, from the missile gap of the late fifties to the "window of vulnerability" in the late seventies.

But what kind of forces should constitute this invulnerable deterrent, and how should they be targeted? In 1959, when the United States had something over a thousand medium- and long-range bombers, and only a few dozen medium- and long-range land missiles, targeting plans were necessarily limited. The weapons were large, inaccurate, and slow to arrive on target. Since it is difficult for a bomber force to prevent an enemy bomber force from becoming airborne, it was not possible even to contemplate a successful preemptive strike against an alert enemy. It was comparatively easy to protect one's own nuclear weapons from attack by becoming airborne on warning of attack. Nonetheless the questions were asked. At the minimum, everyone agreed, the United States should be capable of utterly destroying Soviet society, because that would deter the Soviet Union from destroying American society. But was that the only possible targeting plan?

Assured destruction, the ability to at all times and in any

conceivable circumstances respond to a nuclear attack with a devastating attack on the Soviet Union, was seen by some RAND thinkers as only a necessary and not sufficient principle for deterring war. Bernard Brodie, William Kaufmann, Albert Wohlstetter, and then later thinkers like Henry Kissinger and James Schlesinger, argued that the threat of massive retaliation might deter a massive attack. But it was not plausible, for example, that the United States would destroy Soviet cities, expecting that American cities would be destroyed in turn, in response to a Soviet attack on Berlin or a single American bomber base or a fleet of American warships. The United States should perhaps threaten to retaliate "massively," but Soviet planners, like American planners, might very well conclude that such a massive response was unlikely.

So one question was whether nuclear weapons could be used in small numbers for limited objectives like repelling a Soviet invasion of Berlin or blocking a Chinese push into Korea. Another closely related question was whether an exchange of nuclear weapons with the Soviet Union could somehow be controlled or confined so the destruction would be limited. The first question could not be answered affirmatively unless the second was also answered affirmatively.

As early as 1952, Brodie, in a series of classified papers, had been arguing that the United States needed to find ways of limiting thermonuclear war. But if deterrence no longer meant simply the ability to ensure, at all times and in all circumstances, the destruction of Soviet society, then "deterrence" was no longer a finite number of weapons. It could equally justify an indefinitely large number of weapons of every size and kind, since these could be said to be necessary for a wider range of contingencies. This is exactly what happened to the doctrine of "deterrence." It began as an insight into the nature of nuclear weapons, but came to justify the kinds and numbers of weapons that would be deployed as if they were no different from other weapons, and not doomsday weapons that could never be used without the destruction of both the society against which they were directed and the society that initiated their use.

There were several different schools of thought on how to limit thermonuclear war. The army Chief of Staff General Maxwell Taylor, said in 1956 that the United States should in the first instance respond to a Soviet attack with its conventionally equipped armies, holding its nuclear forces in reserve to deter their use by the other side. General Taylor's prescription required a very large increase in army numbers, one of the reasons he liked it and the Eisenhower administration did not. The following year, the young scholar Henry Kissinger adopted another idea: the United States should rely on its tactical nuclear weapons to repel a Soviet invasion in Europe, and hold its strategic nuclear weapons, which were much more powerful, in reserve. Tactical weapons, which the Eisenhower administration was deploying in large numbers in Europe, had yields as low as a few hundred tons of TNT. They were carried in mortar and howitzer shells, aerial bombs, and naval munitions. The problem with this approach was that tactical nuclear weapons, which may be much smaller than strategic weapons but are still much more powerful than most battlefield conventional explosives, would destroy Europe, would just as likely obstruct the movement of allied troops as Soviet troops, and, in any close combat situation, would pose as great a threat to the side that used them as to the side against which they were used. The tactical nuclear option is one of the very few ideas about nuclear weapons that does not survive today, except in the more obscure reaches of the Department of the Army.

What did emerge from the rethinking of the fifties, when the Soviet Union was clearly achieving the ability to assure the destruction of American cities, was a doctrine which, in one form or another, has come to dominate official thinking about nuclear weapons. Dr. William Kaufman, who would later advise the incoming defense secretary, Robert

McNamara, began work on a "no-cities" strategy at RAND in the late fifties.

The idea of the "no-cities" strategy was that, so long as the Soviet Union avoided bombing American cities, the United States would avoid bombing Soviet cities. Instead, the United States would begin by attacking military targets in the Soviet Union, like armies and missile silos. This became known as "counterforce targeting" or "controlled response."

The doctrine raised all kinds of questions which have proved very difficult to answer, and, as the kinds and sizes of weapons have changed, those questions have become ever more difficult and conjectural. One overriding problem is that it depends on Soviet cooperation. It only works if the Soviet Union avoids U.S. cities in its first attack, then leaves its nuclear weapons on the ground awaiting the American reply.

Yet a threat to attack the Soviet Union's missile sites would encourage the Soviet Union to use its missiles to attack the American cities before the Soviet Union was disarmed. The "controlled response" idea could make uncontrolled war more likely rather than less. The strategy also rested on a misconception of the value of cities. Since they are the centers of industry, skills, and capital, they are not only the easiest but also the most lucrative targets in a general war, and thus there are excellent military grounds for destroying them if war appears likely. The problem with city bombing in World War II was not that it was militarily useless to wipe out all the major cities of Germany and the United Kingdom, but that, in spite of their best efforts, both sides found it impossible to do so. With nuclear weapons, that is no longer a problem.

Proponents of "no-cities" said that it was a deterrence policy, directed at persuading the Soviet Union that no exchange of weapons would be worthwhile; but, like the assured city destruction policy that it replaced, it had to be analyzed in the light of what would actually happen in war.

Examined in this light, it is not easy to see how it improves on a city busting policy, and how it avoids ending up in the same place by a different route. Another problem, which was not serious in the late 1950s but is very serious today—the difficulty of finding an invulnerable base for MX is one result —is that, if one side develops the capacity to strike at the opponent's nuclear weapons, both sides will soon have it, and both sides will be less confident of their ability to deter war. A final problem is that having the ability to reply to a less than massive attack with a less than massive attack lowers the threshold of conflict beyond which either side may contemplate using nuclear weapons.

For the history of MX the city-avoiding strategy contained an important implication. Bombers were too slow and submarine-launched weapons too inaccurate and too difficult to coordinate to credibly attack the nuclear weapons of an opponent, which could be airborne on warning and removed from danger on warning of attack. The development of the "no-cities" strategy into the various forms of "flexible response" and "war-fighting" strategies of the sixties, seventies, and eighties has depended on the development of fast, accurate, and extremely powerful land-based intercontinental missiles, of which the MX is the most advanced and lethal form—a missile developed for the mission of attacking Soviet missiles still in their silos.

The Kennedy administration came to office in 1961, after a campaign largely fought on issues of nuclear strategy. Kennedy alleged the existence of a "missile gap" with the Soviet Union which threatened the security of American nuclear forces. He said "massive retaliation" was not believable, and America needed to find an alternative strategy to mutual suicide.

When McNamara and his RAND advisers began reviewing American nuclear strategy in 1961, they found there was but one plan for nuclear attack—the United States would launch all its weapons immediately after the order was given. The target plan included Soviet and satellite cities. No reserves would be held, and the command and control of the forces was expected to survive only as long as necessary to get the weapons off the ground. The Joint Chiefs computed expected Soviet, Chinese, and satellite fatalities at from 360 million to 425 million.

McNamara and his advisers drew up a new guidance. China and the satellite countries were separated from the Soviet Union, and Soviet cities from Soviet military targets. Reserves of weapons were to be kept, Soviet command and control was to be avoided in the first stage of a nuclear exchange. American command and control systems were to be protected. And, in place of the single spasm attack, the nuclear forces were ordered to prepare a series of optional attacks, ranging from those against Soviet nuclear forces to those against Soviet cities and all military targets. The city of Moscow, for example, was taken off the initial target list in late 1961.

At the time this new plan was drawn up, the United States had fifty-four land-based intercontinental missiles, eighty submarine-launched long-range missiles, and six hundred long-range bombers. The Soviet Union had about ten intercontinental ballistic missiles and a total of a few hundred long-range bombers of questionable quality. The missiles on both sides were extremely inaccurate, and the bombers would take hours to arrive at their targets.

Through the sixties, the numbers of weapons on both sides grew enormously, and all the growth was in missiles. By 1963 the United States had a total of 700 land and submarine-launched missiles deployed, and 630 long-range bombers. In the same year, the Soviet Union had about 80 land missiles and 100 submarine-launched weapons, together with 200 bombers. By 1965, when the Soviet buildup began in earnest, the United States had over 1,300 land and submarine-launched missiles, and 630 bombers, while the Soviet

Union had 300 land and submarine-launched missiles and
200 bombers. Toward the end of the decade, the United
States reached its cap of more than 1,700 missiles and 465
bombers, while the Soviet Union had 1,125 missiles, 150
bombers, and was adding missiles so quickly that in 1970, its
land missile numbers overtook the United States.

Confronted with the buildup of Soviet weapons, the nuclear strategy declared by McNamara in successive Defense
Reports changed year by year. In 1962 the declared strategy
was to deter war through the ability to destroy the Soviet
Union's capacity to make war, even after the United States
had absorbed the first blow. By 1963, when the replanning
of 1961 had been completed, the strategy was to avoid cities
by maintaining a second-strike force big enough to attack
military forces first, holding the cities hostage to a second
salvo. By the following year, the strategy was to "assure
destruction" by maintaining forces capable of destroying Soviet society under all circumstances, and also to "limit damage" by maintaining weapons capable of striking at un-
launched Soviet nuclear forces after a Soviet attack.

By 1964 Robert McNamara realized that a nuclear strategy that sought to cover all important Soviet military as well
as economic and population targets meant unlimited spending on nuclear forces. As the Soviets deployed more forces,
as they strengthened silos and put submarines to sea, American forces would have to get bigger and bigger in what was
clearly a competition without end. It was apparent, too, that
the invention and deployment of long-range ballistic missiles had fundamentally changed the balance between
offense and defense. The army, the air force, and then the
Chiefs of Staff pressed for the development and construction
of an anti-missile missile, a defense against missiles, and
McNamara doubted it was technically feasible or affordable.
Yet only with an anti-missile missile could the U.S. limit
damage to its own society from a nuclear war. Faced with
these results from controlled response and the policy of lim-

iting damage to the United States, he changed course and announced instead that the United States would reply on assured destruction, an invulnerable nuclear retaliation force, as the criterion for deciding on the size of its forces. As President Lyndon Johnson said in February 1965, damage limitation was costly and probably unattainable.

McNamara's switch from controlled response to assured destruction was by no means clear-cut. He did not adopt the idea that the only contingency that America needed to deter was an attack on American cities, for which purpose it would need only several hundred weapons, instead of the thousands it had already deployed. He did not say that America would not respond selectively to less than massive attacks (although the plans were organized around massive attacks), or that America would attack only cities and not the nuclear forces of its opponents (it had and would continue to target both), or that America would respond to an attack with a single barrage of weapons. But there could now be a criterion by which to judge the size of nuclear forces, and that criterion was the number of weapons required to destroy, with complete assurance, at least half the Soviet economy and at least a quarter its people, in any and all circumstances. For that purpose, he said, it was sufficient—much more than sufficient—that America should have the nuclear forces that he had already planned to deploy. In 1968, after an eight-year buildup in America's nuclear arsenal, it had 1,054 missiles in silos, 656 missiles in submarines, and 456 bombers which could each carry sixty thousand pounds of hydrogen bombs. With the important qualification that many of the missiles now have multiple warheads, and 100 bombers have been retired, those are the forces deployed today.

In his final Defense Report of 1969, McNamara calculated that, even if Soviet forces exceeded the highest intelligence estimate in the early seventies, the U.S. missiles alone would be able to deliver six times the destructive power needed for his assured destruction criteria after absorbing a Soviet attack. The McNamara buildup, begun in 1961 with the strong support of the exponents of "flexible response" from RAND, far exceeded the forces developed by the Soviet Union in the first half of the sixties. The secretary himself later judged that the American buildup contributed to the dramatic expansion of Soviet forces which, beginning in the mid-sixties, surpassed the number of American missiles in 1970. The McNamara years, from 1961 to 1968, put down the foundations for the next great shift in thinking about nuclear war. But, if McNamara's buildup and the Soviet response created problems with which planners on both sides have had to deal, his drive to head off the Joint Chiefs' demand for ballistic missile defense through a mutual renunciation agreement with the Soviet Union also led to the first serious talks on the control of nuclear weapons.

The fall of "damage limitation" was caused by the growth of Soviet forces, by the realization that it was an open-ended commitment to more and more weapons, and by the fundamental realization that it depended on the Soviets playing by rules patently not in their interest. By the end of the sixties, American strategic policy had returned to the principles Brodie had declared in 1946. Nuclear weapons could not be used for rational purposes. The only reason for possessing them was to deter enemies from using them. Deterrence depended not on the capacity to strike first but, as Brodie had seen, on "the security of the retaliatory force."

But, while McNamara had come back to "assured destruction," a weapons program that he had blessed was about to pose a fundamental challenge to "assured destruction"—a challenge we still have not met. McNamara had developed a weapon which would, in time, raise the possibility that the side that initiated nuclear war would gain an important advantage. Assisted by his deputy secretary, Cy Vance, and his director of defense research and engineering, Harold Brown, McNamara had fostered the development of a new technology that would place several warheads on a single missile. Instead of a single bomb, each missile would now carry several bombs, and each bomb could be directed at a different target. The technology was called MIRV, for multiple independently targetable reentry vehicle, and its effects would be to change once again the foundations upon which nuclear strategy had been erected. Because one missile could now destroy several enemy missiles, the equation of exchange was once again changing, and, in the hermetic community of weapons scholars with access to classified material, it was already being said that America would need to deploy its next generation of missiles in some kind of mobile or deceptive way to hinder Soviet attack.

2

The Weapons Community

No single system has had a greater effect on the
world balance of power over the last fifteen years
than the ICBM.   —*General Richard Ellis,*
commander-in-chief,
United States Air Force
Strategic Air Command (CINCSAC)

ON a hot, unpleasant August day in Washington, a day
when the sky was yellow and smog settled over the Potomac,
Dr. Albert Latter of the RAND Corporation went to call on
Dr. Harold Brown, the deputy director for defense research
and engineering at the Pentagon. It was 1963, during a series
of difficult hearings before the Senate Foreign Relations
Committee on the proposed nuclear test ban treaty. Like
Brown, Latter was a member of the weapons community,
and though he was somewhat older than Brown, Latter had
been closely connected with him. Both were brilliant theoretical physicists who had been drawn into work on nuclear
weapons design, both had made their professional reputa-
tions in California, both had been prominent in the tiny
group of scientists who staffed the weapons research

50

laboratories around Los Angeles. When Brown was directing the Lawrence Livermore Laboratory, which had designed the hydrogen bomb, Latter was head of the physics department at RAND and a member of the U.S. Air Force Scientific Advisory Board. They had been close colleagues, but today they differed bitterly on an important issue.

The job Brown held in 1963 was in many ways becoming the focal point of the weapons community. His predecessor had been Herbert York, himself a former director of the Lawrence Livermore Laboratory. His successor, in two years' time when Brown switched over to become secretary of the air force, would be John Foster, who had worked with Brown in the Lawrence Livermore lab and had in turn become director. The job at the Pentagon, which grew more powerful as Robert McNamara centralized control over the weapons programs of the three services in the Defense Department, was already becoming more important than the job of science adviser to the president, and would in time overwhelm it.

Both Latter and Brown were among the two dozen or so best nuclear weapons scientists in America, but they had often found themselves on different sides of issues that divided the weapons community since 1945. Now Latter was very strongly opposed to the nuclear test ban treaty between the United States and the Soviet Union. Latter was a close associate of the inventor of the H bomb, Dr. Edward Teller; together they had published in 1958 a breezy little tract called "Our Nuclear Future," which asserted that "an atomic war need not be connected with more suffering than past wars." Because nuclear weapons could more quickly destroy the armies of the aggressor, future wars were likely to be shorter—an argument which rested on the implicit assumption that a nation could emerge victorious from a nuclear exchange. Believing in the possibility of victory, Teller and Latter wanted "flexible refined weapons of all kinds and sizes" and also "weapons to defend our cities" (though they argued simultaneously that cities would not be attacked). One thing that could obstruct that golden future would be a nuclear test ban.

Robert McNamara was overseeing the deployment of a thousand nuclear tipped missiles and the first nuclear missile armed submarines, but he thought of himself as a moderate who was holding the air force back. On August 13 McNamara had testified before the Foreign Relations Committee in favor of a test ban, arguing that the United States had nothing much to gain from further atmospheric testing, which had gradually been building up the level of radioactive particles in the world's air supply. The treaty's opponents argued that America needed to keep testing explosions. One reason was to find out what effect they would have on the newly deployed Minuteman missile. McNamara had told Congress this argument was unsound because "it is clear the Soviets do not have anything like the number of missiles necessary to knock out our Minuteman force."

Latter was angry with McNamara over that statement, and he was even angrier when, a week later, Brown also testified that a test ban treaty was in America's interests. A few years before, Brown had been an influential opponent at a test ban. It was one thing for McNamara to argue in favor of the treaty. McNamara was a manager, not a scientist. But Brown was a scientist, and his testimony hurt. Latter very much wanted to explode more thermonuclear weapons in Alaska, and his argument was one which, even before the technology and the weapons became available, strikingly prefigured the later conflicts over MX. Four months before, in a RAND paper, Latter had raised the possibility that the Soviet Union might put many warheads on the heavy missiles they were beginning to deploy and direct each separate warhead at a Minuteman silo. In this way, they would be able to destroy the whole Minuteman system with relatively few missiles of their own.

Latter was not the only inventor of what would later become known as MIRV, but he was one of the first to make the connection between MIRV and the vulnerability of American missiles. This was the argument he repeated to Brown that day in late August. The United States still had only a few hundred land missiles deployed at intercontinental range: the very heavy Titan and the first Minuteman. The Soviet Union had only begun to deploy its first primitive ICBMS— SS7s and SS8s—the year before. Neither side had MIRVs, and the United States had only just begun to think about the MIRV technology that it would not deploy for another seven years. The Soviet Union would not even test MIRVs for another decade. But Latter could see that the Soviet Union would one day have many hundreds of land missiles, and that they would have many independently targeted warheads, which could threaten America's land-based missiles with a preemptive strike.

Latter could see all this in August 1963, and the conclusion he drew from it—which was perhaps the weakest link in his chain of reasoning—was that the United States should continue nuclear testing to find out what effect a nuclear explosion would have on a Minuteman field. What thickness of concrete really was sufficient to protect against a blast at what distance? How far should the missiles be placed apart to minimize the damage? This was one of the only plausible arguments against the test ban treaty, and McNamara had destroyed it by saying that Soviet missiles were not sufficiently accurate to be used for a one-on-one attack, that to use more than one Soviet missile to attack one American missile was a foolish exchange for the Soviet Union, and that, even if they initiated such a foolish exchange, the hardening programs for the Minuteman silos would save a high enough proportion of American missiles to be able to counterattack the remaining Soviet missiles and submarine pens and bomber bases.

Latter was tough with Brown. He told him he had done a disservice to the United States. In a community where only patriotism can justify spending one's life inventing better weapons, to say you have done a disservice to the United

States is very tough indeed. Brown defended himself, offering some reasons why it would be difficult to put more than one independently targeted warhead on each missile. Brown was already familiar with the MIRVing concept, and later that year the air force began to look seriously at MIRVing the next generation of American missiles. That, so far as Latter was concerned, was the beginning of the American MIRV, and also the beginning of the American response to the Soviet MIRV—the MX. From that time onward, Latter was working both on the MIRV technology for the United States and on different ways to base land missiles to defend against MIRVs. By 1966, in a paper called "Garage Mobility," he described a system for putting Minuteman missiles on trucks and moving them between shelters—a system essentially similar to the system decided upon by President Jimmy Carter thirteen years later.

The meeting between Latter and Brown was characteristic of the "mad momentum" of the arms race which McNamara would deplore. Latter had conceived of both a new offensive technology in MIRV and a new defense against it in mobiles. All this a decade before the mobile missile plan would be presented to Congress. In 1977, fourteen years after this meeting, Latter would reappear in Brown's office to argue against one form of missile sheltering, and propose another.

The history of nuclear weapons and the history of nuclear strategy since 1945 are separable stories, though one profoundly influences the other. It is not true, as the military textbooks allege, that weapons are developed to fulfull a "mission" that is defined by strategy. More often than not, certainly in the case of MIRVing land missiles and in the case of MX, the weapon produces its own rationale. In the early disputes over nuclear strategy, adherents of the different services adapted their strategic reasoning to whatever best suited their service's interests. Thus, when the navy, in the immediate postwar period, was seeking a supercarrier as the central weapons system in its fleet, it argued that carrier-based aircraft, armed with nuclear weapons, could perform limited countermilitary strikes against Soviet targets, which could not be performed by the heavier and more distant air force bombers. In that period, the navy espoused counterforce strategies, and the air force propounded the idea of a single massive attack. A limited attack is synonymous with an attack on military targets, because an attack on population targets invites an immediate attack on one's own cities. And a single massive attack is synonymous with an attack mainly on cities, since there is only one chance and cities are the nearest and most lucrative targets.

Once the navy lost the supercarrier battle and found itself in command of submarines equipped with nuclear missiles, its service ideology changed from counterforce to counter-city, which is to say from envisaging the possibility of limited exchanges to relying on the mutual deterrent effect of city annihilation. The change was brought about not by philosophical speculation in the navy command, but by the inescapable fact that submarine-launched ballistic missiles were, at the time, so inaccurate they could be aimed only at soft, undefended large targets like cities. At the same time as the navy was swinging to mutual deterence, the air force, with increasingly accurate land missiles, was being more influenced by theories of limited nuclear war, which depended on the ability to strike with great accuracy at hardened targets.

This kind of interchange between weaponry and strategy was characteristic of the weapons community and it illustrated the frequency with which a weapons development would proceed quite independently of a strategic theory. But the weapons would present new challenges to the Soviet Union, and the Soviet response to the U.S. would present new challenges to the United States. The clearest example of this is the chain of action and reaction that led from multiple warheads on ballistic missiles to a new concern with ballistic missile defense and to the argument that America needed both a new land missile and a new way to base it.

The idea of deceptive or mobile basing for land missiles was not inspired by the likelihood that the Soviet Union would put more than one warhead on its missiles, and thus theoretically win an advantage from an exchange of missiles that it inittiated. Research on mobile basing for land missiles had actually been conducted long before multiple warheads were developed by either side. But MIRVing revived research that had long since been dormant.

Even before Latter's paper on "garage mobility," there had been a great deal of work on mobile land missiles. The first program for the construction and deployment of single-warhead solid fueled Minuteman rockets, adopted in 1959, included three squadrons of missiles carried in railway boxcars to fool the Russian planners. *Missiles & Rockets* magazine reported in 1959 that it had learned that U.S. strategists had well-advanced plans to mount Minuteman on rails, "camouflaged as ordinary freight trains." The cars would be air-conditioned to protect the crews from radioactive fallout, and the fifteen-car train carrying the Minuteman missiles would include a diner and caboose. The study of the system was financed partly by the American Car and Foundry Corporation, which hoped to build the cars, and the Association of American Railroaders. During tests with army ambulance cars, *Missiles & Rockets* reported, the most popular diversion when the air-conditioned cars, diner, and caboose failed to entertain, was the showing of movies on screens rigged against cattle sidings during nocturnal rests on the empty rails. One problem was that the union crews insisted on changing at each division point. This is what the air force refers to as a "civilian interface" problem, and was one of the reasons that the incoming Kennedy administration killed the rail-mobile Minuteman—this in spite of the fact that Kennedy had said, soon after his inauguration, that "we must provide funds to step up our Polaris, Minuteman and air-to-ground missile development program, in order to hasten the day when a full mobile missile force becomes our chief deterrent and closes any gap between ourselves and the Russians."

By the end of the sixties, the air force had contemplated a bewildering variety of shelters, hiding places, carriers, and methods as invulnerable basing modes for land missiles. In all, thirty possibilities had been considered. These included the "sandy silo" idea, in which one hundred missiles would be buried two thousand feet deep in holes that would then be filled with sand. On command, it was said, pressurized water would be released from tanks, and the missiles would float to the surface through the fluid. The air force examined putting five missiles on each of 167 dirigibles, which would hide behind clouds. Another possibility involved securing missiles to float collars in the open ocean. In 1960 the U.S. Navy developed Project Hydra, which used ships and barges to transport missiles, which were then tossed overboard with float collars and successfully launched.

The most obvious solution to the vulnerability of land missiles has always been to put them to sea. Indeed, that was the original motive behind submarine missile programs, which were at first resisted by the navy as incompatible with the mission of its surface ships and attack submarines. To the navy, more money for submarines carrying missiles targeted on the Soviet heartland meant less money for other ships. When the Polaris was first deployed, it was expressly to provide America with an invulnerable retaliatory force at a time when the air force was only just beginning to harden the silos for its liquid fueled Atlas ICBM. And when Polaris was replaced by the MIRVed Poseidon submarine system, it was justified by the same need to have an invulnerable retaliatory force. As Dr. Alain Enthoven, the assistant secretary of defense, said in 1968, "One of the big factors in the Poseidon development decision made three years ago was the conclusion that Poseidon would be the most effective way possible of guaranteeing against the threat of accurate Soviet missiles."

While seagoing missiles might best secure America's retaliatory power, they were not sufficiently accurate and were too difficult to coordinate to be useful for striking Soviet missiles in their silos or initiating a strike against all Soviet forces. The nuclear age has seen the development of many things never thought possible, but some simple problems have been stubbornly insoluble. One is how to communicate with a submarine when it is cruising at great depths, and a second is how to communicate between distant points while a nuclear war is occurring. The submarine problem is compounded when it is necessary to communicate with all submarines simultaneously.

During the 1960s, other solutions to the problem of missile vulnerability were preferred to mobilizing or randomizing or hiding them. As the Soviet Union began to deploy SS7 and SS8 ICBMs, there were a number of air force reviews, all of which concluded that the most cost-effective protection for a certain number of surviving missile warheads was the deployment of small missiles in single silos.

In 1964 the air force began looking at the technical possibilities of MIRV. In a study of MIRV called Golden Arrow, which began in November 1964 and concluded the following year, the air force decided that the proliferation of warheads in single silos was the preferred solution. But even then a close second was a version of Albert Latter's garage mobility —missiles mounted on trucks moving over unimproved roads in the Southwest, which could hide in horizontal shelters. The important characteristic of this system was that the missiles were relatively small, so they could move quickly from one shelter to another. Since they could hide in any one of a number of shelters and move rapidly between them, each shelter did not have to be as strongly hardened as it would be if the missile had only one shelter. The ability of the missile to "dash" between shelters would be part of the Carter administration's scheme fifteen years later.

The next major Pentagon study was a force requirements study called Strat-X, which began in 1967 and ended in January 1969. The goal of the study was to compare the costs of alternatives in terms of numbers of warheads surviving a Soviet strike. Though Strat-X is sometimes said to be the beginning of MX, it actually focused most on submarine-based missiles, recommending a new submarine with the missiles standing on the hull. That idea was rejected by both Admiral Rickover, whose nuclear propulsion division built the subs, and by the navy. They wanted the huge Trident submarine instead, and they got it. Strat-X looked at the problem of ICBM vulnerability, and agreed it was a long way off because of the accuracies the Soviet Union would need to develop in their missiles. The study recommended the air force strengthen the missile's command and control system, and that the army's developing anti-ballistic missile system should be connected with the defense of the strategic nuclear forces. This began the great debate about anti-ballistic missile systems, which had been going on within the defense department since the mid-sixties and became a contentious public issue at the end of the sixties. At the same time the ABM debate began, Strat-X and studies called Pen X and Intercept X strongly recommended the MIRVing of American missiles to penetrate a possible Soviet anti-ballistic missile system.

At the end of the sixties, although many mobile missile studies had been conducted in the Defense Department and the air force, the center of the stage was taken up by anti-ballistic missile systems to protect silo-based missiles from attack by future Soviet MIRVed missiles; and by American MIRVs to penetrate future Soviet ABMs. The result of this set of circumstances was enormously important in forming the political coalition that would later support MX. This result is that, beginning in the late sixties and continuing into the seventies, the idea of a mobile missile system would be advocated by the doves in Congress and the executive as an alternative to the anti-ballistic missile system favored by the air force. The mobile missile system, which began as a mobile Minuteman proposal and became simply a mobile deployment for a bigger and more accurate system, was conceptually an alternative to the ABM site defense system, the Safeguard. Therefore the story of the development of MX wove in and out of the history of the ABM, waning when ABM rose, rising when ABM waned, until the negotiation of the agreement to ban missile defense systems, with no similar restraint on MIRVs, put a new missile in a new base at the top of the Air Force agenda.

The story of the MIRV prefigured the story of MX. The origins of the technique lay in the impetus of technology, in the momentum of the bureaucracy in the air force ballistic missiles division, in the pressures of contractors, in the insistence of people that you could not stop technology, which really meant you should not stop it. There was no strategic rationale for MIRV, for having many independent warheads on one missile, when it was invented in 1963. The air force set out to find a reason for it when it had already decided to build it. "In 1964," wrote the historian of the MIRV, Ted Greenwood, "the task force supervising it realized that the MIRV system it was developing could not be justified by any existing mission requirements. Its members made a conscious effort to find a strategic rationale. Counterforce targeting and the growth of Soviet missile forces provided the solution." Counterforce meant the targeting of Soviet military forces, and particularly its intercontinental nuclear rocket forces, which were beginning to grow in response to the U.S. buildup and the humiliating backdown in the Cuban missile crisis.

Since MIRV meant a huge increase in the number of U.S. weapons, there must accordingly be a huge increase in the number of Soviet targets the U.S. should now cover. By 1965, counterforce theories of nuclear war were unpopular because of McNamara's change of heart. So the rationale for MIRV changed. Now it was that MIRV was required to make sure a sufficient number of American warheads penetrated Soviet defenses. This rationale was inspired by the gathering debate about Soviet anti-ballistic missile capabilities. MIRV became a "penetration" device, able to overwhelm the Soviet anti-ballistic missile system. And since American MIRV technology was so far along already, and since the Soviet Union could be expected to copy it, a third argument was found for MIRV, which was that it was necessary to defend against the Soviet MIRV. If Minuteman was to be made vulnerable by Soviet MIRVs, then each Minuteman should have as many warheads as possible. This way, each surviving Minuteman could do more damage to the Soviet Union. This last argument was a fine example of the "mad momentum" of the arms race that the military found utterly convincing. In fact, the argument about Soviet intentions was well ahead of Soviet capabilities. The first group of ten MIRVed Minuteman III missiles was operational in June 1970. The first patrol of a submarine armed with the MIRVed Poseidon missile began on 31 March 1971. It was not until August 1973 that the Soviet Union first flight-tested their MIRV.

When Richard Nixon became president in January 1969, the development of MIRV for Minuteman had been completed. Lyndon Johnson had begun but had interrupted negotiations with the Soviet Union over strategic arms limitations, and the Soviet Union was continuing its missile buildup.

As early as June 1969, the president's national security assistant was urging him to review the assured destruction doctrine that McNamara had left behind, and to request the Pentagon to devise strategies to meet contingencies other than all-out nuclear attack. This was, ironically, exactly the request that McNamara and his new team had made eight years before. Kissinger had recanted his conviction that tactical nuclear weapons should be the foundation for NATO strategy, and he was now convinced the U.S. needed more targeting plans, and thus more weapons. Kissinger was drawing on the city-avoiding theories of the late fifties and also on his interest in using nuclear weapons on the battlefield. In 1969 he worked on new criteria of "strategic sufficiency," and, in the president's first foreign policy report to Congress, a document drafted by Kissinger, the president asked: "Should a President, in the event of a nuclear attack, be left with the single option of ordering the mass destruction of enemy civilians, in the face of the certainty that it would be followed by the mass slaughter of Americans?" But, in the face of congressional resistance to an accelerated arms race, the president insisted that there was no ongoing U.S. program "to develop a so-called hard target MIRV capability."

In the SALT talks which had been begun by Lyndon Johnson and suspended after the invasion of Czechoslovakia, Kissinger sought a mutual ban on anti-ballistic missile deployment and a cap on missile numbers on both sides. He did not seek—perhaps could not seek—the one restraint that would have reduced the forthcoming threat to missiles on both sides—a ban on MIRV.

The SALT negotiations, which got under way in 1970, were to have many important implications for the later development of MX. SALT limits depended on both sides being able to verify the numbers of weapons deployed. Because it was impossible to count missiles, which could be in factories or stored underground, the negotiators agreed to count launchers. In the early seventies, "launchers" meant missile silos, submarine missile tubes, and bombers. Knowing it would be difficult to count mobile land-based missiles, the United States repeatedly sought a ban on their production and deployment. Failing to achieve a satisfactory ban, the United States declared their deployment would be inconsistent with

SALT. As U.S. concerns about the vulnerability of its missiles deepened in the mid-seventies, the U.S. reversed its position and rejected the Soviet Union's preferred acceptance of a ban on mobiles. But if mobiles were not banned, they must nonetheless be countable, if only to satisfy the SALT requirement of no interference with the means of verification. Since most mobile missile schemes included many hardened points for which a missile could be launched, it was necessary to separate the idea of "launcher" from the idea of "launch point." This technical and legal thicket was one of the many enduring complications in the MX program.

SALT complicated MX, but it also encouraged it. It codified the basic idea of equality of forces between the two sides, so that "sufficient" no longer meant enough weapons to utterly destroy the opponent's society, but approximately the same number of weapons as possessed by the opponent. The idea of equality in nuclear forces rested upon a fundamental misapprehension about their nature. In armies and navies equipped with conventional weapons, equality of forces implies balance, which implies stability. In nuclear weaponry, this is not necessarily so. It is not a stable situation, for example, if both sides have equal numbers of missiles in fixed silos, and each is capable of destroying their opponent's missiles in a first strike. Nor is there anything commendable about equal numbers for forces when both sides possess—as they do today—vastly more forces than could be justified by any rational requirement.

SALT also encouraged MX because it won for the United States and the Soviet Union the great success of a mutual ban on anti-ballistic missiles but did not win agreement on banning the deployment of multiple warheads on missiles. One without the other meant that land missiles would be vulnerable.

The Nixon administration's chief negotiator in the SALT talks, Ambassador Gerard Smith, had been a Washington insider since the days of John Foster Dulles, a Republican patrician who made his home on the eastern shore of the Chesapeake. Smith was a man of dovish sentiments and wide concerns for the future of the world, sentiments that he camouflaged behind a stern expression, a forward thrusting jaw, and an impeccably orthodox manner. The beneficiary of a considerable estate accumulated by his father, who had been general counsel for Coca Cola, Gerard Smith was perhaps a little too obviously of the stylish, moneyed, upper middle class to attract Richard Nixon, and it was not surprising that Henry Kissinger played all the trumps in the SALT negotiations under the Nixon administration.

But, if Smith was dovish for the Nixon administration, he was also dogged, and he was far-sighted enough to get it into the record. He wrote to both the president and the secretary of state as early as 1969, urging the U.S. ask the Soviet Union for mutual limits on missiles with multiple warheads. He pushed for it at a National Security Council meeting with the president and his advisers on 25 March 1970. He wrote to Nixon toward the end of 1971: "As you will recall, the United States made a determination some years ago to achieve greater targeting flexibility and assured penetration, the important factor was the number of independently targetable reentry vehicles—not the number of launchers. When your administration took office, we had 1,710 independently targetable reentry vehicles. Today, we have more than twice as many. By the end of 1975, we will have between 6,000 and 7,000."

"In retrospect," Smith later wrote, "the weak effort to ban MIRVs was a key aspect of SALT." The American SALT position, developed by Morton Halperin for President Johnson in 1968, had not pushed for a MIRV deployment ban, because the overriding concern then was to carry the Joint Chiefs of Staff along on the central aim of the negotiation—to avert a massive expenditure by both sides on anti-ballistic missile systems. Halperin did not think a MIRV ban was either politically or technically feasible. The Chiefs were hostile to any restraint on MIRVs under Johnson, and they were just as hostile under Nixon, arguing that MIRV was needed for hard target coverage as well as penetration, and that anyway it was the only ongoing U.S. program in which there was substantial U.S. lead time.

Both Kissinger and Nixon agreed to a MIRV ban proposal as one of the options for the Vienna SALT negotiations commencing in April 1970. But, at the insistence of the Joint Chiefs of Staff, the MIRV proposal was absolutely tied to an on-site inspection provision which was known to be unacceptable to the Soviet Union. Since the United States would be giving up penetration aids if it gave up gave up MIRV, the Chiefs argued that on-site inspections would then have to extend to anything that might conceal ABM systems. It would, for example, require inspection of anti-aircraft batteries. This was not a proposal designed for serious consideration, and it wasn't treated as such by either side in the negotiations. In turn, the Soviets tabled a document that called for the banning of the prodution and deployment of multiple warheads, but not their testing. It was to be verified by "national means" and not by on-site inspection.

As the chairman of the Joint Chiefs of Staff, General Jones, recalled of the SALT I package during the SALT II hearings in 1979: "There was some consideration about going for MIRV limits, and the military recommended against that."

That is as far as the MIRV negotiations, which could have prevented the problem of Minuteman vulnerability which led to the MX, ever went. Neither side was really serious about a MIRV ban. The Soviets did not seem to have the same concern about missile vulnerability. The U.S. military did not look far enough ahead. Nixon did not want "too much traffic" on the road. But, as Smith later wrote, the U.S. still wanted to "look good." After the United States definitely withdrew the MIRV ban proposal in July 1970, Smith wrote, "we continued to state for the record that we would press for them in subsequent negotiations."

Could a ban have worked? One big problem at the time was how a ban could be verified, since MIRVs are hidden under the shroud of the missiles cone. But on-site inspection would not have solved that problem, since MIRVs could easily have beeninstalled once the inspectors had left. "It's a screwdriver job," remarks Smith. Kissinger later wrote that the Soviets were only interested in a MIRV ban to the extent that it involved production and deployment, so that it would constrain the United States but not prevent the Soviet Union from catching up with the technology. This is perfectly true but, since they were going to catch up anyway, and everybody knew they would, how much better it would have been to have an agreement that neither side would deploy them! When a similar inspection problem arose in SALT II, it was satisfactorily handled by the formula that any missile tested with MIRVs was assumed to have MIRVs in all missiles from that class of missile, and they are counted toward an agreed number of MIRVed launchers. So technical means proved sufficient. But, in SALT I, by holding on to an evanescent advantage, the U.S. deepened its own strategic problem. As Smith later concluded, since MIRV was effectively not negotiable, there was very little for the two sides to agree on, and there would be no treaty limiting offensive weapons.

Recalling the issue in 1981, Smith said, "I think the chances [of getting a MIRV ban] were slim with the best will in the world on the part of our political masters. I think it was a long shot. I think there were possible compromises that would have allowed Soviets to develop MIRV, but not produce or deploy it. The monitoring would have been limited to what has apparently been satisfactory in SALT II. All launchers that had been observed to be used in testing MIRVs would be presumed to have MIRVs in that type of launcher."

In December 1974, six years after he had been invited to meet president-elect Nixon at New York Hotel Pierre, Kissinger made an unusually candid confession at a press briefing. Asked if he was now sorry that the United States had deployed multiple independently targeted warheads on its sea and land missiles in 1969, he replied, "Well, that's a good question. And I think that is the same question that people faced when the hydrogen bomb was developed. It raises the issue of whether your development of MIRVs or of a weapon produces the development of the other side, or whether, by not going ahead, you simply give an advantage to the other side. I would say, in retrospect, that I wish I had thought through the implications of a MIRVs world more thoughtfully in 1969 and 1970 than I did."

One of those implications was MX.

For the sake of the SALT talks, Kissinger held back both on changes in theory and on the introduction of new weapons other than MIRVs. But the crisis in Jordan in September 1970, which demonstrated to him the impotency of nuclear weapons, led him to press for a review of U.S. targeting strategy. This was an ad hoc targeting study panel, chaired by Dr. John Foster, who had succeeded Harold Brown as director for defense research and engineering. The staff panel for the study was headed by General Jasper Welch, who would later head some of the key MX studies and join the National Security Council staff under Dr. Brzezinski.

According to a participant, the Foster panel was not about countersilo targeting, though it was widely believed that it was. A review of the record of discussions by one participant shows only one forty-five-minute discussion of hard target kill or Minuteman vulnerability. This was partly because Senator Brooke was effectively attacking the idea of hard target kill, which in this context meant attacking Soviet missiles in their silos, and it was inappropriate to pursue what had become a policy issue in a targeting study. The study was linked to the experience of the Jordan crisis, and accordingly the targets and options it reviewed were all connected with theater support or operations outside the main battlefield in Europe. The conceptual point, according to one

participant, "was to bring U.S. strategic forces to bear politically and develop contingency plans for actual use in non-
central campaigns."

The key distinction was between the use of nuclear weapons in regions like the Persian Gulf, and their use on Soviet
territory. The underlying assumption was that it might be
possible to use nuclear weapons to support some kind of U.S.
objective in a region without causing a Soviet nuclear attack
on the United States. An attack on Soviet soil, on the other
hand, even if it was only an attack on a remote missile site,
would call forth an attack on U.S. soil.

The precise message of this study was obscured by the
appointment of Dr. Schlesinger as secretary of defense long
after the study had been completed but before the Nuclear
Weapons Employment Policy based on it had been signed.
The Foster panel had finished a draft that could be signed by
the secretary of defense in May of 1972. It was then sent over
to the White House. Kissinger asked for it to be redone as an
interagency study. This was carried out under the rubric of
National Security Study Memorandum 169, and lasted from
June of 1972 to January 1974. In early 1974 it was codified
for the president as National Security Decision Memorandum 242, which then went to Dr. Schlesinger as the Nuclear
Weapons Employment Policy he signed out in April 1974. At
the beginning of January, Schlesinger had foreshadowed the
changes in a speech to the Overseas Writers' Association in
Washington. The issues in nssm 169 were actually such
things as whether a change in targeting ought to be announced or not, and what would happen if nuclear weapons
were used in regional conflicts. But Schlesinger had believed
for some time that, if nuclear weapons were used against the
Soviet homeland as part of a campaign on the periphery, the
Soviet Union would not escalate but would run for the bargaining table. He had expressed this view in rand reports,
so when he announced the changes in January 1974, most
people assumed that "flexible options" meant limited at-

tacks on the Soviet Union.

The air force and Joint Chiefs were anxious to draw a distinction between counterforce attacks, which meant attacks on Soviet silos, and "flexible response," which in this context meant the ability of the United States to use nuclear weapons in "non-central campaigns." These might either involve Soviet troops, or only the troops of some third nation, but the distinguishing characteristic was that weapons would not be directed at either the Soviet homeland or the territory of America's European allies. It is hard to say now which idea—that the United States should be able to destroy Soviet silos, or that it could initiate the use of nuclear weapons against, say, Syria—was the most threatening and ill considered. At all events, the only weapons that were rationalised by reference to the new targeting policy were the kind of weapons suitable for attacking Soviet silos. The right weapon for a limited war is presumably a single warhead weapon of relatively low explosive power. The kind of weapons developed after NSDM 242 were heavy accurate weapons with many warheads.

The distinction between countersilos and limited attacks was one soon lost in the presentation of the new policy by Dr. Schlesinger. In a press conference in August 1973 he had said that the United States had not foresworn efforts to "acquire precision instruments that would be used in a limited counterforce role," thus straddling both concepts. At the same time Schlesinger repeatedly made public his view that if the Soviet Union was going to place many warheads on its heavy missiles then the United States would have to push ahead with its own heavy missile programs, which meant the MX.

National Security Decision Memorandum 242 focused on flexibility and for the first time included tactical and theater nuclear weapons in the overall targeting plans. Although Robert McNamara had introduced the damage-limiting strategy in 1962, the targeting plans had remained as they were under General LeMay in 1948—a massive strike against Soviet and Warsaw Pact industrial and military installations. The new order listed four categories of targets. The first basic instruction remained as it had under McNamara's policy of assured destruction: Under all circumstances, the strategic forces must be able to destroy 70 per cent of Soviet industry.

An important terminological distinction was introduced by Dr. Schlesinger's predecessor, Elliot Richardson. Under McNamara's directives, the strategic forces were required to destroy a quarter of the Soviet population. As amended by Secretary Richardson in compliance with State Department advice, there was no mention of civilian casualties. Since Soviet industry was in Soviet cities—that, after all, is why cities exist—the deletion of a requirement for civilian casualties made no difference whatsoever to the targeting of forces. Under NSDM 242 this first category of targets was allocated from one hundred fifty to four hundred weapons.

The second category was the political and military leadership of the Soviet Union. Since these leaders would be dispersed and protected in time of crisis, there was a total of two thousand targets in this category. The third category for attack was continental military forces of the Soviet Union, with the number of targets depending on the deployment of forces, and how far they had reached into Western Europe in the most likely war scenario.

The final category of targets, designated 4 Charley, was the nuclear forces of the Soviet Union. This included missiles, bomber bases, and submarine pens, together with command and control facilities—a total of about three thousand targets.

The fact that the nuclear forces of the Soviet Union came fourth in the target list and that the first category of industrial destruction was the only one that specified a required proportion of damage, prompted some insiders who were briefed on NSDM 242 to conclude that the new policy was very like the "assured destruction" policy of McNamara's final years in defense, with the three other categories merely thrown in to provide targets for the much greater number of warheads that came into the MIRV program. This was an important misinterpretation of what NSDM 242 really meant. The first category of targets were those that the targeters must be confident they could destroy in any circumstances, but it was not the category that would necessarily be attacked first, nor did it require anything more than a fraction of the weapons available. There was no longer a requirement for a single massive attack, and accordingly the new doctrine justified the development and deployment of weapons that would be used in a graduated attack—the kind of powerful, quick, and accurate weapons, known as "time urgent hard target kill" weapons in the Pentagon, that threatened the Soviet Union's rocket forces.

Among the people who developed 242 there was a profound difference of emphasis, even on the question of what "flexible response" meant. To some, reflecting one inspiration of the targeting study in Henry Kissinger's realization that the threat to use nuclear weapons had no meaning in a crisis like that in Jordan, "flexible response" meant primarily the ability to use nuclear weapons other than on Soviet territory. One set of options now included in the targeting plans allowed for the possibility of using weapons in these "non-central" theaters. But another and ultimately more powerful interpretation of "flexible response" was that it meant the ability to conduct limited strikes against the Soviet Union, and particularly against Soviet missile silos. This was an interpretation strongly emphasized by Dr. Schlesinger, who added more options for targeting Soviet missile silos to the NSDM 242 drafts.

In a closed meeting of the Senate Foreign Relations Committee in September 1974, Dr. Schlesinger elaborated on his views. He hypothesized that if the United States threatened to use nuclear weapons to stop a Soviet invasion of Western

Europe, the Soviet Union might conclude it should wipe out as much of America's nuclear retaliatory forces as it could. "In effect," he said, "the Soviet Union would be sending a message to the United States that it had badly crippled our military strength and that we had better desist from war— that the Soviet Union has won its objectives. Those are the kinds of circumstances that one could hypothesize."

This was an argument for America having a greater "counterforce" ability against the Soviet Union. But it didn't add up. The Soviet Union would be just as likely, perhaps more likely, to attack America's nuclear forces if they had the ability to attack Soviet nuclear forces. It is an argument for having less vulnerable forces, but not for having more accurate weapons. Confronted with this difficulty, Dr. Schlesinger had an alternative argument, which was that it looked bad if the Soviet Union had a greater ability to attack American silos than America had to attack Soviet silos. It was an argument about the presumed "perceptions" of people who were not sufficiently knowledgeable about nuclear weapons to realize that there was no point in a strike against some but not all American nuclear weapons. And, in the case of American weapons, the proportion of warheads actually at risk from a Soviet rocket attack was always less than the proportion of Soviet warheads at risk from an American attack, since the Soviet Union deployed so many more of its warheads in silos. The only real point in having silo killers is to use them while Soviet rockets are still in their silos, to try and reduce the force of the subsequent Soviet strike. But the problem with this is the problem first seen by Brodie in 1946—even if the counterforce strike is as effective as it possibly can be, there will be more than enough Soviet weapons left over to utterly destroy the United States, and the extent of damage caused by a successful counterforce strike would compel the Soviet Union to respond with a general attack on American cities.

Although Dr. Schlesinger was at pains to assert that the

new strategy did not require more accurate weapons, it clearly did—and all the development of American weapons was explicitly in the direction of greater accuracy.

Dr. Schlesinger added another criterion to U.S. weapons development, which augmented the case for more accurate silo killers. This was that the Soviet Union was developing a hard target kill capability, and the United States could not allow an "assymetry" to develop. "It would be impermissible," he told the Overseas Press Club in 1973, "to allow the Soviet Union to develop a countersilo assymetry."

When Schlesinger walked into his Pentagon office in April 1973, the MX missile was one of several hundred items on the services' wish lists, only a few of which would ever be produced. Henry Kissinger didn't like mobile missiles, and the U.S. had announced at the time of the first SALT agreement in 1973 that the deployment of mobile missiles would be inconsistent with the agreement. Congress had expressed displeasure with any type of nuclear weapon that had the capability to destroy Soviet nuclear missiles and thus diminish their confidence in their nuclear deterrent. In 1971 the conservative senator from New York, James Buckley, had mustered only a few votes on the Senate floor when he moved to fund programs to increase the power and accuracy of U.S. missiles.

The MX proposal had two aspects: One was the greater power and accuracy of the new missile. The other was its mobility. One aspect was designed to threaten Soviet missiles, the other to protect against the threat of Soviet missiles. If the counterforce threat presented by the new missile had a long history, so did the new way of basing it.

It was for Schlesinger to point to the obvious—that, if the Soviet Union married its very heavy land missiles with America's MIRV technology, it would eventually be able to threaten America's missiles with a first strike, and it would ultimately have a greater countersilo capability than the United States.

His appointment coincided neatly with two developments in the Soviet Union that supported his argument for more accurate and more powerful weapons based more securely. The first of these developments was the testing of Soviet multiple independent warheads in August 1973, three months after the Senate had consented to Schlesinger's nomination. He announced the Soviet test with great publicity and the direst warnings, adding that the U.S. could no longer refrain from adding to its arsenal the accurate and powerful weapons required for the "surgical extraction" of selected targets. The U.S. had developed and tested multiple independent warheads a decade before, and at the time of the Soviet test was deploying thousands of these on its Minuteman III and Poseidon missiles, but this precedent was of no significance to Schlesinger and was soon lost in the debate. The second Soviet development was the testing of four new missiles. This was of less significance, because the missiles were lighter than the SS9 already deployed. The only improvement was that they might have multiple warheads. Thus, for Schlesinger to cite both the new missiles and MIRVs as demanding a U.S. response was double-counting.

The Soviet MIRV served a very important purpose for Schlesinger—it was fuel for the assault against Henry Kissinger and the detente policies with which he was identified. Schlesinger argued that the Soviet MIRV and the new missiles illustrated that the Soviet Union was unsatisfied with "essential equivalence" and wanted nuclear superiority—although it had been assumed by the American side in the SALT negotiations that it was only a matter of time before the Soviets deployed a MIRV. He also argued that, since the Soviet Union already had more land missiles than the United States and these missiles had more lifting power than U.S. missiles, the Soviets could one day threaten to knock out land-based American missiles by putting multiple warheads on their missiles and striking first. This was quite true, of course, and it had been predicted by liberal opponents of the

multiple warhead technology. The liberal Republican Senator Brooke had told Kissinger in 1971 that, to produce MIRVs,
would be "to let the genie out of the bottle," and the *New
York Times* had begged the new Nixon administration in
1969 to halt the MIRV program. But the Joint Chiefs had
been, according to Kissinger, "passionately in favor" of
MIRVs, the U.S. had gone ahead, and now the Soviet Union
had caught up.

Schlesinger said that, if the Soviets were to go ahead and
deploy multiple independent warheads, then the U.S. would
have to make its missiles less vulnerable. Thus, the research
into mobile missiles. And if the Soviet Union was going to
have so many quick, accurate warheads, why then the U.S.
must have more, too. Thus, the big missile with many accurate warheads. Together, the two responses could be contained in the one system, which was the MX.

Schlesinger brought all these thoughts together in his February 1974 Report of the Secretary of Defense. Normally a
tedious committee document, important parts of the report
were on this occasion written by Schlesinger, and it still
stands as one of the turning points in the history of nuclear
weaponry. He wrote then that, as the Soviet Union closed its
gap with the United States, more options were needed than
the threat of massive retaliation on cities, which the Soviet
Union could now do equally as well as the United States.
Accordingly, as a first step, Schlesinger had changed the
targeting plans for the U.S. nuclear forces. Before, the targets had included factories and military installations, but
only as part of a "relatively massive response." Now, the
president was to be provided with a wider set of more selective options. The new targeting policy was flexible response
"in such a way as to limit the chances for uncontrolled escalation, and hit meaningful targets with a sufficient accuracy
yield combination to destroy only the intended target and
avoid widespread collateral damage."

However, Schlesinger added, there still remained the

problem of Soviet lifting power or "throwweight," which, "combined with increased accuracy and MIRVs, would give the Soviets on the order of 7,000 one to two megaton warheads in the ICBM force alone. They would then possess a major one-sided counterforce capability against the United States ICBM force. This is impermissible from our point of view. There must be essential equivalence between the strategic forces of the United States and the U.S.S.R. . . ."

This Soviet development, plus the new requirement for flexible response, became the argument for a new weapon. "To enhance deterrence," he wrote, "we also want a more efficient hard target kill capability than we now possess: both to threaten specialized sets of targets with greater economy of force, and to make it clear to a potential enemy that he cannot with impunity proceed to threaten our own system of hard targets."

"To ensure" therefore "a realistic option to modernize our ICBM forces in the 1980s, we are requesting about $37 million in fiscal year 1975 for advanced technology leading to the development of an entirely new ICBM. We are considering the technologies for both a new large payload fixed base missile which could be launched from the existing Minuteman silos, and a new mobile missile, either ground or air launched." It would have, he promised, "a very good capability against hard targets," and would make it clear to the Soviets that they could not "proceed with impunity to jeopardize our own system of hard targets." This program was already referred to within the air force as Missile Experimental, or simply "MX."

3

Peace Is Our Profession

RIGHT up to 1948, the U.S. Air Force base on the outskirts of Omaha, Nebraska, had been too far away from the centers of command and activity on the coasts to be a much sought-after posting. It was home to the 61st Balloon Unit in the First World War and a camp for Italian prisoners of war in the Second World War. But soon after that conflict was ended with the bombing of Hiroshima and Nagasaki, the fact that Omaha was so far away from everything—that it was more or less in the center of the continental United States —became a great advantage. With the invention of atomic weapons and the expectation that the Soviet Union would soon acquire what the United States already possessed, the nature of warfare completely changed. For the first time, the United States itself was vulnerable to a devastating attack, and so the command center for American nuclear weapons had to be moved from Washington to the interior. In 1948 the Strategic Air Command, soon to be headed by General Curtis E. LeMay, moved from Andrews Air Force Base near Washington, D.C., to Offutt Air Force Base, Omaha, one of the first of many such moves in the American nuclear forces that would be made in response to or in anticipation of vulnerability to Soviet attack.

The base is tightly secured. Visitors are driven past the SAC Peace Is Our Profession signs through guarded gates to a guarded entrance hall, where they are issued numbered passes. Security tightens as they proceed under escort by blue-uniformed SAC officers past the public affairs division, the briefing rooms, the service floors, down into the three stories of underground halls and offices. Surrendering their cameras and tape recorders, encumbered by heavy briefing folders, warned to press flat against the walls if they hear emergency warnings, the visitors file along tiled floors and green-painted walls, past red klaxons and hostile guards, down into the dimly lit, cavernous command post.

This underground half of the building is stupendously solid. It has a two-foot thick concrete base, a two-foot thick concrete roof, and two-foot thick concrete walls. Huge steel doors seal off the underground stories from the three stories above. There are enough supplies and enough room down here to feed and water and maintain eight hundred people for two weeks. The command post is fifty feet below ground. It is twenty-one feet high, one hundred and forty-nine feet long, and thirty-nine feet wide, a vast room equipped with six display screens, each sixteen feet by sixteen feet, which can accommodate simultaneously sixteen different sets of graphics in seven colors and two sizes. In front of the display screens, the battle support staff sit before consoles littered with ashtrays, Coke cans, and styrofoam coffee cups, amid teletype boards and switching systems. Those display screens are the center of the center, flashing up-to-the-minute reports on the status of all the missiles and bombers and submarines at sea that carry thermonuclear weapons. From this command post, through a gray phone that connects the controlling colonel with an underground cable and a red phone that connects him with two hundred stations worldwide by two separate surface communications systems, the Strategic Air Command can reach 154 missile launch control centers throughout the United States, the U.S. weather service, the North American Air Defense Command deep in Cheyenne Mountain, Colorado, the air force bomber bases, the submarine communications stations, and the early-warning posts throughout the world. The controlling colonel can also reach the White House and the military aides carrying the "football," the guidance kit for nuclear war, traveling with the president. He can reach the second-story Command Center at the Pentagon, the underground alternative command center at Mount Richie, seventy miles from Washington, the SAC general aloft in the Looking Glass command plane, and he can reach the converted 747 on the apron at Andrews, the Doomsday plane which waits twenty-four hours a day to carry the president, vice-president, and their authorized and designated deputies and successors away from the nuclear detonations below.

Those heavy briefing folders tell of a precise and detailed sequence that would commence were it ever necessary to use the nuclear weapons at the president's disposal. In time of war, the visitors are told, the great steel doors would be sealed, the commander-in-chief of the Strategic Air Command (CINCSAC) and his senior staff would report down here and convene on the balcony overlooking the command post. Battle staff members would take their designated positions on the command post floor. Seated in his lounge chair with his aides and telephones around him, the commander would communicate with the Joint Chiefs of Staff at the Pentagon Command Center, with the president (who would have reviewed the optional battle plans listed in the "football" materials), and he would pass their commands along to the 154 missile launch control centers, the 350 bombers, the submarines at sea. The commanding colonel would relay the orders through the red phone, they would be printed out in the launch control centers and decoded by the missileers, the launch procedures would be activated, and the missiles launched or retained according to their preprogrammed battle computers. As the weapons were unleashed, the SAC automated command control system would record the progress of the strike force, serving—so says the SAC briefing material—as an invaluable aid to the commander in making decisions. Information would be processed automatically, giving the battle staff immediate and continuous updates on the strike force as it flew toward the Soviet heartland.

So go the SAC handouts given to the multitude of tourists and business people and reporters and politicians and congressional staff and television teams and foreign visitors who every day file through the command post, hearing the same warning to press against the wall if the holocaust begins, submitting to the same security checks, listening to the same briefings, sitting in the CINCSAC lounge chair on the dimly lit command balcony, watching with awe as the commanding colonel is instructed by the briefing officer to call up Beale station in California on the Pave Paws network, or the Andersen Air Force Base on Guam, or the general circling the skies over Omaha.

So goes the visit, so goes the briefing. But, as the SAC people cheerfully concede, nuclear war probably would not go so. In a real war, the heavy steel doors and the two feet of concrete and the three stories of underground command post and the two separate above ground communications systems and the below ground system and the radio antennae would be blown away in an instant, along with the hostile guards, the eight hundred people and their food, the seven-color two-size sixteen-panel display board, the ashtrays and coffee cups, the gray phone and the red phone, the CINCSAC general and his lounge chair and his aides—all would turn to dust and gas within the first thirty minutes, and so would the White House, the Pentagon, the underground base at Mount Richie, Andrews Air Force Base, and every fixed terrestrial structure of military interest to the Soviet Union, within the limits of the six thousand to eight thousand warheads it would have at its disposal. All that would remain is the circling airplane, the EC135, with its black-shuttered windows and its commanding general, a plane with seventy-two hours of refueled air life before it burns its oil, its occupants having only the vaguest idea of what forces they have left and what damage has already been done, circling in an ionosphere so distressed they could communicate only within a line of sight, landing and ascending until they run out of oil and fuel and places to land and a sense of purpose.

The Offutt SAC headquarters, the elaborate security, the red klaxons, the warnings to clear the halls, the elaborate video briefings—they are all props for SAC's theater of deterrence, parts of a public relations enterprise intended to win money for planes, missiles, and bombs. What would actually happen after NUDET, the first nuclear detonation on U.S. soil, is one of the underlying issues in the decade-old debate about MX. Whatever it is, it will probably not involve the Offutt Air Force Base, Omaha, Nebraska, and we will not find an answer to the imponderables of nuclear war in the fat briefing folders issued therefrom.

Three decades of controversy in Washington about nuclear doctrine have not meant a great deal in Minot, North Dakota, home of the two strategic missile wings and two bomber wings of the 57th Air Division. Together with its companion base a few miles south at Grand Forks, the U.S. Air Force base at Minot deploys nearly half of America's interncontinental ballistic missile warheads—one hundred-fifty Minuteman III missiles at each base, each with three Mark 12A warheads. Cramped into the six-foot-long cone of the warhead is a hydrogen bomb of recent model which, together with its atom bomb trigger, is euphemistically dubbed "the physics package" by the Strategic Air Command. Since each physics package packs seventeen times the explosive power of the "thin man" dropped on Hiroshima in August 1945, the total explosive power of the three hundred missiles at Minot is twenty-two thousand times the Hiroshima explosion. The missiles alone total three times the destructive power that Robert McNamara's planners calculated was necessary to destroy half of Soviet industry and a quarter of the Soviet people, yet they are only one-tenth of the number of strategic nuclear warheads that the United States now deploys in land and sea missiles and in its B52 bombers. Spread out over the black soil of the wheat and beef-cattle country of the thinly populated northern state, Minot has, along with the Warren Air Force Base near Cheyenne, Wyoming, one of the most powerful concentrations of forces in the history of the world. Were all the missiles at Minot released and all the B52 bombers ordered off to their targets, Soviet industry and cities and armed forces would be decimated. Were the Soviet Union to strike first with its still more powerful missiles, the explosions on and above the missile silos would be of the same order of magnitude, and Minot's black soil, now airborne and lethally radioactive, would poison the northern United States and southern Canada.

That could happen tomorrow, but today Minot Air Force Base is organized around training routines, guard duties, competitions, public relations exercises, graduate study, war games, and ball games—anything that will serve to relieve the boredom of the missileer. The trophy case of the 91st Strategic Missile Wing displays the Colonel Lee R. Williams Memorial Missile Trophy and the Omaha Trophy for the Best Missile Wing. Competitions keep spirits up. A more lachrymose sign of the missileer's life is a verse by Missileer Captain Robert A. Wyckoff, pasted up behind the door of a Minot training room:

> *Behind a concrete door slammed shut*
> *No starlit skies of night*
> *No sunbleached clouds in azure sky*
> *In which to dance in flight . . .*
> *In boredom fluxed with stress*
> *Encapsuled they reside.*

For every ten missile silos there is one underground launch control center and, behind its concrete door slammed shut, a cheerless concrete room, crowded with communications and monitoring equipment. Each launch control center is manned twenty-four hours a day by two missileers of the 91st Strategic Missile Wing.

Today's missileer is a twenty-seven-year-old male college graduate, with a ninety-day course in missile control procedures behind him, who doesn't like his job. A lot of missileers want to become pilots. A good indication of the level of interest in the two jobs is given by the relative cost of training. In 1979 it cost the air force $375,000 to train a pilot in the complexities of flying a B52 bomber. It cost $22,000 to train a missile crew member.

The targets each missile will seek are already programmed into its on-board computer, which can simultaneously retain a hundred targets. One of the duties of the two-man launch control team is to change the targeting kits and execution plans in response to commands from Offutt, which are then transmitted into the missile guidance computer. Most of the training procedures focus on the missile launch order, since the two absolutely essential requirements in controlling missiles are to prevent an unauthorized launch, and, at the same time, to make an authorized launch so routine that the missileers won't be overawed by it. To prevent an unauthorized launch, there are always two men on the launch control team, each of whom has a key. They are separated from each other by a distance of about twelve feet, making it impossible for one to switch his key, overpower the other, and switch his key as well to complete the launch sequence within the required time. Even when the two-man sequence is completed, any other launch control center may countermand the order, and it will need another supporting launch control center to restart it. To make an authorized launch routine, missileers are trained and retrained in the launch procedures, and especially in the procedure of the missile combat crew commander and deputy missile combat crew commander, each unlocking one of the two locks on a red box marked "Entry Restricted To MCCC And DMCCC" withdrawing their orders, and following the sequence to the launch command. Each of the two missileers has before him a brightly colored panel which displays the sequence of steps from the command from Offutt to the missile's blast off. Happily, most orders do not go beyond the "not authenticated" panel, which assures the missileers that the doomsday instruction is just a check on their alertness. Only in the training capsules do the panels light up in changing colors from "stand by" to "launch command," "launch in progress," and the final "missile away."

Once trained in these two vital operations—not sending missiles and sending missiles—the missileer's major problem is not the threat that twenty-five Soviet bombs will explode over his head, but that he will be bored miserable in his bunker. Responding to this problem, the authorities have provided some of the symbols of the romance of the air force. Missileers wear colored silk scarves (yellow for instructors, red, green, and blue for the various grades of missile combat crew commanders), carry .38 caliber revolvers to their subterranean, unmolested workplaces, and use pilot's language. A missile is "a bird," one alert missile a "sortie," ten missiles are called a "flight," and a twenty-four hour tour of duty is an "alert." The launch control center is got up to resemble a cockpit, down to the red seatbelts which, it is said, will assist the missile combat crew commander and the deputy missile combat crew commander ride out, in their gimballed and hydraulically balanced capsule, a nuclear attack above.

Writing more than a decade ago about the life of the missileer, a former combat crew commander recorded that "Capsule life is spartan. Once we are locked in and are in comfortable clothes, we sit. No entertainment is available to pass the endless hours. There is infrequent maintenance activity to relieve the monotony. There is constant equipment noise. The many alarms are loud enough to alert a hangar instead of gaining our attention in a tiny, enclosed capsule. Rube Goldberg contraptions are devised to silence them. A capsule tour is long hours of quiet boredom. To pass the time, crew members place endless phone calls to family and friends. Occasionally an officer takes a game or a model airplane into the capsule." Today, working conditions have been liberalized. Inside the capsule on a typically uneventful day, the combat crew are officially said to be Studying Their Technical Orders, decoding routine alerts, and checking for defects in the missiles under their control. They do these things, which are designed to keep them awake. But, however sedulously they study their orders, they will still have time on their hands. At Minot, the most serious threat to the placidity of the missileer's ride are jack rabbits as big as terriers which frequently hit the defense perimeter of the missile silos. In winter, a big problem is snowdrifts on the defense perimeters that, like the jack rabbits, sets off security alarms. Most of the time missileers are bored. They call their wives and friends, listen to the AM/FM radio, watch TV, play games, and read books. All these privileges have been introduced as the Strategic Air Command tries to meet the dissatisfaction of the crews. At Minot, the missileers frequently work on their business master's from the University of North Dakota. More than a decade ago, SAC General Holloway testified that "the life of the missileer is intrinsically boring and monotonous," but said one good way to relieve it was through the education program. "We now offer to almost all Minuteman crews the chance to get a Master's degree," he said. "I went down to the University of Missouri at Whiteman [Air Force Base], about three months ago, and awarded 167 Master's degrees."

How would the missileers perform in a real war? If the Soviet Union struck first and the United States did not choose to launch its missiles at the first sign of an attack, the missileers would not have a chance to do anything. Each launch control center has an emergency generator and a supply of food and water intended to support the crew when the base above is destroyed. They are provided with digging tools and an escape shaft intended for use when the nuclear exchange is concluded. In practice, the launch control centers, though they are concreted and gimballed, cannot stand either a direct hit or a near miss from a nuclear weapon, so most combat crews will be killed with the first NUDETS.

If the U.S. launches some or all of its missiles first, then the combat crews can be expected to perform their awesome jobs in a routine manner. But there is ground to wonder whether the order will not be processed as automatically as the Strategic Air Command expects. Ted Wye, who was a missileer captain for three years, recalled that "A controller at SAC headquarters once mumbled a missile alert message over a live mike while practicing. Realizing his error, he closed with Oh Shit. Less than half the missile wings responded, even though we were taught to react to any correctly decoded message, no matter how received."

The missile combat crew commander and deputy missile combat crew commander watching television in the launch control center buried underground in North Dakota are the end of a long chain of command which is said, in the briefings to congressional committees, in the annual reports of the secretary of defense, and the promotional literature handed out by the Strategic Air Command, to stretch all the way from the president, through the Joint Chiefs of Staff, to the SAC command room at Offutt, to the pilots and missileers in the United States, the patrolling submarine commanders, and the U.S. commanders-in-chief of Europe, the Atlantic and Pacific, through the worldwide military command and control system.

Planning for nuclear war, the targeting of the forces is said to come from the top down. According to the organization charts, nuclear targeting begins with a National Security Decision Memorandum issued by the president after discussion with the National Security Council, a statutory

body that includes the secretary of defense, the secretary of
state, the chairman of the Joint Chiefs of Staff, the national
security assistant, and other officials in Washington.

It is said that the secretary of defense then examines the
National Security Decision Memorandum issued by the president and gives two documents to the Joint Chiefs of Staff.
One is the Defense Guidance, which tells the forces what
weapons they should procure and maintain. The other is the
NUWEP, the Nuclear Weapons Employment Policy, which
tells the defense forces how they should use their weapons.
The chairman of the Joint Chiefs of Staff then issues a document to the commander-in-chief, Strategic Air Command,
and, in accordance with NUWEP, the Joint Strategic Target
Planning Staff at Offutt prepare the Single Integrated Operational Plan, or SIOP. Single, in this sense, does not mean
that there is only one plan—actually there are hundreds and
hundreds of plans—but that there is only one command covering the use of weapons held by the navy as well as by the
air force and by the NATO armies in Europe. The essential
SIOP directive is to "employ forces to control conflict and
quickly terminate on terms favorable to us." That simple
sentence, of course, conceals a lot of arguments about how
the forces ought to be employed, and what those forces
should be.

This is the briefer's description of reality, with the emphasis placed on orders coming down from Mr. President. In
practice, the president makes very little contribution to the
details of nuclear targeting, and the broad outlines of the
strategy are determined by the characteristics and numbers
of the weapons. The decision that comes down to the secretary of defense has, in practice, gone up from the secretary
of defense some weeks or months before, and he is in turn
advised by the Joint Chiefs and the war gamers, analysts,
combat commanders in the Strategic Air Command, and
civilian strategists in the Pentagon.

Publicly visible people, like secretaries of defense and national security advisers, like to give the impression they are in charge of these matters, but the officers at the Strategic Air Command, who have control over the actual plans, have always done things pretty much their own way. On the great question of targeting cities versus targeting Soviet military forces, for example, SAC has been far more influenced by the number of weapons it has at its command, their accuracies, and the amount of intelligence available on the location and vulnerabilities of Soviet forces, than it has been by the intermittent, ferocious debates in Washington. SAC has always targeted as many military sites as it could. As General David Jones, a former SAC officer who became the chairman of the Joint Chiefs, told the Senate Armed Services Committee SALT hearings in 1979, "We have always targeted military targets," and while one heard "a lot of rhetoric" in Washington, "the strategy always stayed the same in the implementation of targeting." Omaha is a long way from Washington.

Even as long ago as 1962, according to research by nuclear strategist Desmond Ball, the first and second attack options in the SIOP were aimed at the destruction of Russian nuclear and conventional forces. The mix of targets has remained much the same. Today, of the forty thousand targets listed in the SIOP—a tedious schedule of Russian names and map coordinates—more than half are military targets, compared to fifteen thousand economic and industrial targets. But if the mix has not changed, the number of targets and the number of weapons have grown hugely—with the target number always growing faster than the number of weapons available. From the Half Moon Joint Emergency War Plan in 1948 to the latest SIOP (5D), the number of targets has increased from ninety to forty thousand. At the same time, there has been a very big increase in the number of nuclear weapons available, from fifty atomic bombs in May 1948 to more than nine thousand thermonuclear bombs and missile reentry vehicles in the SIOP forces today.

Most of the increase has occurred over the decade of the

seventies, when the arms race was said to be controlled by SALT agreements. In 1974, for example, there were twenty-five thousand targets, compared to the forty thousand today. At the beginning of the seventies, the United States had less than 5,000 deliverable warheads. It had 1,910 separate warheads on its missiles in silos and at sea, and 2,800 gravity bombs and hound dog air-to-surface missiles, which are carried on the B52s. But, by 1976, the United States had 9,000 warheads, mostly because of the multiplication of the numbers of warheads on land and sea missiles in the Minuteman III and Poseidon submarine-launched ballistic missile programs. The Minuteman III carries three independently targetable warheads, compared to one on the Minuteman I, which it replaced. And the Poseidon missile carries between ten and fourteen warheads, compared to the three on Polaris.

The improvement was not just in numbers, but in accuracy as well. In 1970 the circular error probable (CEP) for the single warhead Minuteman II missile, which is the radius of the circle into which half the warheads are likely to fall, was two thousand feet, and three thousand feet for the Polaris submarine missile. There is no single CEP for a system—it depends on the reentry angle—but these figures represent what could be achieved. By 1980, with new guidance systems, the accuracy had been whittled down to six hundred feet for the land Minuteman III and twelve hundred to fifteen hundred feet for the Poseidon.

By 1980 the command and control had improved as well, with a new worldwide military command and control system, satellite communications systems, and improved communications for the submarine fleet. The decade of SALT witnessed an explosive growth in the number, accuracy, and control of the nuclear weapons in the American inventory.

The American effort was paced by the Soviet Union, which began deploying its first MIRVs in 1975. The number of warheads available to the Soviet Union increased from three thousand in 1975 to seven thousand in 1980, while the accuracies of its land missiles improved from a circular error probable of fifteen hundred to two thousand feet in 1975, to eight hundred fifty feet for its best land missile in 1980, to six hundred feet, the same as Minuteman, in the latest series of tests.

According to briefings before congressional committees, the Nuclear Weapons Employment Policy, NUWEP, sets up the requirements for the level of damage on the Soviet Union. One requirement, for example, is that the U.S. nuclear forces must in all conditions be able to destroy 70 per cent of the Soviet industry that would be needed to achieve recovery after war. The document is said to set out the planning assumptions, attack options, targeting objectives, and damage levels needed to satisfy the Defense Guidance.

The forty thousand locations on today's target list include military, industrial, and civilian targets. There is so little point in concealing the obvious that a defense official gave the Senate Armed Services Committee a sample target list in 1980. It looked like this:

SOVIET NUCLEAR FORCES

ICBMs and intermediate range ballistic missiles, together with their launch facilities and launch command centers.
Airfields supporting nuclear capable aircraft.
Nuclear submarine bases.

CONVENTIONAL MILITARY FORCES

Kasernes.
Supply depots.
Marshalling points.
Conventional airfields.
Ammunition storage facilities.
Tank and vehicle storage yards.

MILITARY AND POLITICAL LEADERSHIP
Command posts.
Key communications facilities.

ECONOMIC AND INDUSTRIAL TARGETS

War Supporting Industry:
Ammunition factories.
Tank and armored personnel carrier factories.
Petroleum refineries.
Railway yards and repair facilities.

Industries That Contribute To Economic Recovery:
Coal.
Basic steel.
Basic aluminum.
Cement.
Electric power.

Officially, the United States no longer aims at population "per se," but, since many of the forty thousand targets are in cities, the people will be destroyed anyway. As a defense official said in 1976: "Cities are economic targets."

We know from congressional hearings that these targets are now divided into four general categories of options by what the SIOP planners call a "ladder" process. The four general categories are Major Attack Options (MAOs), Selected Attack Options (SAOs), Limited Nuclear Options (LNOs), and Regional Nuclear Options (RNOs). Within each set of options is a wide range of further options, including the option to "withhold" some kinds of targets so there is a chance of ending the exchange. Four general categories of withholds have been publicly identified: national command and control centers; population centers; particular countries targeted in the SIOP; and "allied or neutral territory." There are also categories for preemptive strikes against the Soviet

Union, launch on warning or launch under attack options if there is unequivocal warning of a Soviet attack, and a general base plan for a massive retaliatory attack on the Soviet Union.

The really big job for the Joint Strategic Target Planning Staff, JSTPS, and the reason it needs banks of computers and highly trained programmers, is to choose the weapons for the various targets. This is difficult because the land missiles, submarine missiles, and B52 delivered bombs all have different characteristics. Land missiles are accurate and quick, but limited in number. Sea missile warheads are most abundant, but less accurate, hard to coordinate, and less powerful in their explosions. The B52's bombs are the most powerful and reasonably accurate, but the slowest to arrive on target. Although there are forty thousand targets, only a proportion of these can actually be attacked, since the United States has, at the most, ten thousand warheads. There would probably be many fewer in an actual war, since if the Soviet Union strikes first and catches United States nonalert bombers or submarines in port, about two-thirds of the bombers and nearly half the submarines will be destroyed. Nor will the remaining numbers of weapons be equal to the number of targets, because the planners cross-target their weapons, aiming a number at the same target to maximize the chance of destroying it. A percentage of missiles will not work when they are commanded to launch, a percentage will go awry on the flight to the Soviet Union, and a percentage will miss.

The planner's job is to match weapon range, yield, accuracy, and timeliness to target range, vulnerability, and time sensitivity. Not a simple job, when there are nine thousand weapons with different characteristics and forty thousand possible targets.

There has always been a very big difference between the way nuclear planning is seen at Offutt and the way it is seen in Washington. The first and biggest difference is that the Strategic Air Command has always targeted Soviet nuclear forces and other military installations as well as cities. Even when Washington was talking about relying on assured deterrence, the Strategic Air Command was targeting as many Soviet rockets, bombers, and submarines in port as it possibly could. The second and equally important difference is that the Strategic Air Command has never been very receptive to the idea that strategic nuclear war can be limited or controlled. Among civilian strategists, most people who favor targeting military sites in the Soviet Union do so because they think this is one way of controlling the war—by confining it to "countermilitary" exchanges and, at the same time, reducing the potential for damage to the United States. Their opponents, the city-busting school, argue that nuclear war cannot be controlled, and the best way to prevent it is threaten a single massive country-city attack. The Strategic Air Command didn't go along with either school. From General LeMay's first plans in 1948, SAC was committed to a single massive strike that would include both cities and military forces. When the Nixon administration took office in 1969, it found that, in spite of all the debate in the McNamara Defense Department, the actual strategic plans remained much as they were in 1960, when Defense Secretary Thomas Gates had first asked the services to come up with a joint plan for using nuclear weapons. One important result of this thinking at Offutt is that the Strategic Air Command does not favor weapons that could best be used for small exchanges. This is one explanation for the fact that MX is much more powerful than a weapon designed for limited nuclear war. It is a countersilo weapon for total war. SAC wants weapons that are big enough and accurate enough to take out Soviet missiles before they can all be fired. The only weapon capable of doing that now programmed for the SAC forces is the MX, which SAC first requested in 1971 with a requirement for "a system oriented advanced technology program for a replacement strategic missile for the 1980's."

In the mid-sixties, the Strategic Air Command, which has never departed from the idea that nuclear weapons, like any other weapons, are designed to destroy certain particular targets, had demanded a huge warhead for a new missile, accurate enough to would blow away the hardest of targets. Although studies continued under the code name WS120, the big warhead idea was refused by McNamara, who even refused a briefing on the subject. As MIRV technology was perfected in the late sixties, the Strategic Air Command leadership was persuaded that greater numbers at more accurate warheads were more valuable than smaller numbers of very big warheads, and it, too, began to support the MIRV program. Like MX, MIRVs had both offensive and defensive aspects, both hawkish and dovish proponents and opponents, and the arguments shifted about, as those for MX later would, depending on the audience and the political atmosphere. MIRV was designed to penetrate Soviet defenses against missile attack, and thus secure America's retaliatory capability and deter war. But MIRV was also designed to increase the number of American warheads to cover more Soviet targets, and thus had the effect of intensifying the arms competition. MIRV was both a soft target weapon and a hard target weapon, just as MX was to be both more mobile and more accurate, more threatening and less threatened, stabilizing and destablizing.

4

Senators and Generals

The dilemmas of ICBM survivability are devilish.
... Most proposed solutions for this problem seem
to have at the center seeds of new dilemmas.
—*Senator McIntyre, April 1977*

IN January 1974 John W. Hepfer, a diligent and thorough officer of the Air Force Systems Command, was sent from the Rome Air Development Center at Griffiss Air Force Base, New York, over to the West Coast to take charge of the growing MX program at Norton Air Force Base near San Bernadino, California. Hepfer, then fifty, had last been at Norton four years before, when he had taken over and successfully concluded a program to design and develop the all-important guidance system of the first MIRVed land missile, the Minuteman III. Hepfer, a Pennsylvanian who had flown combat missions as a navigator against the Japanese in the Pacific war, had earned his science degree after the war and first worked on the Navaho missile in the early fifties. He had risen quickly in an air force that was rapidly expanding its need for research and development specialists, and particularly specialists who knew about missile guidance.

Hepfer was not then and would never be a political general with the breadth of mind and capacity for deception that would take him to the front rank. He did what he was told, within reason. He thought the country was probably going to the dogs, he thought people who advocated minimum deterrence were probably communists or close to it, he thought Australia and South Africa were the last frontiers, and he read with interest and admiration the accounts of the rugged and enterprizing life of white South Africans described in South African government magazines which followed him, he knew not how, from one posting to another. But this lack of guile had its admirable side, and, when the time came for John Hepfer to retire at age fifty-five, he did not look for consultancies to industry or good jobs selling hardware to the air force or even a research job with an aerospace corporation. John Hepfer and his wife went down to Florida, where he amused himself building a computer.

Hepfer retired a general but, like most air force generals, he didn't look like a general. Not exactly short but certainly not tall, not exactly thin but certainly not imposing, General Hepfer had an intelligent, interesting, but not forceful presence. His job was to produce the weapons, to bring together the hundreds of workers, dozens of high-technology contractors, the various levels of the air force and defense hierarchy above and below him, and so far as it could be done smoothly with a system as contentious, as inherently difficult as MX, Hepfer did it.

When he arrived at Norton in the winter of 1974, MX had "category 1 importance" for the air staff, and the air force could see that the land missiles would one day be vulnerable —the Soviet buildup beginning 1965 promised that—and the preferred way around this was to put a new heavy missile in a long, covered trench—a four-thousand mile trench stretching over backlands in Utah, Nevada, and New Mexico, with a new missile on tracks every twenty miles or so. The trench would be built out of concrete one foot thick, and the missile on its transporter could be remotely controlled by above-ground operators. The idea had certain advantages—the trench was hidden, required few people to run it and consequently few would know of the missile's location. Once built, it would be invisible to the American public and to Soviet satellites. That, at least, is how the theory went. But if the idea appeared then to be technically feasible, it was, like most MX basing ideas, "counter-intuitive." That is to say, it sounded crazy. Certainly John Hepfer thought so when he was briefed by his subordinates on the project, and he told them very firmly, in that first week, that if they thought he was going to take the idea of a four-thousand mile trench to Washington, to the high-level Defense Systems Acquisitions Review Committee meetings in the basement of the Pentagon, and explain it there to the assembled chiefs of the air staff, the director of defense research and engineering, and the Joint Chiefs of Staff—well, they had another think coming.

The trench system had solid support at the top of the air force and at Strategic Air Command in Omaha, however, and so John Hepfer came in time to see its virtues. They were political rather than military, but they were persuasive. The continuous trench would become a series of shorter trenches, and it would always have its adherents in the air force.

The Norton command, which would soon be redesignated the Ballistic Missile Office, was one of the most complex in the service. It was supposed to supervise the development of weaponry, but, since the ultimate user of the weapon would be the Strategic Air Command, SAC insisted on following the development from inception to completion. So a SAC team, a representative of what is a semiautonomous barony in the air force, attended all the important meetings at Norton, and they could veto at an early stage any design specifications distasteful to the war-fighting mentality of Offutt. If there was a case for a lighter missile or a shorter missile or a less threatening missile or a basing mode that put more importance on allowing Soviet Satellites to verify the numbers deployed, then it wasn't considered seriously at the BMO. The politics of the cooperation with SAC, which had always wanted a big missile with countersilo capability, precluded it. SAC's job, specified in the program management directive issued seven months before Hepfer took command, was that "SAC will continue its effort to define and develop supporting rationale for mission requirements and derived ICBM capabilities." That meant SAC could say what the missile should do, and it could exclude candidates that didn't do what SAC wanted. It also meant that once the missile was being developed, SAC had to think up good reasons why it should be developed.

Norton was supposed to be an air force office, and officially it was, but the fact was that the air force didn't have and couldn't recruit the range of technical talents and managerial skills necessary to produce a highly sophisticated weapon. So another complexity in John Hepfer's command was the constant presence of a civilian contractor who actually handled most of the project. It was still up to the air force to decide what it wanted, but it was the civilian contractor who managed the program from day to day, who brought the various components in on schedule, and who controlled the performance of the subcontractors. Early on in his new command, Hepfer decided that TRW Corporation should have that job, and not the air force's own Aerospace Corporation, which had been set up for just that purpose. It was a difficult decision, made on the ground that TRW had better people and a better idea of the job, and Hepfer would have to fight back several times over the succeeding years as Aerospace counterattacked.

The Ballistic Missile Office was supposed to report directly to the Air Force Systems Command headquarters at Andrews, which in turn reported to the air staff, which in turn were supposed to deal with the office of the director of defense research and engineering. That was the formal chain of command, but it had long been subverted by more informal ties and would be again in the MX program. The fact was that the Ballistic Missile Office at San Bernadino and the director of defense research and engineering on the third floor at the Pentagon knew much more about the job in hand than any of the intervening commands, and so in practice agreements made between those two offices determined what happened with the program. This had been the case with MIRV, and under the Carter administration it would be the case with MX. Twice during the Ford administration, the air force staff intervened to direct changes in the Norton program. On neither occasion would the changes actually be put into effect.

The public perception of the air force is that its appetite for spending on missiles and advanced nuclear weaponry is unappeasable. From within the air force, however, and especially from within the Ballistic Missile Office at Norton, the perception is quite different. These people see themselves as fighting a daily, precarious struggle to extract funds for missile development from an air staff that would far prefer to spend the money on pilots and planes. The total program cost for the FA-18 fighter, for example, which is only one of several fighters, is equal to the total MX program cost.

Because it worked so closely with the private aerospace corporations, the Norton Ballistic Missile Office had always been a proponent of new and improved technologies. The standard argument for this was the need to catch up with the Soviet Union, but actually, since the equivocal Soviet lead with intercontinental ballistic missile tests in 1957, the U.S. had led in every technology in every department of nuclear warfare. It had been the first to miniaturize the H bomb for delivery by the ICBM, it had been the first to field nuclear-tipped ICBM's, it had led in increasing the accuracy of warheads and in multiplying the number of independently targetable warheads a single rocket could carry. When the

Ballistic Missile Office didn't have anything to do, it was an unhappy place, and when Hepfer arrived in 1974 it was only just beginning to recover its good temper. The Minuteman III program had ended at the beginning of the seventies. The MX program had not officially begun as a separate program until June 1973. They had been barren years for the office, and there was now a sense of élan and purpose as it began work on the most sophisticated weapon mankind had yet produced.

One day in early Spring 1974, three months after John Hepfer arrived at Norton, a policeman stood outside room 224 of the Russell Senate Office Building in Washington, D.C. A few moments before, the room had been swept for listening devices. It was a small room, wanting the Doric grandeur of the larger hearing rooms in the Russell, but it was quite adequate for the purpose of the day, which was to take evidence in closed and secret session on a new missile program proposed by the United States Air Force.

Considering the immense importance the program would later have, the air force had sent relatively junior officers up before the Research and Development Subcommittee of the Senate Armed Services Committee. The first of these witnesses was Major General Richard D. Cross, who enjoyed the title of director of operational requirements and development plans in the office of the Deputy Chief of Staff for research and development in the United States Air Force.

General Cross explained that $37 million was being requested for the following fiscal year for the "advanced ICBM technology program." This program, he said, had been reorganized during 1973 from a "device and piece part technology effort to the pursuit of focused technology in a system context." What this meant, though General Cross didn't spell it out, was that up until James Schlesinger had become secretary of defense a year before, the program had funded bits and pieces of research on ways of making missiles more accurate and powerful. It was now to fund research on an entirely new missile, incorporating these improvements.

Having introduced the "reoriented" program, General Cross turned the briefing over to his assistant, Colonel Virgil W. Munsey. The colonel explained that it was "prudent" to examine alternatives to the existing force of Minuteman missiles, and that the program under discussion was intended to provide an alternative "systems technology capability" by 1977. Most of the $37 million requested, he said, was for studies of rocket propulsion and improved guidance —the latter meaning increased accuracy.

Under questioning, Colonel Munsey explained that the air force had been studying a new missile for nearly two decades. However, "while there have been a number of internal Air Force studies, this is the first formal ICBM systems technology program which is focused towards a jumping-off point that has been submitted to the Secretary of Defense."

A missile, identified as MX for Missile Experimental, had first been mentioned in the USAF magazine *Air Force* in March 1973. It was then an idea for a new missile that would be ejected from an aircraft before it launched itself toward its target. It was then a long-term option—a possibility, not a probability. "We have no plans at the present time to initiate a program for the development of MX," an air force witness had told a Senate committee in April 1973, following disclosure of the idea in *Air Force*. But if it was officially no more than an idea, in practice the missile proposal had already come a long way in the internal planning of the air force by the time General Cross and Colonel Munsey came up to Capitol Hill. The Strategic Air Command had asked for the missile in 1971 with an official Required Operational Capability request, and Colonel Munsey would explain in 1974 that "the milestones of the program" were "laid out in internal Air Force planning" in November 1971. These milestones specified that the new technologies that the missile would incorporate, the guidance and propulsion, should be ready by 1977. This planning took place long before the program was submitted to Congress, and long before the appearance of accurate Soviet missiles which the new American missile was supposed to match. As General Cross observed, with the implacable logic of the arms race, "the ROC as it was submitted from the SAC was in anticipation of what any potential enemy might do." The SAC request followed the rejection of an earlier demand for a still larger MIRVed missile code named WS 120A.

By 1974, when some details of the MX program were explained to Congress, the air force had already done considerable work on the new missile and its base. It had been testing shelter doors for a tunnel-based missile, and it had been testing in wind tunnels suitable designs for a missile-carrying aircraft. The focus of work was on carrying missiles in aircraft or concealing them in land shelters, and these would remain the major alternatives right through the Ford and Carter administrations and into the Reagan administration. The air force was also looking at a long list of other alternatives. Colonel Munsey explained to the Research and Development Subcommittee that these included hauling the missiles on trucks, ferrying them on barges on inland waterways, loading them on railway cars, submerging them in pools, hiding them in hard-rock tunnels or soil tunnels. The air force was working on a new guidance technology that would make the missile more accurate even though it would not be launched from a fixed silo.

Explaining the program to the Research and Development Subcommittee, Colonel Munsey said he expected the total cost of the advanced development of the new missile to be $150 million, concluding with a missile design that could go into full-scale development in 1977.

Only one senator had attended this briefing, and he for only part of the time, though Colonel Munsey had been telling Congress about the beginnings of a program that was destined to become an insuperable political problem to three successive presidents.

The only senator to attend the hearing was Tom McIntyre, Democrat of New Hampshire, chairman of the Research and Development Subcommittee of the Senate Armed Services Committee. A slight five-foot-eight, with sparse hair combed over his bare head, black-framed spectacles, and a manner people thought timid until disturbed by his very direct green-eyed gaze, McIntyre was easy to underestimate and difficult to predict. He liked collecting shells and stamps and old bottles, and he liked playing golf, but he also liked to find out as much as he could about nuclear weapons, nuclear strategy, and how the Pentagon went about its business. And if he seemed polite and deferential with generals and undersecretaries during the hearings of his subcommittee, there were many generals and undersecretaries who later found that Tom McIntyre had politely cut their program.

An attorney from the small New Hampshire town of Laconia, McIntyre seemed to be in the Senate more by chance than destiny. He had been mayor of Laconia, Laconia city solicitor, and ultimately he had been director of the Laconia Industrial Development Corporation, but that had seemed the summit of his career. In 1954 he had won the Democratic nomination for his local congressional district, lost to a Republican opponent, and announced his retirement from politics. It required, he told the local newspaper, too much conflict between people. Eight years later, an unexpected split among Republican candidates in a special Senate election put McIntyre into the most powerful legislative chamber in the world.

Throughout the sixties, Senator McIntyre gave no evidence of the exceptional qualities of personality he would display in the seventies. He was an undistinguished member of the Banking and Armed Services committees. He supported President Kennedy and then President Johnson, voting loyally for Great Society programs and for the war in Vietnam. But, toward the end of the sixties, McIntyre's mood began to shift. In early 1968 he had conducted a write-in campaign for President Johnson in the New Hampshire Democratic primary. By late 1968 he had announced that he would vote against increased funding for the war in Vietnam, and quite soon he was opposed to American troops being in the war at all. At the same time, his senior colleague on the Armed Services Committee, Stuart Symington, was beginning his remarkable swing from hawk to dove on the issue of ballistic missile defense. Symington's conversion split the hitherto solid Armed Services Committee, and very soon the lines were drawn on whether or not Congress should fund a nationwide defense against Soviet missiles. The cost was huge, the issues complex. Senator McIntyre wavered.

At the beginning of the seventies, McIntyre got his chance at national reputation and he took it. Old Senator Richard Russell, who had headed the Armed Services Committee through decades of uncomplaining fidelity to what the services wanted, fell ill with emphysema, and Senator John Stennis of Mississippi, who had been there almost as long and who was almost as conservative, took over the committee. For the first time in the history of the committee, which authorized the largest single slice of money spent by the federal government, Senator Stennis divided its responsibilities. He asked McIntyre to be chairman of a subcommittee on research and development, and McIntyre accepted.

The committee was officially titled the Research and Development Subcommittee of the Senate Armed Services Committee. It was more commonly referred to, among the people who followed its doings to learn what the military would be deploying a few years hence, as R and D. The full committee had been divided by the conversion of Symington, who, as second ranking Democrat, had made opposition to defense spending respectable, and this division percolated downward to Senator McIntyre's subcommittee. He didn't think of himself as a dove, and was particularly concerned

that the voters of New Hampshire didn't think of him as a
dove, but, one way or another, he often found himself in the
company of doves on the Armed Services Committee. He
preferred to call it "good old Yankee common sense," and,
whatever it was, it often put him on the other side of Mr.
Barry Goldwater of Arizona and Mr. Jake Garn of Utah, who
were the minority members of his subcommittee. It also put
him on the other side of Senator Stennis, who described
himself as "warmly friendly" to the services, and to another
fellow Democrat, the man with whom he would lock horns
over nuclear strategy and the new missile for the air force,
Scoop Jackson.

From the late sixties to the mid-seventies, McIntyre was
to work closely with another senator deeply concerned about
the nuclear arms race, Edward Brooke of Massachusetts.
Both senators were advised by aides who combined political
astuteness with an increasingly commanding knowledge of
Defense Department nuclear weapons programs. For Senator Brooke, the aide was Alton Frye, an intellectual interested in arms control who put together a framework of ideas
against the counterforce doctrines that were becoming increasingly important in the Defense Department.

Frye believed strongly that the only sensible purpose of
nuclear weapons was to prevent your enemy from using
them against you, and this condition could only be met if
both sides were confident of their ability to destroy their
opponent's society. He believed that if one side was to field
weapons that could defend against a missile attack, then the
other side would field such a system also. Since no system
was anywhere near perfect, and, in the nuclear age, a system
had to be perfect to be any good at all, both sides would be
locked into an endless competition to build more and more
weapons to defend against ballistic missiles, and more and
more ballistic missiles to overcome the defenses against ballistic missiles, and, when the treasuries on both sides were
drained and their landscapes cluttered with rockets, neither

side would be one whit more secure than it had been before. So Frye and Brooke and McIntyre and the powerful Stuart Symington were opposed to America developing and deploying an anti-ballistic missile system. They wanted the U.S. to negotiate a mutual renunciation of the ABM with the Soviet Union.

Frye also believed, for the same reasons, that if America made missiles that became as accurate as a missile could become, and if they deployed them in numbers sufficient to threaten the Soviet Union's missiles with a disabling first strike, then that too would endlessly prolong the arms race and risk the very grave danger that, in a crisis, neither side could be confident that the other would not see great advantages for firing first. So McIntyre and Brooke, with their congressional allies, also led the fight against the increasing accuracy of American weapons, programs that, by and large, were recommended by the Defense Department when James Schlesinger was secretary.

For Senator McIntyre, the aide was Larry Smith, a former Dartmouth historian who combined a scrupulous regard for the politesse of the military with a keen understanding of the subtle ways by which the Defense Department and the air force got what they wanted from Capitol Hill. Larry Smith always addressed generals with courtesy, but it was soon well known in the Pentagon that Larry Smith's deference didn't go much beyond calling them "Sir."

Frye was Smith's intellectual companion and teacher on arms control issues until he left Senator Brooke's staff in the early seventies. He left behind a capable pupil, who advised Senator McIntyre during the secret sessions of the Senate in 1974 and 1975 when McIntyre pleaded for the renunciation of increased accuracy for American land missiles, and even after he left the senator's staff to work for the full Armed Services Committee in the middle of 1975, Larry Smith was still thought of as a staffer very close to the influential senator from New Hampshire. By the mid-seventies, Frye's pupil was freely acknowledged by the air force officers whose programs he scrutinized to be the best informed staffer on the Hill on nuclear weapons and nuclear strategy.

Brooke and McIntyre fought the Nixon administration to two successive compromises on the anti-ballistic missile debate in 1969 and 1970, forcing a furious Henry Kissinger to postpone plans for development and deployment until he was able to achieve agreement to ban all but a vestigial ballistic missile defense in both the Soviet Union and the United States. They fought the Trident submarine program, and in the mid-seventies they fought to prevent the United States from developing a suite of technologies that would improve the accuracy and power of American missiles, reasoning that to endanger the Soviet Union's deterrent was to make both sides more vulnerable to nuclear war. And, as the seventies progressed, Senator McIntyre's Research and Development Subcommittee became the only obstacle to the air force's determination to have a new and accurate missile, whether or not they could find a place to put it.

None of this was clear at the beginning of the seventies, when Senator McIntyre took over the Research and Development Subcommittee. The air force was then deploying its MIRVed Minuteman III, and, while the future vulnerability of American missiles was already an issue, the preferred solution in 1971 was not mobile missiles or concealed missiles, but a ballistic missile defense system called Safeguard. Funds for investigating mobile or concealed missile deployments were actually refused by the Senate Armed Services Committee in 1971 and 1972, reflecting Senator Stennis's doubts that missiles carried on trucks would be popular on American highways, or missiles concealed among many shelters would be acceptable to any administration that wanted the Soviet Union to be able to count missiles for arms agreements.

At the top of the Defense Department, the officials in charge also had doubts about mobile or concealed missiles.

That neither the Senate Armed Services Committee nor the air force were much interested in the mobile option in 1971 was clear in a question asked by Senator Stennis during the regular March hearings. "You do not indicate," he asked the Defense Department research and development chief, John Foster, "that any efforts are being made this year on the concept of a mobile Minuteman. I understand the decision not to pursue this system was made not on technical grounds but because of a Defense Department assessment that political opposition would be great and because of Service opposition. Could you elaborate on that and discuss the technical possibilities of a mobile Minuteman?" Foster replied: "The major limitation connected with a land mobile ICBM is that it must be deployed over a large area of countryside in order to be survivable, and, since land vulnerability is to some degree a political issue, the problems with land mobility could be said to be political problems."

In one colloquy in April 1971, McIntyre had asked Colonel E. Coy of the air force missiles division what was "the present thinking regarding the possibility of increasing the Minuteman force as an alternative to either playing the shell game, hiding the missiles in shelters, making them mobile, or further increasing their hardness."

Coy replied that there was always the possibility of proliferation, but the United States had not seriously addressed it lately, "because of President Nixon's foreign policy address wherein, on February 18, 1970, he indicated he did not want to make major changes in strategic and defensive forces. And of course also considering the fact that we are at present trying to negotiate a SALT agreement with the Soviets."

McIntyre then asked, "The idea of a mobile Minuteman or the shell game—are those sort of in low key?" Coy responded, "Yes sir, they are in low key."

As the seventies progressed, these circumstances changed remarkably. From a barely noticed and sometimes unpopular set of programs at the beginning of the seventies, the MX program would emerge to become, within six years, the most important priority for the air force and the most expensive single program ever contemplated in the Defense Department.

This great change was brought about by a number of unrelated circumstances which together produced MX. One important factor was the anti-ballistic missile agreement with the Soviet Union. Both sides agreed not to deploy any system capable of making a useful defense against missile attack. But since it was not also accompanied by a MIRV agreement, it left unsolved and increasingly serious the problem of the threat to land missiles. Another important factor was the momentum of the air force and its Ballistic Missiles Office. It had created and carried through the MIRVing program for Minuteman, and now it needed a fresh project to engage the talents of its team of scientists and engineers. With the greater popularity of counterforce doctrines in the early mid-seventies, the missile makers could easily promote the idea of a replacement missile for the eighties. These were reasons that were important in the air force and the Defense Department and came to be important in the White House. In Congress, a more unexpected set of forces supported the MX program. For different reasons, it attracted the support of both hawks and doves, first as an alternative to ballistic missile defense, and then as a way of both reducing the threat to American missiles and increasing the threat to Soviet missiles. The story of MX in Congress in the seventies is one of agreement between the most unlikely legislators that the program should go ahead.

Senator Stuart Symington of Missouri, a blunt, acerbic senior Democrat on the Armed Services Committee saw a mobile missiles as an alternative to the proposed "safe-guard" ballistic missile defense system. On 4 May 1971, for example, he grilled John Foster about mobile missile programs: "As you are no doubt aware," the senator began, "in their column last Friday, Evans and Novak reported that 'the threat of obsolescence to Safeguard is now under top secret analysis at the highest levels of the Nixon Administration. As a result, defense planners are on the verge of a crash program to make the U.S. long-range missile force mobile, possibly by putting part of the force of giant missiles on sea barges and keeping it moving.' Is there any truth to these statements?"

Foster replied that no, there was not. Symington said: "More and more, it would appear that, if we find it necessary to continue with this type of character of all-out destruction potential, we should put missiles out to sea, or make them mobile on land."

Symington's views were accepted by McIntyre and Brooke, who would consistently oppose the accuracy programs like the Mk12A warhead and the advanced inertial reference sphere that were to be incorporated in the new missile, and consistently defend research on hiding or concealing the next generation of land missiles.

In the June 1974 debate, for example, McIntyre asked Congress to delete money for the more accurate Mk12A warhead, which was to be fitted to the Minuteman III and would later be adapted for MX. Yet both Senator Brooke and Senator McIntyre *supported* the MX program, though MX would turn out to be the most wonderful silo killer built. Senator Brooke argued that the improvements to Minuteman were not necessary because the air force was developing "the advanced ICBM, which could provide a new missile, less vulnerable than Minuteman, in time to counter the hypothetical threat."

During this debate, Senator Stennis, who had deplored increased counterforce capability when Senator Buckley had sought it three years before, reasoned that "you do not kill many birds that way. The hunter has to swing with the moving target. . . . I think we must improve the accuracy and yield of the weapons we have." (McIntyre later remarked that he had tried to stop the trend to increasing accuracy during these closed-chamber debates, but had met too much misunderstanding on the other side.)

A year later, in June 1975, McIntyre again tried to stop counterforce programs—but not the MX. He opposed money being spent on Mk12A, on terminally guided warheads, and on an advanced reentry vehicle. But of MX he remarked: "I have also supported this year continued R and D on mobile missile systems."

According to Senator Brooke, who joined McIntyre in opposing counterforce programs, "one can identify programs in the Defense Department budget request that conform to the defensive criterion. The MX program emphasizing land mobility for our ICBM is one such program."

Thus the MX emerged during the mid-seventies, from the bits and pieces of earlier programs, as one with the support of both hawks and doves. The doves were attracted by its mobility. The hawks were attracted by its countersilo capability. To the doves, who were opposing other counterforce programs, support of MX was evidence of their hardheadedness and toughness. As later, when the Carter administration doves like Cyrus Vance, Paul Warnke, Leslie Gelb—Carter himself—would go along with MX because it seemed to be the way to get SALT II approved, so, in the mid-seventies, the doves applauded MX as a safer alternative to other counterforce programs. Mobility was the doves' answer to Soviet accuracy, where the hawks' answer was better American accuracy and perhaps ballistic missile defense; that MX was itself to be more accurate than the most accurate of Soviet weapons was a congressional battle that could, perhaps, be fought another day.

As the air force encountered more and more problems with the basing schemes, its emphasis shifted to the missile itself. By 1976, the year before the Carter administration came to office, the air force had decided that efforts to find an acceptable base were prejudicing the building of the missile itself, and this preference for the missile over the base led to increasingly acerbic conflicts between Senator McIntyre and the air force witnesses who appeared before him.

In the early seventies, work at Norton Air Force Base proceeded quickly. In the first two years, Hepfer's office let contracts for the development of the upper-, lower-, and third-stage motors for the three-stage missile, it had let contracts for an advanced computer for guidance and control and another contract for the advanced inertial reference sphere that would make the missile the most accurate of any missile, and it had also let contracts for designing the protective structure and the canister for deploying the missile.

By April 1975 the air force was able to confidently report that it had successfully tested the feasibility of launching the missile from the air, and narrowed the possible air-mobile carriers down to two. It had also narrowed the land-mobile ideas down to one—the covered trench—and it had tested this trench with high explosives. It had tested a missile transporter suspension system with pleasing results.

In 1975 the program sounded good, but out at Norton it didn't look so good. Behind the official reports to Senator McIntyre's committee were quite a lot of problems, and the bulk of resources was being devoted to a system that would prove unworkable. The air-mobile version was still officially being considered, but it had no support in the air force. Since B52s were now forbidden from carrying nuclear weapons while aloft, it was hardly likely that planes carrying missiles would be allowed to cruise on alert in peacetime. That meant missile-carrying planes would be just as vulnerable as the B52s and would have the same command and control problems. It was a messy idea to the air force, and the interest in it was purely formal.

The real interest was in the land missile—the trench— and there were problems of forbidding complexity. The first was to find a way of cheaply digging four thousand miles of trench. Ultimately, a way would be found, a way that did it for one-sixth of the cost of ordinary trench digging, but it took some finding. Another problem was designing doors to protect the canistered missile against blast propagated along the trench by its concrete walls. If there was no blast protection, then the canistered, transported missile needed blast doors, and these would have to ride along with the vehicle. Ultimately, a solution was found to that, too, but not one that proved satisfactory to the critics in the Carter administration.

General Hepfer's problems were not just with the recalcitrance of the trench, but also the pessimism of the air force staff and the Defense Department under the new secretary, Donald Rumsfeld. The air force's highest priority was the B-1 bomber, and it had troubles enough in Congress. The Vladivostok accord of 1974, which was the basis of SALT II, had capped missile numbers on both sides, and the momentum of negotiations could be imperiled by the rapidity of American programs that threatened Soviet land missiles. The MX program lost its priority as the air force's Research and Development Office fought with the Defense Department over funding levels and schedules, resulting in a cut in General Hepfer's budget for the fiscal year 1976. His funding was cut by the Defense Department from a request for $105.6 million to $41 million, and the projected date for the initial deployment of the system was put back to 1981. After the ballooning of the program in 1974, 1975 turned out to be a step backward for MX.

The excuse for the cutback by the Ford administration was the 1974 Vladivostok accord. "As a result of the Vladivostok agreement," Malcolm Currie told the full Senate Armed Services Committee, "we have moderated the pace of deployment of some of our strategic systems. . . ." Amplifying for the air force, Walter La Berge explained that "the pace of MX development is strongly dependent on Soviet threat projections. The Vladivostok accords impacted these projections by setting a numerical limit on the number of MIRV boosters, thus placing a cap on one of the most important parameters affecting the strategic nuclear balance."

Questioned by Senator McIntyre, another defense official said that the secretary for defense "decided not to pace the MX program at this time to any fixed initial operating capability. I think last year we were talking about the MX program based on an IOC in about 1981. That time has been relaxed now, and it has been primarily, I think, as a result of the Vladivostok and our ongoing negotiations, our desire to see how the Russians constrain themselves and how they react in these negotiations."

But in a hearing before McIntyre on 5 March, 1975, John Walsh, deputy director of strategic and space systems under the director of research and engineering, was able to offer a more pertinent explanation for cutting the MX program: "I think there is a fairly narrow reason for that particular decision with respect to the size of the funding for the MX program," he said. "That reason is, we have not yet decided what is the best or most appropriate mobility mode, and we could not spend money efficiently at a greater level than is now being spent. If we were to try and hold open the options for differing modes before making the decision, we would end up just initiating development on two or more mobility modes, one of which would have to be truncated or thrown away."

But if the Department of Defense wanted to slow down MX, the air force had found a way to speed it up. As Colonel Munsey explained in April 1975, "the basing mode has been selected, as the Secretary of Defense stated in his report to Congress. We envision that the missile will be initially deployed in a silo. It will be a universal missile so that it can be redeployed subsequently in a mobile basing mode if that should become necessary due to the evolving Soviet threat." Their work on basing systems, he said, had allowed them to select hardened launch point ideas—buried trenches, multiple aim points and pools—and discard road mobiles and rail

mobiles, as well as silos. They were, however, still looking at
air-mobile versions.

The following year, 1976, was the last year of the Ford
administration, and it witnessed a dramatic recovery in the
fortunes of MX. The Defense Department was now clearer
about the time of deployment—it wanted an early initial
operating capability. And it was clearer about why it wanted
the system—it wanted to be able to take out Russian silos.
Both moves were related to the changed political tone at the
beginning of 1976, as Gerald Ford fought off a challenge from
the Right in his own party. During the year, the Defense
Department would also decide the size and the preferred
basing mode of the missile—they wanted the biggest of the
sizes proposed, and they wanted it deployed in a tunnel.

The markedly different tone of the 1976 round before the
Senate Armed Services Research and Development Subcommittee was clearly apparent. Whereas a year before, the pace
of the MX program could be decided by the pace of Soviet
programs, this year the Department of Defense argued that
"the need for MX with an early IOC remains, regardless of
further Soviet effort, in order to counter Soviet initiatives
which are now ongoing and thus to insure our deterrent
capability. The number of Soviet military and industrial
targets grows modestly by 1985, but they are hardening
those targets to a significant extent. In addition to the ICBM
numbers preponderance they now hold, they are improving
the quality of their ICBMs and placing them in superhardened silos. This represents a significant threat to the U.S. if
not balanced on our side." Schlesinger's innovation, the assymetry theory, survived his departure.

Where a few years ago air force witnesses had barely mentioned the increased accuracy of a new missile, in 1976 it was
flaunted before the R and D subcommittee. "Although the
Minuteman is the best we have," Walsh told the committee
in March, "the system is not as effective as we would like
against the harder targets. That is why we regard the devel-

opment of the MX, with its many reentry vehicles and precise accuracy, as so important."

This excitement over accuracy was not at all to Senator McIntyre's liking, and he began to probe the relative importance of the two characteristics of MX.

In March 1976 McIntyre asked: "Shouldn't the primary concern regarding our land-based ICBM force be survivability? If that is the case, shouldn't we be concentrating on survivable basing options rather than a new missile?"

He was told, by the Department of Defense: "Survivability of the land-based ICBM is an extremely important consideration. However, the primary factor behind MX development is the need for a more effective missile to meet an escalating Soviet threat. Increased numbers, hardness, and dispersal of Soviet economic recovery targets are exacerbating the existing shortage of high quality weapons . . . the constraints of both SALT I and the Vladivostok understanding clearly establish the need for a more capable ICBM to meet projected requirements for coverage of time-sensitive hardened targets."

Two years after his appointment to command the project, Hepfer brought his conclusions to Washington for the first Defense Systems Acquisitions Review Council meeting. He was now familiar with the problems of where to put the missile that worried air force planners since the rail-mobile Minuteman of 1958, and he tended to think, like the rest of the air force, that the important thing was to get the big missile itself into development and work on the basing problems at the same time. If the worst came to the worst, he reasoned, and the new missile had to be deployed in Minuteman silos, the fact that it had ten warheads instead of Minuteman II's one or Minuteman III's three meant more would survive, and they would in turn do more damage to the Soviet Union. So his idea—supported by General Slay at the Systems Command—was to get the missile going and work on the base at the same time. He felt the air-mobile idea was worthless and, while he brought it along to the DSCARC meeting, he had no intention of recommending it. He thought the solid trench idea was still the best, and the second-best idea, a backup, was some kind of surface shelter in which the missile would be parked horizontally. This was the garage idea of Al Latter's, and it would eventually be the idea adopted by the Carter administration in September 1979. But there were big uncertainties about both ideas. A problem with the trench was the blast door and the mechanism to break the missile out of the concrete to fire it. A problem with the shelters was the design of a cantilevered door to allow the missile out through tons of debris after a Soviet barrage. On missile size, Hepfer thought a big missile, with a 92″ diameter, would be best, though he acknowledged that it would preclude joint development of a missile with the navy, because the air force missile was too wide for the Trident submarine firing ports. But Hepfer resisted the demands of some air force officers for an even larger missile, arguing that the new missile had to be compatible with the size of Minuteman silos, with a bit of "rattle space" all round. Those were Hepfer's ideas, but air force research and development chief, Walter La Berge, had others. He decided that the base and missile decisions should not merely be separated, but that the air force should press for formal agreement to have the new missile deployed in the first instance in existing Minuteman silos.

Hepfer responded to La Berge's direction, and reworked his briefing to demonstrate the advantages of deploying the MX's silos until the threat from Soviet missiles became so severe that there was no advantage in having them in fixed silos at all, even with the extra number of warheads. Presented to the director for defense research and engineering, Mal Currie, in March 1976, the air force proposal was accepted, and the new scheme was explained to Senator McIntyre's committee.

With the Defense Department now eager to increase funding for an early deployment for the new missile, major obstacles began to appear on Capitol Hill. Senator McIntyre's probes had clearly established in his mind that the air force was more interested in having the ability to strike at Soviet rockets than it was in the protection of American missiles from Soviet strikes, and both he and Smith were more alarmed still when they learned, at the beginning of 1976, that the air force proposed to deploy three hundred of the missiles. A force of that size, with each missile equipped with at least ten warheads, was more than sufficient to cover the eighteen hundred or so counterforce targets in the Soviet Union—its rockets, launching command centers, submarine pens, and bomber bases—so there was no other interpretation to place on the MX program other than that it would do the gravest injury to the stability of both sides in any crisis. Smith reasoned that the counterforce debates of 1974 and 1975 had represented the high point of congressional sentiment against the increasing accuracy of American weapons, and that it was time to accept that all future American weapons would be as accurate as they needed to be to destroy Soviet missiles in the hardest of silos. Accordingly, McIntyre and Smith changed priorities. The fight now had to be on the number of missiles deployed and the vulnerability of the base. It had been a gallant but losing battle, and now it was time to change tactics.

The president asked for $70 million for fiscal year 1977 for the MX program—somewhat less than the $90.8 million requested by the air force, but still a sizable increase on the year before. The program called for a decision to enter full-scale development in fiscal year 1978. The missile was to be initially deployed in silos, until a visible rather than projected Soviet threat became clear.

McIntyre had not been able to stop the Mk12A warhead, which would increase the accuracy of the Minuteman III and which would later be fitted to the MX. He had not been able to stop the technology upon which it depended, the advanced inertial reference sphere. But he was still in a powerful position as chairman of the Research and Development Subcommittee, and still the best informed senator on nuclear weaponry. In the spring of 1976 he and Larry Smith began to fashion a political compromise that they hoped would force the air force to either produce a missile that was invulnerable, or not produce one at all, and that would force the issue of the numbers of missiles deployed up to the White House and on to the president's agenda.

There were three issues up before the committee. The Defense Department wanted the B-1 bomber; it wanted a sea-launched cruise missile that would be deployed on surface ships; and it wanted to develop the MX for initial deployment in silos. McIntyre and Smith felt strongly that the sea-launched cruise missile would perhaps enormously complicate SALT negotiations. It was difficult to distinguish a sea-launched cruise missile, capable—because of its range and the power in its warhead—of striking at Soviet targets, from conventionally armed sea-launched cruise missiles intended to sink other ships. Once the United States began to deploy them, they argued, all cruise missiles at sea would have to be counted, or none counted, and thus the SALT negotiations would be blocked. The key Republican on the committee was Senator Barry Goldwater, who accepted the logic that the sea-launched cruise missile had no advantages not already possessed by the submarine-launched ballistic missiles, and that it would make any kind of arms control impossible. He was perhaps the strongest supporter of the B-1 on Capitol Hill. So, working through their staff aides, McIntyre offered to withdraw his objections to B-1 if Goldwater would agree to kill the sea-launched cruise missile and also agree to impose a requirement on MX that it be deployed in a base less vulnerable to Soviet attack than the silo. Goldwater agreed, and, when his fellow Republican Strom Thurmond of South Carolina protested that the Senate would approve B1 anyway, McIntyre threatened to throw all his prestige behind a floor fight against the bomber.

The staff reported to their principals and came back with agreement to Larry Smith, who flew to Boston to get McIntyre's agreement to the package. Later accepted by the full Senate Armed Services Committee, the Senate chopped funding for a fixed base for the missile and required the secretary of defense to undertake a comprehensive study of the future of America's ICBM force and its role in America's national security policy. This was intended to force a study of the number of land missiles that would be deployed. With the House Appropriations Committee expressing similar sentiments, the Authorization Conference Report for the 1977 fiscal year, written in 1976, expressed the view of Congress's armed services committees at the end of the Ford administration: " . . . the rationale behind the development of a new missile system (M-X) is to provide a land-based survivable strategic force. The development of an alternate basing mode as opposed to a fixed or silo-based mode is the key element in insuring this survivable force. The conferences are in agreement that providing a survivable system should be the only purpose for this effort, that the design of this system should not be constrained for silo basing; that none of this program's funds shall be expended in fixed or silo basing for M-X; and that none of the program reduction shall reduce the Department's proposed investigations of mobile deployment.

"The Senate in its committee report directed a comprehensive study of our ICBM force and its role in our national strategic posture. The conferees agreed to this review, with the stipulation that it be accompanied by a statement from the President that this study reflects national policy."

The report explicity prevented the air force from spending one cent on fixed silo basing for the new missile, or from designing the missile so that it could only be based in a silo. Six years later, the air force would argue in the Reagan administration that the Congress had already forbidden the silo scheme that the new president preferred. And the 1978 report for the first time insisted that the president clearly state the role of silo killing weapons in American nuclear strategy. That requirement would never be met.

With the Senate demonstrating resistance to the air force plan, Hepfer's office went back to the development of the basing ideas. No base, no missile, the Senate had decided, and some of the best minds of the air force were called in to consider this new crisis. But, by mid-'76, with Jimmy Carter much further in front in the polls than he would actually be in the election against Gerald Ford, the Republican administration began to die on its feet, and uncertainty surrounded all the major weapons programs. Toward the end of 1976, when the fate of the Republican administration was becoming clearer, Air Force Secretary Tom Reed told the air staff he wanted the MX program speeded up. Planning for full-scale development of the missile should proceed forthwith, he told his staff, and he went out to Norton and told Hepfer to pump up the MX budget for full-scale development. The decision was purportedly related to a sudden increase in the Soviet threat, though a year before the threat had been sufficiently distant to allow the missile to be put in silos. In reality, the decision was related to the imminent end of the Ford administration. If the Ford administration was to lose office, let it leave behind a fat defense budget. When the Democrats cut it, as they did, they could be accused of disarming America.

5
One Step Backward

The craziest idea I ever heard.
—*Jimmy Carter, 1978*

JIMMY Carter came to office as a president unlikely to approve—as he did thirty month later—the biggest buildup in America's nuclear arsenal for two decades. During the election campaign, Carter had denied the possibility of limiting nuclear war to selected, contained attacks on military or isolated industrial targets. He said that both the United States and the Soviet Union had far too many weapons already. He seemed to imply that the right policy was mutual assured destruction, a policy of minimum deterrence. All that was needed were the submarines at sea, with their powerful but inaccurate warheads aimed at big, soft Soviet cities. "There would be no possibility under the sun that a first strike capability could be adequate in preventing mass destruction of the country that initiated the strike," candidate Carter said in November 1976. "There is no way to prevent a massive retaliatory strike because, for all practical purposes, atomic submarines are invulnerable."

Later, even as late as five months before deciding to add five thousand more warheads to the American arsenal of ten

122

thousand warheads, Carter would still be saying that American nuclear power was "overwhelming" and that a small fraction of the missile force could destroy "every large and medium-sized city in the Soviet Union." What Jimmy Carter said was one thing, what he did another. It was not so much that Carter was a hypocrite as that he happened to be president when the implacability of the arms race with the Soviet Union demanded a decision. By 1979, when Carter and his advisers examined the choices for the last time, they felt they had no choice. Yet if the decision had to be made, it was also in another sense unmakeable. This final turn in the arms race was the most difficult of all. The competition had become technically and politically indigestible.

If the MX builders in the Ballistic Missile Office at Norton Air Force Base, California, or at the Space and Missile Systems Office at Andrews Air Force Base near Washington, D.C., had reason to worry about Jimmy Carter, they also had some reason to worry about the new defense secretary, Harold Brown. A former chief of research and engineering at the Pentagon under McNamara, a former secretary of the air force under Lyndon Johnson, one of the outstanding minds of the weapons community, Brown was familiar with all the issues and seemed to have come down on the opposite side of the debate from James Schlesinger and the United States Air Force.

Brown's had been a perfect career profile for a member of the weapons community. He had been a child prodigy, graduating from the Bronx High School of Science with an average of 99.52 per cent and some of the highest scores ever achieved in the New York State Regents Exam. He had won his bachelor's degree at eighteen and his physics doctorate at twenty-two. He had filled almost every one of the jobs on the weapons community ladder. He had been deputy to Edward Teller at the Lawrence Livermore Laboratory in California where, according to another eminent member of the weapons community, Herbert York, he had originated more of the ideas that have gone into thermonuclear weapons development than any other person since Teller's original concept. He had been director of the laboratory after Teller, and he had been deputy director of defense research and engineering in the Kennedy administration, the third highest civilian official in the Defense Department and the person, in McNamara's time, who controlled the budgets and directed the programs for all the weapons research and development of the services. He had gone on, in 1965, to become secretary of the air force. He had been one of McNamara's civilian whiz kids, an abrasive and shy thirty-four year old who had helped kill the B-70 airplane, the predecessor of the B1, and the skybolt missile and the army's Nike Zeus missile system.

Brown was remembered now as a tough analyst who had demanded "more bang for the buck" but, like Cyrus Vance, Brown had been not only a participant but an active supporter of those policies that had lead to so many difficulties for America's defense: the decision to MIRV, and the war in Vietnam.

Brown's connections in the weapons community were the key to the development of MIRV. He was the link between its inventors and the upper reaches of the Defense Department. Under Brown, the directorate for defense research and engineering became more of an advocate of new technology in weapons than it had been under his predecessor.

As air force secretary during the bombing of Vietnam, Brown was inevitably involved in the bombing decisions. The Pentagon Papers showed that he had sent up three papers by staff members recommending more bombing over a wider area, though Brown had since claimed that a covering letter, not printed in the Papers, had made clear his disagreement with the views of his staff. Roger Morris, who had served in foreign policy jobs in the Johnson administration, wrote that "Brown was perhaps more than any other single second rank official the architect and executor of defoliation and bombing technology in Vietnam." As air force secretary, he had advocated bombing the North, and continued to advocate it within the administration when it had been suspended. Brown had since recanted on Vietnam, though in a characteristically ambivalent and diffident way: "It was a very catastrophic time in American history," he said, and "what I think I, as an individual have learned, and one of the things our nation should have learned, is that we should be very cautious in expanding our foreign policy commitments beyond our vital security interests. What I have also learned is the limitations of military force in a politically circumscribed, highly ambiguous situation." These were careful judgments, the conclusions of an analyst accustomed to weighing the facts in the light of the end desired. No moral retraction was involved; it was enough for Brown to have admitted a miscalculation.

Brown left the administration with President Johnson to become president of the California Institute of Technology, but he had kept a strong involvement in the weapons community, working on SALT with the Nixon administration. It was no surprise when, with the election of Jimmy Carter, a candidate he had informally advised during 1976, Brown was invited back to Washington as secretary of defense.

Shy and intense, with a spare figure, graying, neatly brushed hair, an habitual slight ironic smile as though he was expecting a satirical repartee and did not want to be thought to have missed it, Brown was softly spoken and inclined occasionally to show, by a smile expressing despair or amazement, that everyone else was a little slower than he was. He was not happily remembered from his earlier Pentagon experiences: "His mind worked so quickly, he was always way ahead of everyone else," an official who worked with him recalled. "He would show his boredom, he was very impatient." So intense was Brown that he had written on his Columbia application, in the space marked "Objective": "I intend to let all my actions be dictated by the answer to this question: will this step help more than any other action in winning the war against fascism and in winning the peace that will follow?" For a man of such intensity, the ceremony in his job was agony. Visiting Korea in the summer of 1977, he was obliged to review a parade of American troops. "How do you like it here?" he asked one soldier. "I like it fine," the soldier replied. Brown smiled, looked down, and then looked back up at the young soldier, saying with a nervous laugh, "Well, I guess that's about all I have to say."

Like Carter, Brown had changed his opinions about nuclear strategy and nuclear weapons. In late 1964 he had been advocating a MIRVed submarine-launched missile because "technical studies had indicated that significant gains could be made in high accuracy reentry vehicles and MIRVs. The high accuracy would be very effective against undefended hard point targets." Brown then liked the idea of counterforce weapons. Yet in March 1975 he told an audience in the Soviet Union that, while it was important to have options other than striking at cities, a full-scale nuclear war would almost inevitably follow any exchange. He thought that "the facts of the indefensibility of each of our countries against nuclear attack by the other, and the open-ended nature and unlimited costs of countermilitary strategy, are clear." He concluded that "counterforce capabilities, especially because the limitations on their effectiveness are not matched by limitations on their costs, will not be carried very far on either side. Facts do in the end prevail, whatever doctrine may assert."

Before Senator Stennis's committee in 1977 Brown several times took issue with the Schlesinger doctrine that it was possible to have nuclear war without erasing the Soviet and American societies. Any exchange, he believed, would inevitably escalate to holocaust. Even a year later, in his February 1978 Defense Report, Brown said that it was not "at all clear that an initial use of nuclear weapons—however selectively they might be targeted—could be kept from escalating into a full-scale thermonuclear exchange, especially if command control centers were brought under attack. The odds are high, whether the weapons were used against tactical or strategic targets, that control would be lost on both sides and the exchange would become unconstrained. Should such an escalation occur, it is certain that the resulting fatalities would run into scores of millions."

And a year later, when a series of presidential decisions had been drafted which intended to enhance the ability of the United States to conduct the kind of wars he believed impossible, and when he was about to recommend to the president a decision on the MX, he would say that "I do not wish to pretend that anyone has found a way of conducting a strategic nuclear exchange that remotely resembles a traditional campaign fought with conventional weapons. . . . Admittedly, counterforce and damage limitation campaigns have been put forward as the nuclear equivalents of traditional warfare. But their proponents find it difficult to tell us what objectives the enemy would seek in launching such campaigns, how these campaigns would end, or how any resulting assymetries could be made meaningful."

Brown might have believed that limited war was impossible, but, in his four years as defense secretary, he did more to make it possible than any of the secretaries who had preceded him since 1945. Four years after Brown had declared limited war an illusion, and had said that the facts would prevail, nuclear strategy had yet again been revised and recodified as Presidential Decision 59, which increased the number of selective strikes in the war plans. Decisions had been made to improve communications and civil defense during nuclear war, the United States was pressing ahead with the development of MX and the deployment of cruise missiles and Trident submarines.

An administration that had come to office with a promise to cut defense spending by $5 to $7 billion, that wanted to concentrate on energy problems at home and human rights

abroad, and that made as its principal issue against the
Republican challenger, Ronald Reagan, his opposition to the
strategic arms limits agreement with the Soviet Union,
nevertheless left as its principal monument an extraordinary and little-noticed buildup in nuclear weapons.

When it was all over, four years later, officials who took
part in those decisions would recall them as logical, as rational and properly paced responses to a sequence of challenges
presented to the administration. Yet every official had his or
her own different recollection of what these challenges were,
and which were more important than others, which mattered and which did not. Each could point to an orderly
"decision process" through which MX had been carefully considered and the alternatives weighed. For some, the process
was the committees of Congress, the Defense Systems Acquisitions Review Committee (DSARC) meeting in the Pentagon,
and the Missile X Committee meetings between the air force
and the office of the secretary of defense. For others, the real
meetings were White House meetings on the budget, sub-
committees of the National Security Council, and formal
meetings with the president. For others, the real meetings
were informal conferences between staff.

The truth is that in this penultimate moment of the long,
protracted decision to build MX, there was no orderly decision process. The decision process was in fact a lot of different people and organizations going their own ways, reacting
to different impulses, thwarted by different setbacks and
encouraged by different victories, until a set of temporary
pressures forced the administration into making the decision in a rush, with studies no more satisfactory and for
reasons no more compelling than they had been when the
administration arrived in office four years before. It was a
final decision that was to be just as fragile and untenable as
the final decisions that had preceded it. It was also an egre-
giously wrong decision, though it may be there is no right
decision on MX and no way to deal with the problems it

addresses. The Carter administration saw itself taking charge and putting its stamp on nuclear policy. In reality, the MX decision had been determined a decade before, when the United States deployed multiple independent warheads on its land missiles.

The many different elements that contributed to the MX decision were apparent in what policy people in Washington call "tracks." At one time, for example, the missile decision was in "the SALT track," which meant that political decisions about it were being made by the people negotiating SALT. At another time, it was in "the budget track," which meant that political decisions about it were being made by people who drew up the administration budget for the next financial year. There was also the research and development track, the congressional track, and eventually MX would have its own track, which meant that a top-level committee was appointed to consider it and it alone. Each of these tracks considered the missile in a different light and dealt with a different set of pressures.

In the SALT talks, the incoming administration began with an attempt to make deep cuts in the nuclear weapons of both sides, which would have involved a particularly deep cut in the number of heavy missiles deployed by the Soviet Union on land. This would, as David Aaron, deputy national security assistant, remarked, "stave off the strategic problem" presented by American vulnerability to Soviet missiles, and thus might have staved off MX. But if the Carter round of SALT talks started off with an attempt to make deep cuts, it concluded by accepting a big buildup in the forces of both sides. And not only did these negotiations not stave off MX, the chances of getting the agreement through the Senate actually came to depend on the administration proposing MX as well. The first SALT agreement had seen a vast increase in the number of weapons on both sides; the second agreement would encourage this trend to continue.

Another important influence was the technical progress

on the missile shelter. All along, for the two decades during
which the air force had studied mobile or deceptive basing,
there had been problems with costs and vulnerability and
command and control. Now there were problems with the
environment, which had not been an issue when the Minuteman was deployed in underground silos, and problems with
the verifiability of the number of American missiles. Most of
the problems had been worked over since Eisenhower had
agreed to put Minuteman missiles on railway cars, and most
of the problems were no nearer solution in 1977 than they
had been in 1959. At the beginning of 1977, the air force had
substituted for a single three thousand mile tunnel a series
of twenty mile long tunnels, and it was working on a still
shorter trench with spurs.

In all weapons programs, the most prominent public aspect is the threat that it meets. The degree to which Minuteman was actually threatened, and the time at which that
threat would become a real one were issues hotly contested
within the Carter administration. In the end almost everyone came to agree, but when Carter came to office, there was
no agreement. In the CIA, Admiral Turner found a threat
projection heavily influenced by the hawkish Team B, which
claimed that the Soviet Union would be able to destroy
America's land missiles within a few years. Later, two studies by Carter analysts would dispute that conclusion before
Soviet missile tests offered evidence that Soviet accuracy
was indeed increasing swiftly and threatening American
land missiles.

Even in his fiscal year 1979 Defense Report, delivered in
February 1978, Brown had not been too deeply distressed by
the problem of Minuteman's vulnerability. "Even if we did
nothing about it," he wrote, "it would not be synonymous
with the vulnerability of the United States, or even of the
strategic deterrent. It would not mean that we could not
satisfy our strategic objectives. It would not by itself even
mean that the United States would lack a survivable hard

target kill capability or that we would necessarily be in a worse post exchange position in terms of numbers of weapons, payload, or destructiveness."

But, as time passed, "Minuteman vulnerability" became the most important strategic problem seen by the administration. Two months before the National Security Council meeting, which was convened to decide on MX in June 1979, Brown told the Council of Foreign Relations that "the growing vulnerability of our land-based missile forces could, if not corrected, contribute to a perception of U.S. strategic inferiority that would have severely adverse political—and could have potentially destabilizing military—consequences."

When the Carter administration took office, the MX had already passed what the air force called the "first milestone" in its official history. In the official accounts, the air force had presented a set of land missile options to the Defense Systems Acquisitions Review Committee (DSARC) in March of 1976. That committee was chaired by the deputy director for defense research and engineering, Malcolm Currie. The options included hardening Minuteman silos, and changing the Minuteman booster so it could carry more warheads. For the MX, the air force presented both an 83″ diameter missile that would be compatible with the navy's Trident II missile, and a 92″ missile that could carry more warheads. The air force had formally concluded that none of the alternatives except the big missile could meet the "targeting requirements" of the 1980s and "reverse the trend of growing imbalance between U.S. and Soviet ICBM capabilities." The air force had also concluded its study of the basing alternatives and it had come down to three: air mobile, and two land deception ideas—multiple shelters and covered trenches. Everything else was ruled out. General Hepfer, who was in charge of the program, would later testify that "in March of 1976, when we had our DSARC, we had not even looked at the vertical shelters." It was not until November of 1977, according to General Hepfer, that the air force began to consider the silo-based multiple system that became the favorite in 1978.

After the March 1976 meeting, Currie had accepted the recommendation to validate the big missile design and continue studies on the three basing alternatives. The Ford administration also accepted that the new missile would be based in existing or new fixed silos until the new base was ready. This meant that, even in 1976, the submarine alternative and many land-mobile alternatives had already been rejected because the 92″ missile was too big and too heavy to move around, except in specially built vehicles on specially built roads. It would not move quickly. Nor could it ever be deployed in the Trident submarine, since its diameter was greater than that of the Trident firing ports. Effectively, the decision to build it in that size put back work on the D5 submarine launched missile. Another very important implication of the March 1976 decision was that the Ford administration had gone along with the idea of deploying the missile in fixed silos before the new bases were ready. Since the new bases might never be ready, this was a lurch in the direction of the air force's declared preference for accuracy and firepower first, and invulnerability second. In the outgoing administration's lame duck budget, the MX project reached a level of priority it would not reach again for another two years. It was recommended for Full-Scale Development—the first time the program had broken out of the formal research and development status. After a crushing reversal in 1975, the air force now had the makings of the missile.

For the air force it was a fleeting victory.

In written testimony prepared for Senate hearings at the beginning of 1977 but never actually delivered, Lt. Gen. Alton Slay, deputy chief of staff for research and development in the air force, was to have declared that "the new MX development schedule represents an acceleration of the program I described to you a year ago. The decision to request this acceleration was based on several months of detailed study of Soviet activity in the strategic area. Deep personal involvement at the highest levels of the air force and the Office of the Secretary of Defense characterized this study and the eventual decision. Very broadly, it was determined that acceleration of the MX was necessary to assure the United States will be able to maintain a high confidence deterrent posture in the face of a concerted drive by the Soviet Union to achieve unquestioned strategic superiority over us within the next five years."

The air force was focusing on the trench concept of deployment, with the shelter as a backup. Confronted with continuing problems in designing a cheap tunnel to conceal the missile, the air force had decided that the missile should be built anyway, while work continued on a new base. Ultimately, the air force would have the missile, and the administration would have to find a place to put it. It was, an air force general ruefully conceded some years later, "a strategy of desperation—we knew that."

But Harold Brown and his staff were determined not to be trapped into a program they had not yet examined. The Ford-approved air force budget request for MX was chopped from $289 million to $132 million, and its status changed from "full-scale development" to "advanced development." In April, Senator McIntyre convened his subcommittee and introduced the MX missile hearing with a statement of extraordinary prescience: "the dilemmas of ICBM survivability are . . . devilish, he said. "Most proposed solutions for this problem seem to have at their center the seeds of new dilemmas."

He explained that the active defense of American ICBMs would require the abrogation of the one durable and broadly supported achievement of SALT I, the ABM treaty. A mobile ICBM force would pose difficult issues of arms control verification and the problem of local acceptance of such a system, while possibly solvable, would be by no means as easy as it was when the Minuteman sites were first chosen. The missile itself was designed to multiply dramatically the efficiency of America's own ICBM force in destroying Soviet missiles in their silos. "I think," he concluded, "we can agree that the MX as it is currently designed would, like the Soviets' own ICBM buildup, lock both sides into a new, much more dangerous and frightfully expensive arms race, an ICBM arms race, in which a minority of either side's ICBM force could endanger most of the ICBMs of their adversary."

At the beginning of 1977, Harold Brown shared McIntyre's concern, and when the secretary designate had come up to the Hill before his nomination hearings, he had listened closely to the senator's misgivings. In both 1977 and 1978, the new administration cut funding for MX below the amount requested by the air force. The reason it offered was one that strongly appealed to Senator McIntyre. This was, as explained by the incoming director of defense research and engineering, Bill Perry, to keep "the basing and the missile development in synchronization with each other." At the end of 1978, however, under increasing pressure to build new weapons, the Carter administration would decide to separate the basing and missile development decisions, and today, while the missile development runs ahead of schedule, there is still no agreement on where to put it. By the end of 1978 there was no Tom McIntyre in the Senate to dispute the decision. After a tough and bitter campaign against him, launched by a New Right candidate, McIntyre had lost his Senate seat and, with it, his chairmanship of the one Hill committee that had been critical of the new missile.

If Harold Brown had overall responsibility for MX, his undersecretary of defense for research and engineering, Bill Perry, was to work at it day to day, arbitrating between the services, reaching agreements on proposals that would be put to Brown, directing one line of work and discouraging another. It was in Perry's Pentagon office that the many

currents of information and dispute about the new missile
mingled: the intelligence about Soviet abilities, the physics
of the shelter tests, the requirements for verifiability and the
need for concealment, the pressures of the White House and
Congress and the air force.

A brilliant mathematician who had worked on electronic
reconaissance systems, who had won an army medal for
top-secret work on what was blandly described as "the development of systems for the collection of vitally important
intelligence through the use of advanced electronics," Perry
was fifty when, after once declining it because of the loss of
income and the disturbance of moving his family from California to Washington, he was finally persuaded by Harold
Brown to take the second most important job in the Defense
Department. Like so many in the weapons community,
Perry was an easterner, a Pennsylvanian who had moved
west to work at Stanford, returned to Penn State for his
doctorate, and then gone back out to Santa Clara to work in
the electronic defense laboratories of a major military sup-
plier. But, unlike others in the weapons community, Perry
was also an entrepreneur. He had been one of the founders
of a high-technology corporation in California, and he had
worked there on the analysis of missile systems and the
design of electronic reconnaissance systems. Perry had
known Brown since Brown had the job Perry now held in the
Pentagon, and Perry was a Defense Department adviser.
Perry didn't know Carter, but when Brown asked—and per-
sisted—Perry came.

Even long after he had left the job four years later, people
in the weapons community would still speak of Bill Perry's
extraordinary quality of persuasiveness; of the way, for example, he could go into a meeting of hostile Mormon students on the Brigham Young campus in Utah and win them
over, convince them that the missile and the forty-six hundred concrete shelters and the ten thousand miles of roads
over Utah and Nevada that went with them were necessary,

inevitable, and reasonable. Bill Perry addressed people by
their first names, and made a point of repeating their first
names in conversation with them, he looked them directly
in the eye, and had a way of suggesting, in this candor and
familiarity, that he believed you were as capable of seeing
the truth as he was of explaining it.

He was soft-spoken and amiable, modest and serious, and
so plausible that, in four years of almost incessant appearances before congressional committees, his good faith was
never queried. But Bill Perry left the Defense Department
in 1981 with a forehead weary beyond his fifty-four years.
For all his knowledge, for all that experience in science and
management, Bill Perry didn't get the missile he wanted,
and when he was once again in private business, a merchant
banker in a San Francisco firm, tending to a flock of high-
tech corporations from an office decorated with the memora-
bilia of successful stock floats and bond issues the MX which
had preoccupied his days in the Pentagon would still not be
under construction in the states of Utah and Nevada; all the
many alternatives he had examined in his Pentagon office
were once again being examined by his successor as Perry's
predecessors had examined them before him, and the deployment of the missile on American land was as far away as it
had been when he entered the administration in 1977. The
protest of local ranchers over Bill Perry's rational, carefully
formulated scheme had been so great that it could never be
built the way he had wished, where he had wished, when he
had wished.

When Perry walked into his Pentagon office he had, he
would later recall, very pessimistic feelings about the MX
program. He did not question that America would eventually need a new land missile, or that it would eventually
have to be deployed in a way the Soviet targeteers could not
easily overcome. What he questioned, as did Harold Brown,
was the tunnel design the air force was then developing, and
the actual likelihood of an early threat to Minuteman.

Perry thought there was no urgent need for MX, and its development could wait study of the alternatives. He wondered whether Soviet guidance accuracy on its current generation of missiles was sufficient to threaten Minuteman. He concluded that, at that time, it was not. The best estimate of the intelligence community at the beginning of the Carter administration was that it would not be until the Soviet rocket forces deployed their next generation of missiles, in the late eighties, that they would have sufficient accuracy to reliably destroy Minuteman in its hardened silos. That seemed a reasonable estimate to him, putting the threat ten years in the future. Even with increased accuracy, Perry believed, it would have been necessary for the Soviets to spend two or three warheads against every Minuteman silo to have a reasonable confidence of destroying them. Some missiles would miss, others malfunction. By using two or three warheads, the Soviet targeteers would automatically solve the reliability problem and compensate for near misses as well. But if the Soviets were to use two or three warheads, they would have to solve the problem of fratricide—that is, the probability that incoming warheads would be thrown off course or be destroyed by the explosion of the warhead that preceded them.

Perry's skepticism about the urgency of the Soviet threat gave him and Harold Brown time to reflect on what they would later find was a seriously flawed basing design. In March 1976 Malcolm Currie had agreed that the air force should focus on the design of a long, covered trench, in which one missile on a transporter would be able to move backward and forward, as the most promising base for the missile. The idea was strongly favored by the air force Chief of Staff, General Jones, and by SAC chief, General Ellis, because of its political simplicity. Once the missile was covered up, it would no longer attract public opposition. Out of sight, out of mind, was the principle. It had worked very well in the case of Minuteman. But the trench system had formidable problems. One was that a nuclear explosion in any one part of the trench would be carried along the trench and would destroy the missile, wherever it was. Another problem, which was common to any system of deceptive deployment, was that the number of missiles in the trench could not be verified by Soviet satellites, and it would therefore violate the SALT agreement.

The man who had to work through Perry's pessimism was Seymour Zeiberg, Perry's deputy for strategic and space systems. A forty-three-year-old New Yorker who had, like Perry, made his career in the West Coast weapons community, Zeiberg had joined Al Latter's R and D Associates soon after it had broken away from the RAND Corporation. Zeiberg became one of the foremost American experts on the design of ballistic missile reentry systems. He had been an engineer working on high-temperature gas flows, and that led into work on penetration aids with Aerospace Corporation, an arm of the air force. Zeiberg was close to John Walsh, who was his predecessor in the job, and Walsh had recommended him to Brown as his successor. A direct, informal, funny man, a New Yorker with a snappy wit, with a more cynical and candid manner than Perry's, Zeiberg was to arbitrate between the air force and Perry for four years, so that MX in the end preoccupied his time.

Zeiberg was already familiar with the problems of land missiles when he arrived in the Pentagon. At R and D Associates, he had been program office director for strategic studies, and he was close to Al Latter, who had devised the "garage mobility" scheme in the mid-sixties. Nor would his association with MX end when he left the Pentagon. His next job was to be vice-president for research and engineering for the aerospace group of Martin Marietta Corporation, builder of MX.

A big, relaxed man with close-cropped gray and black hair, Zeiberg decorated his Pentagon office like an aerospace hobbyist's den: tiny model planes on attack trajectories threatened visitors from their ceiling sky; and the inevitable display board of Soviet and American missiles, known as "the Russians are coming display" among air force lobbyists—the American rockets tiny, defenseless and white, the Soviet rockets huge and mighty and black—poised for blastoff behind his heavy, dowdy, Pentagon-issue desk.

Zeiberg wanted MX, understood and agreed with the air force reasoning, but, through 1977, he faced formidable obstacles. His mind was of a practical cast, and he shared with Al Latter an impatience with political obstructions to what he felt was a technically correct course of action. He would disagree with Perry over whether or not a common missile with the navy was practicable. He would disagree with the White House people over whether there was any chance the Soviet Union could detect the one American missile in a cluster of silos. He was confident of his technical competence and scathing about the pretensions of the political people to technical knowledge. Nonetheless, Zeiberg understood the politics very well. He understood the need to be seen to have gone through the forms and ceremonies, and the need to clearly separate forms and ceremonies, like Defense Systems Acquisitions Review Committee meetings, or congressional hearings, from actual decisions. He was also a pragmatist, willing to bend and change course when that seemed necessary, willing to go along with his boss and his boss's bosses when disagreement was no longer useful. Zeiberg was the perfect man for his delicate job of arbitration between technical people and political people, and the fact that there was a technically plausible option available when the time came to decide on MX is as much his doing as it was anyone in the administration's.

Zeiberg wanted to move ahead with MX just as soon as he could. He had no doubts about the need for it, and he did not share Perry's pessimism about its urgency. But two major studies during 1977 gave the MX critics reason to set the timetable back.

The first study was an exercise by Sam Huntington on the National Security Council staff. A Harvard specialist on civilian-military relations, a long-time colleague and collaborator of Zbigniew Brzezinski, Huntington was a hawkish academic who took charge of an early study dubbed Presidential Review Memorandum 10. It assessed the adequacy of American military forces and the strategy that was to guide their use. One important conclusion from his study, which broadly argued that America needed to build up its conventional forces, was that the Minuteman vulnerability problem was not as urgent as the air force wished the administration to believe. Accordingly, the MX program was not as urgent. But the PRM 10 studies resulted in Presidential Decision 18, which confirmed the existing nuclear strategy. This in turn led to three other studies which would later be important in the development of MX.

A second study was conducted by Frank Press, the president's science adviser. A soft-spoken, graceful, cool geologist, who was as well known for his advanced research as for his popular geology textbook, Press unexpectedly proved to be a formidable bureaucratic player in the Carter White House. Press was a scientist of impeccable credentials, but he was also a scientist-politician who would later become president of the National Academy of Sciences. In the Carter White House, he was the most prominent of the Cambridge scientific community, the Harvard MIT scientists who had always supplied the arms controllers in Democratic administrations, and it was a tradition he took seriously. He was close to the president and he cultivated him assiduously, the dry and ironic charm of the Cambridge scientist who thought before he talked, who had no aversion to silences, mingling well with the energy and curiosity of a president who, all his life, would be a student, an imitator, a too-great admirer of others' excellence. Press knew how to appeal to this aspect of the president and the importance the president attached to scientific advice. Thus, of all the doves in what was said to be a very dovish administration, only Press was able to substantially delay the MX program.

Press was a brilliant geologist whose career path was not unlike Brown's. He, too, was a Jewish boy from Brooklyn who had won his first degree at Columbia, who had been at grad school together with Brown, and who had gone over to the California Institute of Technology and ultimately come back east to the Massachusetts Institute of Technology. As a geologist, Press had become an expert on the remote detection of physical phenomena like earthquakes, and because of this he had been invited to advise U.S. officials preparing for the nuclear test ban negotiations. Press had been drawn into the arms control community, which overlapped but generally stood separately from the weapons community. As a member of the arms control community, as a scientist interested in the various MX basing schemes that crossed his desk, Press was critical of the practicality of all the basing schemes proposed for it.

Press's office had been recreated by Carter in March 1977, seven years after the incoming Nixon administration had abolished it. Under Eisenhower, the job had been a powerful one, perhaps the most powerful job in the weapons community. It had been the president's assistant on science and technology policy who had pushed the air force into the first ICBM program, who had arbitrated the services disputes over new weapons systems, and who had coordinated the scientific community into the great weapons research projects of the fifties. All this had changed when McNamara became secretary of defense, and power went back into the Department of Defense to the deputy director for defense research and engineering.

Press's style as a bureaucrat depended on his credentials as a scientist, as a member in good standing of a community that respected intelligence and training, even where it disputed political views. To revive the office of president's science adviser, and the companion but congressionally mandated job of director of the Office of Science and Technology Policy, to reestablish the office to the importance it had over weapons decisions in the days of Killian and Kistiakowsky. Press needed to work closely with Brown and Bill Perry.

Press was fortunate. The air force loathed him. They knew him from his days as a SALT adviser, as one General explained, as someone with "a history," which meant that he was known "minimum deterrer," and there was nothing worse than that. Press in his turn loathed the air force. He thought their tactics tricky and intellectually dishonest. But he liked and respected Harold Brown and Bill Perry, and they in their turn liked and respected Press. Brown and Press had known each other since graduate school, and later they had worked as advisers on the SALT delegation. Brown was now in the weapons community and Press in the arms control community, two groups that did not always respect each other, but Press was later to say that he and Brown got on well as professional colleagues, "as scientists," and Brown actually expressed gratitude to Press for discovering flaws in the MX basing system. Press, in turn, always consulted Brown.

In the spring of 1977 Press asked Carter if he could conduct a study of what he could clearly see was the central issue in the nuclear arms race—the vulnerability of land missiles. Carter agreed. Press also asked if he could study the tunnel basing mode proposed by the air force for MX. Carter agreed to that.

The Office of Science and Technology Policy panel, which included both hawks and doves, concluded that a follow-on missile to the aging Minuteman would indeed be necessary, simply because the Minuteman would one day begin to become unreliable. It also concluded that land missiles in fixed silos would one day become vulnerable to Soviet attack. The panel did not contest either of the two major premises of the argument for MX. But it did question the timing of the threat, the degree of the threat, and, most importantly, it questioned the protection offered by the tunnel base that the air force proposed as an alternative to silos. Minuteman would be vulnerable some day, but probably not until the mid-eighties at the earliest, and even when it was vulnerable, there would be so many uncertainties associated with an attack on it that it was not a serious military option. That line of argument was a nuisance for the air force, but it was not difficult to rebut. It came from people with backgrounds, people known to be minimum deterrers, and they would say that sort of thing, no matter what. The argument about the tunnel, however, was devastating. For four years the air force had developed this concept because it was most easy to segregate, it had the least "public interface," the least trouble. But the Press study pointed out that the tunnel was not invulnerable and it was not verifiable, and either objection was enough to stop the tunnel and send the air force planners back to design studies. Press's report proved fatal to the air force request for full-scale development at the end of 1977. In September 1977, when the annual budget review came round, the Office of Management and the Budget pointed out the problems to the president, who agreed that work on the missile should slow down until work on the base caught up. Jimmy Carter cut the air force funding request by $100 million.

For Press, the stay on MX was short-lived. In early November 1977 American satellite intelligence recorded a series of tests of what appeared to be a new guidance system on the SS18 missile, one of the most modern in the Soviet armory. This suggested that the Soviet planners were not going to wait for another generation of missiles to increase the accuracy of their missiles. They would retrofit their existing missiles with a better guidance system, as the United States was already doing in retrofitting the Mk12A warheads to its Minuteman. For Bill Perry, this was critically important news, because it brought closer the time when Minuteman would be vulnerable. It was a good reason to raise the whole question of MX's urgency again.

Perry wrote to Brown, in hand, that the new intelligence meant that the threat to Minuteman would be advanced. The information reached Brown shortly after he had read a preliminary version of Press's report on Minuteman vulnerability. The new intelligence did not really make a great deal of difference. Press and his team acknowledged the eventual threat, they had agreed that a replacement for Minuteman was needed. It was still the case that no missile in a new base could be deployed until long after the Soviet threat became real. And Press's objections to the trench were just as cogent after the SS18 tests as before. What the tests did mean, however, was that proponents of the missile had reason to raise the issue once again and to undermine Press's credibility as an opponent by characterizing him as too sanguine about Soviet plans.

Harold Brown had come to his new job, he would later recall, convinced that America needed a new land missile in a new, invulnerable base. He wasn't persuaded that a three-thousand-concrete tunnel was the right base, however, or that the 92″ missile was the right size. When he had to, Harold Brown spoke the air force brief for MX. He asked for funding, he explained its purposes to Congress. But the feeling at the White House was that Harold Brown wasn't putting his weight behind the missile program.

At the same time as Brown was pondering the program, Al Latter began to revive his interest in mobile missiles. It had been twelve years since he had offered the idea of a garage-based mobile missile on a truck. Still associated with the Air Force Scientific Advisory Board, Latter gave a talk in 1977 ridiculing the trench deployment idea. He didn't concern himself much with the shock tube effect—there were ways that could be handled. He didn't concern himself much with the verification problems—actually, he thought the trench could be verified all too well. The Soviet Union could find out exactly where the missile was, because its huge weight and nuclear warheads gave off radiation signatures that satellite or difficult-to-detect ground sensors could register. Latter had another objection, which was crucial but discussed only in secret sessions. This was that even if the blast could be directed out of the trench, the electromagnetic pulse could not be. It would be conducted along the tracks and soundlessly, invisibly, damage the missile guidance system.

Latter's talk began a major split within the services. General Lew Allen, the physicist who headed the Air Force Systems Command, could see the merit of the argument, and he took up Latter's alternative. This was for a deception system with shelters and a smaller missile—either the Minuteman or a missile like the Minuteman. Latter recommended silos rather than horizontal garages, favouring concealment over mobility. General Jones, who was then air force Chief of Staff and would later be chairman of the Joint Chiefs of Staff, and General Ellis of the Strategic Air Command, continued to favor the idea of trenches, essentially because it presented fewer problems of manpower and public contact once it was operating. They believed that detection problems could be met by putting the missile on tracks, so it could move quickly on warning.

Latter's appearance before the Air Force Scientific Board created enough interest for word of it to reach Harold Brown, who called Latter into his office in the fall of 1977. It had been fourteen years since the two had met on the question of multiple warheads, when Latter had told Brown he had done a disservice to America, but this time Brown was very responsive to Latter's criticism. He readily asked the program office at Norton to study the alternative of basing in vertical shelters or silos, and at the end of 1977 he appointed a Defense Science Board panel under Dr. Michael May of the Lawrence Livermore Laboratory to conduct a parallel study.

Michael May was then fifty-two, and one of the most widely respected minds in the weapons community. Born in Marseille, May still spoke English with a French accent, even after twenty-six years in the heart of the weapons community, the Lawrence Radiation Laboratory in the rural town of Livermore, behind San Francisco. It was at Livermore that Edward Teller, Harold Brown, and others had worked on the hydrogen bomb, and it was at Livermore, through the fifties and sixties, that Michael May worked on and then directed the development of the hydrogen bombs for the Poseidon and Minuteman missiles. He had been associate director for nuclear design and, from the mid-sixties until the early seventies, director of the laboratory, as Herbert York and Harold Brown had been before him. After resigning as director, May took the more flexible job of associate director-at-large, and began to interest himself in the arms control negotiations being pursued by Henry Kissinger in Washington. He had been appointed a member of the U.S. SALT delegation in 1974 and a personal adviser to the then secretary of defense, James Schlesinger.

Slightly built and unobtrusive, his bright brown eyes nestled in finely lined pouches, May commanded attention simply with intellect and diffidence, and it was with intelligent diffidence that May approached the task of reviewing, in the fall of 1977, half a dozen years of work on a base for the new missile. It was a problem on which he had not formally worked before, but with which he was familiar. For thirty years, May had been a friend and collaborator with his fellow physicist Albert Latter, and he had many times listened to Latter's discussions of Minuteman vulnerability, of his garage mobility scheme. Most of the basing schemes had at one time or another been discussed around the halls and seminar rooms in the Lawrence Livermore Laboratory, which was tightly protected against outsiders but relatively open and unconstrained for those inside.

In his discussions with Harold Brown, May raised the

problem of the compatability of the various basing schemes
with the expected strategic arms limitations agreements.
May argued that, since the agreement was not finalized, and
it was in theory possible to verify any base so long as one
could agree on the appropriate inspection, he ought to examine all possible bases without excluding those that presented
greater verification problems than others. Brown agreed,
and excused May from the need to use verifiability as the
governing criterion, though May's Defense Science Board
panel was to comment on the ease or difficulty of verifying
the number of missiles deployed in the various basing systems.

May and his panel set to work. All the schemes they considered then were already old, already well known within
the confines of the weapons community. Albert Latter's garage mobility scheme was now more than a dozen years old,
and most of the other alternatives had in one way or another
been canvassed in the 1967 Strategic Bases X study. The
small submarines, superhardened silos, missile-launching
aircraft—the thirty or so alternatives awaited May's
bemused inspection. He was not asked to recommend how
many missiles ought to be deployed, or how they would fit in
with the other legs of the triad, or whether land missiles
were necessary. He was asked to find the best way to protect
them on land.

May and his panel took only a few months to reach their
most important conclusion. They looked at the air force proposal to put the missile in a buried tunnel, and they rejected
it. It was unnecessarily expensive—that was the principal
objection—and it raised too many uncertainties. The shock
tube effect, the vulnerability of the tunnel to electromagnetic impulse—they were uncertainties unnecessarily in-
curred, May thought, and there must be a better solution.
Like many who had looked at the problem, May thought the
best solution, certainly the least expensive and most effective, was to build a light missile and carry it around the

Interstates on semitrailers. But, like everyone else who had looked at the idea, he also concluded that the American people would not care for it, and it had no hope of adoption. The panel then looked at missile-carrying airplanes and small missile-carrying submarines. May thought both these ideas had some advantages, but they both had an overwhelming disadvantage. Planes carrying missiles were vulnerable to the same sudden nuclear attack as were bombers. Submarines carrying missiles shared the same vulnerability as the Polaris submarines already cruising the Pacific and Atlantic oceans. Since submarines are slow and relatively fragile, they are vulnerable to an area barrage attack if they can be located. The Soviet Union cannot now locate U.S. submarines, but since the U.S. can usually locate Soviet submarines, analysts argue that having too much of the deterrent at sea makes it dangerously dependent upon the pace of Soviet antisubmarine technology.

Both planes and submarines protected the new missile in ways that land systems could not duplicate, but neither were any less vulnerable than the comparable systems already deployed. Nor would they have the same advantages as those now given by the Minuteman—the planes could not fire almost instantly after the order was received, as the Minuteman missiles could. The planes would have to take off, release their missiles, which would then fire. If the United States ever had to strike Soviet missiles in their silos, the scrambled aircraft observed by satellite might give warning of the attack. And the submarine missiles had the same problems as existing submarines. It was difficult to communicate with them and to concert all submarines in a combined instantaneous attack. For those reasons, May and his panel could see little advantage in either airplanes or submarines as carriers for the new missile.

The May panel then looked at alternatives to the large missile, the 92″ diameter missile proposed by the air force. The bigger missile could carry bigger warheads, so the more megatons the planners wanted to survive a first strike, the more desirable was the bigger missile. For mobility and invulnerability, there was no doubt that the very smallest missile, even a single-warhead small missile, was the best option. But if the missile was to be put in hardened shelters, which was the only alternative left, then the bigger the missile the better. May personally favored the smaller missile, but there was no cost-effective argument for it, since it would have to be moved on specially constructed roads.

May's panel also looked at the possibilities of defending the missile with a hard point anti-ballistic missile system. This had been one of the recommendations of the 1967 Strat-X study. May was not persuaded that the system would work sufficiently well to justify either the cost of constructing it or the damage to arms control from unilaterally renouncing the anti-ballistic missile treaty between the Soviet Union and the United States.

By a process of elimination, May concluded that the best system was a variant of the 1964 Latter proposal—neither a continuous trench which depended entirely upon concealment; nor a fully mobile system which depended entirely upon unpredictability—but a mobile system with many more hard points than there were missiles. This system combined the advantages of concealment, deception, and mobility, and could perhaps do it at reasonable cost. Because an upright silo was harder than a flat shelter, May's team recommended a series of silos concealing a smaller number of missiles which, given a lag of a few hours, could be moved from one silo to another. This was the multiple aim point or discrete vertical system proposed in earlier studies but never tested or recommended by the air force.

May's report was qualified in a way that would later become important. He had been persuaded that the shelters could be constructed cheaply. If they could be constructed cheaply and in great quantities—not just four or five thousand, but eight or ten thousand—then the United States could stay ahead of any Soviet bid to build more warheads than the U.S. was prepared to build shelters. But if the shelters could not be built cheaply, then the U.S. would lose this race. It depended critically on the cost of the shelters and also on the cost of the roads. And the bigger the missile, the more expensive the roads. So, by a process of tradeoffs, May had finally decided to recommend a system that was very close to the point where it was no longer a good idea.

May was not happy about any of the alternatives. It was a question of "picking the least rotten apple from a barrel of rotten apples," he told his colleagues. If there was to be a new land missile, then it would have to be deployed among a great number of shelters. These could be either flat shelters or upright shelters, but upright shelters were stronger. The critical cost was the road network, he told Brown at the beginning of 1978, and if the costs increased rapidly then it would not be worthwhile competing with the Soviet Union. The Russians would be able to add warheads more cheaply than the United States could add shelters.

While Michael May was looking at the alternatives for Harold Brown, General Lew Allen was conducting his own review for the air force. He appointed a team from his own command under General John Toomay. It examined the tunnel that was being developed out at Norton, and it examined Latter's objections and his alternative of a smaller missile deployed deceptively among many shelters. Toomay's group, known as the Tiger Team, concluded that the smaller missile was much easier to move and hide, and that, while it could not carry as many warheads, it was only in the very long run that the big missile would be cost-competitive, even in terms of warhead numbers, compared to the smaller missile. This was a very striking departure from the position the air force had held since the beginning of the seventies, and it remained so unpopular in the service that Toomay's small-missile recommendation was never widely known. John Toomay and Michael May consulted closely on their studies, and the Toomay study also recommended the tunnel system be dropped in favor of a form of deceptive sheltering, preferably upright.

With the Press, Toomay, and May panels all throwing doubts on the trench idea, Bill Perry was not at all optimistic about an early decision for full-scale development when he testified before Senator McIntyre at the beginning of 1978. "We have made a very intense assessment of where the so-called trench program stands today," he told McIntyre on 28 February. "I have to report to you that we think there are very significant technical difficulties in the program as now conceived. As a result of this, we are not today in a position to recommend going into full-scale development on this program, nor do we have any confidence that we will be in that position this October, which is the date that the full-scale development decision was originally scheduled to be made." However, he added, "we have no significant technical problems with the development of the missile," and the issue is "more of a requirements issue, as it has to do with whether a large throwweight high accuracy missile is desirable. That debate will be engaged in both the legislative and executive branches during this year."

Perry did not think a full-scale development decision could be taken by October. Yet it would be taken by October, with no better idea of a suitable base than Perry had had at the beginning of the year. Just as it had been by Gerald Ford at the end of 1976, the system would be recommended for full-scale development with no certainty about where it was to be put.

For the air force at the beginning of 1978, the problem was to agree on something, on one single base that could be presented as a united solution, or risk losing the program entirely. This was difficult, because the air force itself was now split between the Tiger Team, which wanted a vertical shelter with maybe a smaller missile, and the Ballistic Missile Office at Norton, which wanted a trench with a big missile. As Toomay explained air force thinking in March 1978, "With MX, our approach will be to obtain a broad consensus on the important technical issues before we pick up the banner of advocacy for deployment. Such a system is mandatory for a system as expensive as any new strategic weapon will be, whether a submarine, a bomber, or a missile."

By April 1978, the air force had reached this broad consensus: It wanted Al Latter's vertical shelters, with a big missile.

In time for the spring Defense System Acquisitions Review Committee meeting, the program office capitulated and produced a new costing of the vertical shelter idea. It was cheaper than the continuous trench, and harder to attack. The problem remained that it took twenty-four hours to move the missile from silo to silo. The vertical shelter now became the air force position, agreed by all the fiefdoms and stoutly defended outside the service. After the April meeting in the E ring of the Pentagon basement, a meeting attended by Perry, the Joint Chiefs, the air force secretary and assistant secretaries, and briefed by General Hepfer, the whole Pentagon position settled around a silo shelter system, with earth barriers to assure the Soviet Union of the number of missiles inside the ring of empty silos. This was the system recommended by May, by Latter, and now by Hepfer and the air force. It had not previously been examined—indeed, Hepfer was to remark that the air force had not looked at silos before the March '76 Defense Systems Acquisitions Review Committee—because it had appeared to the air force likely to be unacceptable on grounds of the time it took to move the missiles (twenty-four hours) and the fact that the Soviet Union was likely to say that silos were missile launchers and therefore countable under SALT.

Once Harold Brown had a position everyone was agreed upon, and with the new intelligence reporting Soviet retrofitting of more accurate guidance systems, he went very strongly with MX. At the White House, he began to press for the program.

6

A Flight of Doves

THERE was never any substantial doubt, after the tunnel idea was thrown out, that America would nonetheless have a new, more accurate and more powerful missile. Even Frank Press's panel readily agreed a new missile was necessary, if for no other reason than that the Minuteman was getting older. His panel was not asked to review the capabilities of the weapon, or to examine the fundamental question of whether America needed an improved silo killer. Nor were the May or Toomay panels asked to look at this issue. That was a given, an issue beyond the scope of the committee. If it was to be examined at all, it would be examined in the three Presidential Directive 18 follow-on committees, and they were all under the control of the Pentagon.

In the State Department, which had sometimes contested new weapons decisions in the past, the director of politico military affairs and thus the officer responsible for taking a policy line, was one of the most liberal of the arms controllers in the Carter administration, former *New York Times* national security reporter Leslie Gelb. Gelb might have been expected to raise objections to MX, but he did not. He thought a new missile was necessary, that if the Soviet

153

Union was going to improve the accuracy of its weapons, the U.S. ought to also, and even though he pointed out to congressional committees that the Soviet Union could consider America's MX just as threatening as America viewed the accuracy improvements to the Soviet force, he did not contest the MX proposal in the administration.

In the Arms Control and Disarmament Agency, Paul Warnke, who was perhaps the most prominent and consistent of the administration doves, and who would later become a firm public opponent of the MX, could already see a close political connection between MX and the SALT II treaty—no missile, no treaty—so he did not raise objections to the new missile either. Warnke would later say that the SALT protocol left open the possibility of a mutual agreement to prevent a new generation of missiles on both sides, and his secret strategy was to allow the generals to have MX now and take it away from them later in return for equivalent concessions from the Soviet Union. Warnke saw MX as a bargaining chip for SALT II, and he would ruefully reflect, when the Carter administration was out of office, that the bargaining chip had become a very concrete weapons program, and the treaty it was intended to buy had been withdrawn from Senate consideration.

When the MX decision finally came up to the president for approval, neither Warnke nor Gelb were any longer in the administration. Warnke had left for what he insisted were personal reasons of health and family at a politically convenient time for the administration. Gelb, after a series of bruising defeats by Zbigniew Brzezinski, which made it clear to him that arms control was no longer a winning issue in the administration, left for the Carnegie Peace Endowment and, ultimately, his old job as national security reporter on the *New York Times*.

One other official in the administration might have raised objections in principle to MX and did not. Cyrus Vance, the secretary of state, privately objected that the missile would be "destabilizing." But he did not speak out against it within the administration. Vance, then sixty-two, was a veteran of countless long-forgotten troubleshooting missions for Democratic administrations since Kennedy's—a Wall Street lawyer who had made his reputation patching up quarrels in Panama, in the Dominican Republic, and in Cyprus. At the Paris peace talks on Vietnam, Vance had intelligently and discreetly defended the interests of the United States. He was himself a former Defense Department official, general counsel, then army secretary, and finally under secretary of defense to Robert McNamara in the Johnson administration, and he was—with President Carter—one of the voices for caution and restraint within the government of the United States. Vance was so unobtrusive and his speeches so flavorless that, as international events became more threatening and Carter's popularity dropped, the control of American foreign policy was gradually being lifted out of the hands of the secretary and away from the State Department, into the hands of the national security assistant, Zbigniew Brzezinski, and his National Security Council staff. As time went by, Vance would be left with only the appearances and the day-to-day administration of policy made elsewhere, until in March 1980 he would resign and return to practice law on Wall Street.

Vance knew that MX would directly affect the strategic arms talks with the Soviet Union, if not this round then the next, and he also knew that the decision would affect Carter's standing on Capitol Hill and his ability to get the Strategic Arms Limitations Treaty with the Soviet Union through the Senate. One of the very few unambiguous responses Vance had made in reply to questioning by congressional committees was to agree without qualification that the MX, deceptively based, would be "very destablizing" for America's relations with the Soviet Union—an opinion he became increasingly reluctant to express.

Vance was in an unhappy position, not simply because the

administration was becoming more hawkish and he was losing some of his old allies, like Paul Warnke, but also because Vance had himself in earlier times made decisions which in a sense foreclosed the options on MX.

Vance had come to Washington twenty years before. As old Senator Stennis would recall during hearings on the SALT treaty in 1979, "twenty-two years ago this fall Sputnik went up into space and within a few days thereafter Cyrus Vance went up too, went up to Capitol Hill for his first official duty." Vance had come down as counsel on Lyndon Johnson's Preparedness Subcommittee. He was there from 1957 to 1960, years in which the committee had done so much, with so little evidence, to convince people that the Eisenhower administration had allowed a "missile gap" to open up between the United States and the Soviet Union. Like Brown, he had been an exponent of the "no-cities" strategy within the McNamara Defense Departmant.

As a Defense Department official, Vance had been one of the architects of the MIRV program. Once each side MIRVed, the side that struck first could destroy more missiles than it lost. It would therefore have a relatively larger number of warheads left over, which produced what the Pentagon called "post attack imbalance." Once each side MIRVed, there was no stable situation. This was the source of the vulnerability of land missiles, which was forcing a new decision about America's nuclear weapons arsenal, and which threatened a new and vastly more dangerous round of nuclear weapons competition. Vance could not now plead ignorance of the effect of MIRVs, the consequences of which were still being worked through in Washington and Moscow. Seeing the certainty of competition, he had written in an October 1966 Defense Department memorandum: "I do not want any potential Soviet MIRV capability to be accelerated by our lack of attention to proper safeguarding of information about the concept and its strategic advantages. . . ." In another memo, he warmly advocated these advantages.

Vance's embarrassment on MIRVs was not unlike his embarrassment two years before over Vietnam. In 1966, the same year he had urged the advantages of MIRV, Vance, according to the Pentagon Papers, had been overwhelmingly in favor of prosecuting the Vietnam war with more men and material, with intensified bombing of North Vietnam, and with increased efforts to create a viable government in the South. More than a decade later, he told his congressional confirmation hearing that "in the light of hindsight, it was a mistake to intervene in Vietnam"—a view he could equally take of MIRV. It were better if it had not been done, but, unlike the experience of humiliation in Vietnam, from which people could draw useful lessons, MIRV inexorably led to greater and greater instability. If, in October 1977, he had thought MX in trenches would be "very destabilizing," he would think differently by July 1979. He would then think the decision to develop MX "wise and sensible." When the MX decision came up to the National Security Council in June of 1979, Vance was silent.

Vance, Gelb, Warnke—the three likely opponents—were mute. One of the most powerful reasons for this was the Soviet response to the March 1977 proposals for deep cuts in the missiles on both sides, proposals that included a ban on a new missile on either side. The Soviet counterproposal was for one new missile on both sides, but a single warhead missile only, instead of a MIRVed missile like the MX. The Soviets wanted a single warhead missile and the U.S. did not, so they could not agree.

By the time the Soviet foreign minister, Andrei Gromyko, accepted the U.S. offer of no new missile in May of 1978, the U.S. was already too far down the MX road to accept its own suggestion. The Soviet tests at the end of 1977 and the beginning of 1978 showed they could achieve, in their present rockets, the accuracies necessary to threaten America's land missiles, and so the need for a new land missile for America increased at the same time as the disadvantage of the Soviet

Union having a more advanced missile decreased. Carter rejected Mr. Gromyko's offer to ban any new ICBMs through to 1985.

The really big objections to the MX program came not from the people most likely to be a problem for the air force, but from Frank Press, from the cost analysts in the skeptical Office of Management and Budget, from Admiral Turner at the CIA, who would produce the most powerful arguments against land deployment, and from Jimmy Carter himself. It was Carter and usually Carter alone who kept coming back to the question of verification, and when Zbigniew Brzezinski and his deputy, David Aaron, raised the problems of verification, as they often did, they were frequently and literally speaking for the president.

If there was no substantial objection to the new missile by those who might have made it in the early days of the administration, nor was there any strong objection to the targeting and strategic policies which justified it.

In April of 1977 the Carter administration had explicitly confirmed the nuclear strategy of its predecessor, which was the strategy of NSDM 242, which was the strategy of Henry Kissinger and James Schlesinger. It provided for flexible options, for limited attacks, and for countersilo attacks, and thus implied the need for weapons capable of achieving its requirements. Noone had objected in the Carter administration when this strategy was reconfirmed, and, though both Vance and Brown would later try to slow down the push to codify an even more detailed and sophisticated version of the doctrine in a new presidential decision, neither had any powerful objections to the idea of flexible response. That battle was still sometimes fought in the press; it was no longer fought by sophisticated insiders. The only real battles over MX were over timing, over the size of the missile, and over the way in which it would be based—though these disputes were often seen by their proponents as substitutes for disputes about fundamentals. A smaller missile, for example, could be based in the air or at sea, and, if it was smaller and in the air or at sea, it was much less likely to be mistaken for a first-strike weapon than would be the large missile deployed on land. The disputes between arms controllers and the hawks were more over the size of the missile, the number deployed, and the degree to which its numbers needed to be verified by the Soviet Union.

Yet, one of the most ironic outcomes of the long disputes on these issues, of the debates in 1977 and 1978 which ranged within the administration over verifiability, missile size, mobility, and deception, was that, when a decision was taken the following year to build the missile, it would be in a base that was not verifiable and in a size that was not easily transportable.

After the spring Defense System Acquisitions Review Committee meeting, Bill Perry and the air force agreed that they should have a new missile, and that it should be based in thousands of upright shelters. But they did not agree on the size of the missile. Perry wanted a lighter missile, one that would be compatible with the Trident II missile planned for the navy's Trident class submarines. John Hepfer feared he might have put the idea in Perry's mind one day when, more than usually dispirited about the program, he had told Perry that "we need that missile so bad we'd even build it for the navy." Hepfer worried unnecessarily. The common missile idea had been around for a long time, and it had certain important advantages. Since it was lighter, it could be more easily borne aloft in planes, or put on trucks. And if it ultimately proved impossible to deploy the missile on land, then it could be put to sea. Perry wanted to keep the air-mobile option open, and he thought there were cost advantages, too, and he persuaded Brown to authorize a series of studies to work out the figures.

In a 14 April memorandum, Perry thought the savings if the two programs were run together would be about $2 billion to $4 billion, with a saving of $1 to $2 billion for a mostly common missile and about $0.5 billion for a partly common missile. Perry also thought that the biggest missile that would still fit through the Trident submarine firing ports, an 83″ diameter, would have pretty much the same capability as the air force 92″ missile, particularly under the SALT treaty limit of ten warheads on each weapon. The 92″ might be able to carry a few more warheads, but it could not carry more under SALT constraints. Air force objections to the common missile idea were vociferous and adamant. A common missile would mean that either the navy would build it or the air force would build it, but both could not build it. It would probably mean that the air force bought its missile from the navy, which was not at all a pleasing thought to the Ballistic Missile Office at Norton. Still worse, a common missile would upset the whole strategy that underlay air force planning. This was to get the missile produced whether or not a base had been decided upon, because, once it was produced, a place would have to be found. But if it could be put to sea, the pressure to do so might well become irresistible, and the air force would ultimately lose its land-based missiles. At the MX project office at Norton Air Force Base, General Hepfer's teams studied the two missiles, and concluded that the environments in which a sea missile and a land missile had to work were so different the whole job of building the missile would be complicated. That complication led to the conclusive argument against the common program—that the program would have to be set back two to three years.

Perry was not convinced. The air force had persuaded Malcolm Currie and the Ford administration to endorse the 92″ missile, but in April 1978 Perry publicly insisted the Carter administration had made no decision on missile size.

Dr. Zeiberg, Bill Perry's deputy, was firmly in favor of the bigger missile, as was the Ballistic Missile Office at Norton. Zeiberg's view was that if America was allowed only one new missile under SALT, let it be the biggest. And commonality essentially meant the air force would buy a missile from the navy, which meant trouble.

While John Hepfer worked with the former navy Trident program commander, Admiral Wertheim, on the proposal, Zeiberg called in two of the grand old men of missilery to look it over. They were Admiral Levering Smith, the originator of the Polaris program, and General Sam Phillips, a Minuteman program manager. Both senior retired officers agreed the savings would never be realized. They said the air force would demand so many modifications to the navy plan that the cost would be greater than a completely new design. The experience of navy/air force cooperation on the TFX fighter, which eventually became the F-111 fighter bomber, demonstrated the problems, and designing a common missile, Zeiberg concluded, would be very much more difficult than designing a common plane.

Between a naval and an air missile there were differences in guidance systems and differences in testing procedures. Although Brown and Perry continued to press for the 83", and although Victor Utgoff, on Dr. Brzezinski's staff, succeeded in interesting the president in the idea, it was overborne by the solid weight of service opposition. It was not merely that the air force did not want it. The navy did not want it, either, though the ultimate result of choosing the bigger missile was to delay the Trident II program. So effective was the opposition that the important question of whether a smaller missile was desirable simply on mobility grounds was not examined, though the first Albert Latter proposal for a garage mobile had depended on having a small transportable missile.

The decision to proceed with the full scale development of MX would not come before the president until June 1979, and no base would be agreed on for it until another three months after that. Nonetheless the Carter administration decided to keep open the option of proceeding with a new missile by rejecting the May 1978 Soviet offer to ban a new missile on either side in the SALT II treaty. A year before the administration had made this very proposition to the Russians. Now it rejected it. Soviet missile tests demonstrated, according to the Defense Department, that it could achieve counter silo accuracies on its existing missiles by retrofitting new guidance systems. This meant that the United States had less to gain by agreeing to no new missile on either side. Another reason for rejecting the Soviet offer was that only by keeping the option to develop a new missile open in the new agreement could the administration hope to sell SALT to its critics. But keeping the option open effectively meant that the United States would exercise the option, since it otherwise would be preferable to agree to no new land missile on either side. This decision was taken in the "SALT track," the most senior and political of all the forums where the MX decision was being debated, and for a long time the people lower down, disputing the base and the need for the new missile, were not aware that for all intents and purposes the decision to build some kind of new missile and put it in some kind of land base had already been made. As Warnke would say some months after his departure the following year "SALT II will permit each side to go ahead with one new type of ICBM. The reason for that is to protect the MX option. We would have been able to negotiate an agreement under which neither side would have been able to deploy a new ICBM." Asked whether he would have been able to negotiate such an agreement, Warnke said "certainly."

But deciding that MX was necessary to placate opposition to the proposed SALT agreement raised a whole new set of problems for the MX project, since whatever basing mode that was adopted had to be compatible with America's obligations under the treaty. One problem was that the treaty counted not missiles but "launchers," and the Soviet Union could declare that the thousands of empty silos in the multiple aim point network were "launchers" to be counted toward the total limit on the number of launchers. The problem was to make it clear to the Soviet Union what the United States intended doing, and then interpret Soviet consent to the treaty as consent to the basing scheme the U.S. had foreshadowed. A second problem was far less easily manageable. The treaty forbade both sides from interfering with the "national technical means of verification," which predominantly meant satellites, used by either side to count the other's weapons. Since the multiple silo system was intended to make it impossible to find the missile, it also made it much harder to count the number deployed. The first problem was dealt with, so far it could be, by a series of unilateral U.S. statements. The second problem became an insuperable difficulty for the silo system, and led to its cancellation by the end of fall 1978.

By mid-1978 the Carter administration had concluded that the MX program would be necessary to placate objections to the upcoming SALT treaty. At the beginning of July, officials at the SALT Special Consultative Committee decided that the upcoming SALT agreement must not only preserve the option of a new missile, but must also clearly allow a deceptive basing system. Since the SALT agreement counted "launchers" rather than missiles, a way had to be found to exclude the multiple shelters from being described as "launchers." This was the reason the launcher-canister in the mobile systems considered to date moved around with the missile. The problem was to make sure the Soviet side understood this, and could not later declare that it was an infringement of the SALT treaty.

The administration's concern that SALT would allow MX in the kind of deceptive deployment then being considered was heightened at the end of July 1978, when General David Jones, at his first press conference as chairman of the Joint Chiefs of Staff, foreshadowed military opposition to any kind of treaty that did *not* allow for MX. "I would have deep reservations," said Jones to the press, "about any kind of arms control agreement that did not allow the United States to make its land missiles less vulnerable." He also said: "I consider mobiles are authorized and therefore MAP is authorized. And to me that is not a subject for discussion or negotiation." MAP, an acronym for multiple aim point, generically described all bases that had a single missile deployed among a number of hardened shelters.

Chief Jones might not want to discuss it, but the Special Consultative Committee guiding the U.S. SALT delegation did. Carter's anxiety that the Soviet Union recognize the legality of the multiple mode led it to draft some sentences to be used by Harold Brown in a speech in New Orleans in August. He duly made his speech, asserting the American view that the SALT II treaty draft allowed the deployment of a mobile ICBM system "of the type we are now considering."

Later that year, the outgoing chief of the Arms Control and Disarmament Agency and chief SALT negotiator, Paul Warnke, was instructed to raise the issue with the Soviet deputy foreign minister, Vladimir Semenov, at the SALT talks in Geneva. Since there was no agreed basing mode, and since the U.S. SALT delegation deemed it inadvisable to ask for explicit Soviet consent, all Warnke could do was to draw Semenov's attention to the distinction between shelters and launchers. All he could say of the MX system's characteristics was that the missile and its launcher would move from point to point. He told the Russians, he later recalled, that verifying the numbers of mobile launchers carrying a missile from point to point was no different in principle from verifying the numbers of ballistic missile submarines, and that the Russians were entitled to know how many launchers there were, but not where they were. He added that any system the U.S. decided to deploy and any system permitted by SALT would be one which permitted the Soviet Union to determine how many launchers there were.

Unwilling to seek Soviet agreement to a system whose outlines were only tentative, and risk an almost certain rejection, the U.S. had no choice but to assert the legality of MX in a mobile mode by unilateral statement. The theory was that, if the U.S. asserted that something was consistent with the treaty, and the Soviets went ahead and signed, the Soviets could not later say the system wasn't legal. Perry put the argument before the Senate Armed Services Committee in March 1979: "if we make a unilateral statement where we say the United States is going to proceed to do such and such a thing and the Soviet Union still elects to sign the treaty, that is their risk, that is not our risk." Of this, Senator Nunn remarked: "We had better start reading Tass and see what unilateral statements the Soviets are making, if that is our theory of legal commitment."

By August 1978 the silo based missile plan agreed to by Bill Perry and the air force at the April Defense Systems Acquisitions Review Committee meeting had made its way up to the level of the president, where it ran into the gravest difficulty. Because the president was committed to SALT, he insisted the numbers of missiles in any system be verifiable by the Soviet Union. And, at the same time, his aides insisted that there be no doubt that, while the Soviet Union would know the total number of missiles, it must never know exactly where the missiles were. These were the two conditions for any deployment idea, and they proved irreconcilable.

A meeting in August 1978 at the presidential retreat of Camp David was critical for the whole MX project. It was there that Brown firmly pushed for the MX and there that the president's attention was engaged. Brown was forceful, Carter critical. Brown argued that the Soviet threat to American missiles was increasing more quickly than had been expected, and that the U.S. would have to respond to it quickly. He said he was unhappy with the design work on the trench, but that the upright silo option now being developed by the air force and the Defense Science Board, looked like an effective and reasonably strong alternative base.

Carter was critical, and so was Brzezinski's deputy, David Aaron, who also attended the meeting at the Cacoctin mountain retreat.

Aaron argued that the silo-based missile was vulnerable to a sudden loss of security, which could instantly change it from America's greatest asset in a nuclear confrontation to America's greatest liability. The concept was PLU—presentation of location uncertainty—and he argued that the silo version did not have any protection if PLU was broken. There had been a security breakdown at TRW only a few years before, he pointed out, which resulted in Soviet agents learning details of a classified satellite program. TRW was now managing the MX program. If there was ever a catastrophic breakdown in MX security, he asked, if the Soviet Union ever learned of the location of the missiles in their silos, what could the United States do? If the two nations were in a crisis, and the Soviet Union suddenly revealed this knowledge, how would the United States react? This was not perhaps the most interesting scenario, since in informing the United States it knew where the missiles were located, the Soviet Union would offer the U.S. an inducement to fire first. The fear Aaron appealed to was the fear that the United States would never know for certain that the Soviet Union did not know where the missiles were.

Brzezinski argued with Brown, insisting that MX could be moved around frequently. He favored a truck mobile, able to roam around American highways and deserts, secure from Soviet destruction because, though it could be observed by satellite, its movements would be unpredictable. It was an idea that found some support in the Senate—John Glenn, for example, backed it—but that had some fundamental problems. It could use American interstate highways, which theoretically gave it a vast deployment area. But there was other traffic on those roads, and it was unlikely that, over the course of many years, there would not be public protest at the idea of thermonuclear weapons trucking on the nation's highways. As General Ellis observed to a White House staffer, "You begin with a missile on a truck, and pretty soon you find it's too tough to move it between Dubuque and Kansas City. There's too much protest. Then you move to other areas, but it's the same, and you find yourself moving into deserts. Once it's in a single area, it can be barraged, so you begin building shelters for it. Then you create roads or tracks between the shelters, and you end up with a deceptively based system and not a true mobile."

Brezezinski stuck to the true mobile idea with fidelity, not always aware, apparently, that the biggest size missile, which he also favored, could not be carried on a freely moving truck that could drive on public highways.

The meeting had before it the views of another panel set up by Press's office, strongly disputing the Defense Science Board's endorsement of the multiple silo base. The Press group believed that there were doubts about American ability to keep the missiles hidden from Soviet sensors, that it would be complicated by SALT constraints, and that it would not be effective until most of the shelters were built. All were strong criticisms. The panel recommended that research and development continue on surface multiple shelters, but that, in the meantime, the missile be based in the air. This had been the air force concept in 1973—before the difficulties became apparent.

The president had other problems with the missile system. He wanted to know why the U.S. could not rely on a policy of launch under attack, or at least the threat to launch under attack. Press's people and Arms Control Agency officials argued that the Soviet threat to Minuteman was fictitious since, although they could one day persuade themselves they could confidently hit the missiles, they could never be sure the U.S. wouldn't fire on warning or "launch under attack." If that was so, the Soviet missiles would explode over empty holes, minutes before U.S. warheads began to destroy Soviet factories and airfields. The air force secretary, Hans Mark, was a strong though discreet proponent of this view, and he was not alone in the administration. In response to it, Brown argued that "warning" was itself unreliable in a realistic war situation. Both sides would actually attack each other's warning systems first, so that the only warning each would have of an impending nuclear strike was a malfunctioning warning system. Was the president to give a fire order if all he knew was that warning systems malfunctioned? They malfunctioned for reasons other than nuclear attack—when communications computers broke down, for example—and it would be impossible, within the twenty or thirty minutes during which the president would have to make the decision, to distinguish between a Soviet attack and an electrical fault at, say, a satellite communications station in Australia.

"Camp David was critical," Zeiberg would say later. "That's when people decided something had to be done." But Carter clearly had questions about the silo multiple aim point He was concerned that it would be impossible to confidently verify the number of missiles in a field of thousands of silos, and on this point Brown failed to move him. The primary thing that killed MAP was verification. "The President was clearly opposed to MAP on verification grounds," a participant later recalled.

At Camp David, Carter was convined that MX was necessary, that the threat was real, and that a decision had to be made—but he said he needed more options than the silo, which was then the favorite.

By the end of September 1978, after a budget review meeting that had confirmed the president's doubts, Perry knew that, once again, the MX shelter was a dead duck. The president wanted to be sure about verification, and the doubts raised by Press had been sufficient to convince him the vertical silo wasn't the way. A few months later, the *New York Times*'s Richard Burt, who was close to the National Security Council staff, would report Carter as having remarked that the shell game "is the craziest idea I've ever heard."

Certainly he did remark to a news conference in September
that there were big problems with multiple protective shelters—"One is, how do you verify all the holes that don't have
missiles in them? It's obvious that we would keep the agreement, we would not violate it, but we do not know that that
would be the case on the other side."

When General Hepfer returned to Washington for a Defense Systems Acquisition Review meeting in early December 1978, he had already heard word of unhappiness in the
White House. Again the meeting was attended by the Joint
Chiefs, by the air staff, by Perry and his staff. It was again
held in the windowless basement briefing room in the E ring.
    Hepfer reiterated the confidence of the air force in the
vertical shelter system, explained how security could be
maintained and verification allowed. But everyone at the
meeting knew it was just another try at an already doomed
basing, the thirtieth in the tally of unacceptable alternatives. Perry thanked Hepfer for his presentation, and com-
plimented him on a fine job. It was not often he had seen such
a professional analysis, and he wanted the Ballistic Missile
Office to know he appreciated it. But it wasn't going to fly.
He did not explain all—he did not explain Carter's objections at Camp David and later at the fall budget meetings.
Nor did he explain that he and Zeiberg had already agreed
they would have to look at another alternative. He simply
said the air force would have to go away and look at the
air-mobile alternative and come back, and they would see if
the political climate was brighter. But they were going
ahead with full-scale development of the missile and would
soon make a decision on the base. So now was not a time to
let the effort flag.
    The good news for the air force, and it was very good news,
was that, while rejecting the silo and asking for a study of
the air mobile, Carter had given in on the single most important issue sought by the air force. He agreed to a budget

supplement request for full-scale development that would speed up work on the MX. According to Zeiberg's recollection, at the end of 1978 "we collectively agreed that we would submit a proposal for full-scale development for fiscal '79, but not identify the choice except it would be either an air mobile or a multiple protective shelter system."

This meant that the Carter administration went into 1979 committed to a new missile without knowing its size or where it could be put, making exactly the error that, years before, McIntyre said was disastrous. The trench had been queried by Frank Press and the silo scheme by the president, and this increased the pressure to quickly make an alternative decision to satisfy the SALT waverers and the increasingly strident defense lobby. In the end, the decision would be as irrational as any of those rejected hitherto.

7

The President Decides

BY the beginning of 1979, the changes that had begun the year before were beginning to make themselves felt. In January, Harold Brown, who had reservations about the counterforce concept he inherited from the Ford administration three years before, endorsed that same idea when he announced that "a strategy based on city destruction is no longer wholly credible." Behind this change of direction lay two years of studies, flowing from the Presidential Directive 18 decision in mid-1977 and now completed. There was the ICBM modernization study, which had recently concluded that a triad of land missiles, submarines, and bombers was no more expensive than the diad of bombers and submarines, and was less vulnerable. There was a targeting study, completed in December 1978 and already altering some nuclear war plans, which more than a year later would be publicly revealed as Presidential Directive 59. Using the study the target planning start at Offutt had drawn up single integrated operating plan 5D. It was not so much a change in thinking about nuclear war as an affirmation that the Carter administration was beginning to think about nuclear war in the same practical, detailed way as its predecessor had begun to do. What do we actually do when we find ourselves in a nuclear war? was the opening question, and one of the answers was to increase the number of targeting options.

Now, with the targeting studies and ICBM studies completed, the U.S. strategic policy was changing again. Brown instructed Perry to put together an acquisition policy based on the new targeting requirements and instructed the Joint Chiefs of Staff to put together operational plans to implement them. This last instruction meant that the Joint Strategic Planning staff at Offutt was asked to come up with more targeting options for the president, and existing targets were to be changed to include new economic, political, and military objectives.

At the same time, in the complete renovation of nuclear war planning, three other directives were being prepared. One, PD53, was a directive on a national telecommunications policy designed to increase the endurance of communications during nuclear attack. The other two, PD's 57 and 58, to be signed in the spring and summer of 1980, set planning guidelines for the reconstruction of America after nuclear war.

The PD18 targeting study had concluded, Perry explained in February 1979, that the strategic forces required greater flexibility in targeting than they presently had, and there should be more options available. The Joint Chiefs, he said, were then preparing those options for consideration by the president. The study had also concluded that both the forces and the command, control, and communications and intelligence that controlled the forces should have much greater endurance than the present system. Finally, the study concluded that the targeting emphasis should be shifted from a primary emphasis on population and economic targets to a primary emphasis on military targets, and that, for that targeting emphasis, the priorities should be to maximize the damage to those targets while minimizing collateral damage.

Brzezinski, who was the major proponent of renovating the theory as well as the weaponry, pushed for presidential approval of the new draft directive based on the targeting studies conducted by the Pentagon. Vance and Brown resisted, however, and PD59 was not formally approved by the president until the following year. Nonetheless, the studies had strengthened the case for a quick accurate missile. The studies included a history of U.S. targeting and war plans, an examination of new targeting concepts, escalation control, and war termination, major war and postwar objectives for the U.S., and communications control and constraints. These service studies were supported by a number of other studies farmed out to major think-tanks in the weapons community. RAND did a working note on the termination of nuclear war, Science Applications studied population targeting, Analytic Assessment Inc. reviewed recovery targeting, and the Systems Planning Corporation, the University of Miami Center, Stanford Research International, and General Research Corporation studied various aspects of Soviet thinking about nuclear war, including the Soviet concept of national entity survival and Soviet perceptions of U.S. nuclear strategies and strategic forces. RAND conducted a key study on ways to politically dismember the Soviet Union with nuclear weapons.

All these studies were directed at finding more effective ways to target U.S. weapons, so that, for example, the key links in the Soviet economy could be destroyed, and the war would leave the Soviet Union's regions independent of Moscow and Soviet territory vulnerable to Chinese attack. Another important aspect was meshing the U.S. strategic attack with the allied objectives in a general European war, so that American intercontinental weapons would cripple the Soviet advance. All these changes were refinements of the NSM 242, refinements designed to increase the efficiency of U.S. targeting, maximize the postwar strength of the U.S., and minimize the postwar strength of the Soviet Union. And while the earlier studies had focused on using U.S. weapons outside of the Soviet homeland, the new studies concentrated on big game—the attack on the Soviet Union.

Brown did not want the draft to go forward because he saw that, by raising again the question of countersilo strikes and limited nuclear war, the decision to deploy MX would be complicated. He believed that MX should be presented as a means of stabilizing the arms race, of making U.S. missiles less vulnerable, and that the countersilo, damage limitation, first-strike implications of a system that would be able to take out the entire Soviet missile force in one thirty-minute attack, should be hidden. Vance was equally vehement in his objections, for quite different reasons. He knew the Soviet Union was likely to be very unhappy with U.S. announcements about its refined ability to conduct nuclear wars, and that it would complicate the last stages of the SALT negotiations. Together, the two cabinet secretaries forced Brzezinski to delay the drafting of what became Presidential Directive 59.

But if Brzezinski was thwarted with PD59, he was able to press for action on less obvious improvements to U.S. nuclear war fighting ability. Accordingly, the NSC staff worked on improving the national telecommunications system for strategic war fighting and defense, an effort that resulted in Presidential Directive 53 in November 1979, and on civil defense and the survival of national command authorities, which resulted in PDs 57 and 58 in the spring and summer of 1980. These last directives were designed to strengthen the interagency planning effort for strategic war and postwar recovery and to establish a more credible set of alternative governments to ensure continuity in the face of a large-scale attack.

As these changes in nuclear war planning were being made, the MX project was accelerating. Perry and Brown had persuaded Carter to agree to increase the missile's funding in the 1979 calendar year with a fiscal '79 supplementary. For the first time in this administration, it was accepted that the decision about the base would have to be separated from the development of the missile. Indeed, there was no clear decision even about the size of the missile. All basing options remained open, and particularly air, trench, and silo. Behind the sudden acceleration was the strengthening influence of the president's national security assistant, Zbigniew Brzezinski.

A personality alternately cold and arrogant, charming and childlike, Brzezinski was dubbed "Woody Woodpecker" by the Georgia boys close to the president, partly because of his staccato diction and immense volubility, and partly because his sharp nose, narrow eyes, and hair swept along his brow and brushed up behind suggested the cartoon character. Polish aristocrats, Brzezinski's family was posted to Canada when he was ten. When the Communists seized power in 1945, his diplomat father decided the family would stay where it was. Zbigniew Brzezinski became a brilliant student at Harvard, and later taught there, before moving down to Columbia and his own research institute on Soviet affairs. Later, Brzezinski had founded the Trilateral Commission, an organization funded by David Rockefeller, with the announced purpose of drawing Western Europe, Japan, and the United States closer together. Through the Trilateral Commission, he had met Jimmy Carter, then governor of Georgia, and through 1975 and 1976 he cultivated the Southern candidate for the presidential nomination, offering him advice on foreign policy. He happily accepted the job of national security assistant when it was offered by the successful nominee.

Brzezinski was a man of swift and facile intellect, and he adopted and expounded ideas new to him with an enthusiasm that his staff and his two more experienced colleagues, Vance and Brown, sometimes found amusing and sometimes found disturbing. Like Carter, and like Brown, he had been the brightest boy in his class, and, in his different way, he showed it still. For Carter, his job was "synthesizer, analyzer, coordinator. . . . I might also be alerter, energizer, implementer, mediator, even lightning rod," a description that characteristically and perhaps correctly failed to include the prosaic but useful job of counsellor. His job, he said, "was just one endless race" with three or four hundred pages of material to look at each day, so that every morning he could competently brief the president on the world as it was.

As a briefer, Brzezinski was superb; as a thinker, he was less remarkable. He had been a loyal, indeed fervent, supporter of President Johnson on Vietnam. In February 1968 he had written that "whether we like it or not we are involved in something very long term . . . we must make it clear to the enemy that we have the staying power—we are willing to continue for thirty years, and we happen to be richer and more powerful. . . ." In 1969 he had discerned "a certain degree of political vitality" emerging in South Vietnam. Later he claimed that "it makes me puke how some others who were strong supporters of the war are rewriting history. I'm not going to do that; it's too self-serving. But someday I'll tell you the story of my own efforts in 1969 to end the war." The world waited.

As national security assistant to the president, he had joked with his Chinese hosts about attacking the Russian bear while on the Great Wall, and in Pakistan he waved a rifle in the direction of Soviet troops across the border. Brzezinski was jolly rather than witty, and his jokes often fell flat in the cool Washington social climate.

Although Brzezinski had published two hundred articles and books, it was difficult to say just what his view on the employment of nuclear weapons was. The drift of his many publications had actually been that the content of U.S. foreign policy ought to turn away from its obsession with the Soviet Union because the world was now "multipolar," there were "new influentials" like Saudi Arabia, Indonesia, and Mexico, and U.S. policy ought to be more concerned with them and less with a bipolar global power struggle. He thought the U.S. should make policy more with Japan and Western Europe, a community of developed nations. He also thought, he told an interviewer when his new job was announced, that he would have an architectural rather than acrobatic approach to the job of making foreign policy, a dig at his predecessor, Henry Kissinger.

In office, all these ideas seemed to have little relevance. Beneath the verbal fireworks, Brzezinski was resolutely anti-Soviet, and, as it turned out, his simplest road to the dominant position in making foreign policy was to be more aggressively and consistently anti-Soviet than his rival Cy Vance. Since the Soviet Union was developing missiles which could destroy American missiles in silos, he argued, America must build missiles to threaten Soviet missiles. It was a matter of perceptions, but perceptions were all-important. Brzezinski now wanted the biggest missile possible, as soon as possible. He believed, he said, that "the most urgent problem we face is the growing vulnerability of our Minuteman." If Brown had a problem with Brzezinski, it was perhaps that Brzezinski was a little too eager for the biggest, soonest, and a little too eager, later, to spread the word that he had been the leader on the MX decision.

For Brzezinski, the urgency of a decision on a new missile was dictated not by technology or need but by the upcoming summit between Carter and Brezhnev in Vienna. In late 1978 he persuaded Carter to pull the funding for the project off the budget track, where the Office of Management and Budget could stall it on grounds of financial prudence, and put it onto a decision track of its own, with a special series of National Security Council subcommittee meetings to examine it. He argued that Carter must have an MX decision before he went to Vienna, so he could deal from a position of strength. When he signed the SALT agreement and invited Brezhnev to sign it, it would be in the knowledge that America was proceeding with a new land missile in a deceptive employment.

Neither argument had anything other than a passing psychological significance—Brown had already made it clear that the U.S. considered some form of deceptive basing okay, and Paul Warnke had already informed Semenov that the U.S. thought silos and launchers could be separated. And since the missile would not actually be in the field for another decade, it mattered very little whether Carter knew in Vienna that he had already made a decision, or would make it soon after he returned. Brzezinski's urgency, which contributed to the muddle that the MX decision was soon to enter, was entirely contrived and inspired by a drive to rush a decision through before the missile's opponents could prevent it. China recognition behind, the Vienna meeting in front, the MX between—that was Brzezinski's agenda.

To Carter, a more compelling reason for accelerating an MX decision was not the need to deal from a position of strength with the Soviets, but to deal with the opposition to the SALT treaty in the Congress and the Pentagon. The CJCS General Jones had declared a year before that MX was necessary for the air force, and authorized under SALT. "This is not a matter of debate," he had said then. The Joint Chiefs had not given their endorsement of SALT (they would not do so until the week after the MX decision was announced), and, without their endorsement, there was no prospect of getting SALT through the Senate.

And in the Senate, the administration was being pressed not only to make a decision about MX basing, but to make a specific commitment to the largest-sized missile that could be built under SALT limits. Behind the closed doors of the Senate Armed Services Committee executive sessions, the senators themselves were fighting out Senator Jackson's amendment, designed to compel the administration to build the 92″ missile.

On Tuesday, 9 October 1951, the thirty-nine-year-old congressman from Washington State's first district rose from his seat in the chamber to declare a national crisis. Over the next four decades, the Congress of the United States would become familiar with Mr. Jackson's speech.

Russia had just exploded another atomic bomb, he said, and "one thing should now be clear to all of us—the Kremlin is moving heaven and earth to develop more powerful and more destructive nuclear weapons. Stalin means business." Only America's atomic superiority held Stalin in check, Mr. Jackson declared, and "falling behind in the atomic armaments competition will mean national suicide." Mr. Jackson wanted Congress to spend not the requested $1 billion on atomic weapons, but from $6 to $10 billion. He could not imagine, he said, "any member of this House going before his constituents and saying that he is not in favor of making every single atomic weapon it is within our power to produce." He believed then that "the hour is drawing close when atomic weapons tailored to all types of combat situations can be made available—when they can be produced in quantities and types sufficient to serve as the paramount instrument of deterrence either against all-out war or against future Koreas."

Mr. Jackson's thinking on the universal efficacy of nuclear weapons, a conviction that was to dominate his life in politics, was no doubt influenced by his experience earlier that year witnessing an atomic explosion on a Pacific atoll. "We learned," he confidently told newsmen on his return, "that troops can follow on immediately over an area destroyed by atomic blast with no fear of lingering radiation." It would be another decade before the cancers developed in the bodies of those Army victims of the tests in the Pacific and Nevada.

Henry Jackson of Washington, who was still called by the nickname "Scoop" that his older sister had given him thirty years before, was then at the beginning of what would become the most celebrated modern congressional career in the politics of national security. He had been first elected to Congress in 1940, the same year as German troops invaded his parents' homeland of Norway, and that conjunction seemed to guide his subsequent conduct.

Jackson would never be said to lack vigilance. When he reached the Senate in 1952, he was already known as a highly knowledgeable legislator on atomic energy matters and a hawk on defense spending. In time, Scoop Jackson would become one of the three or four most powerful people in the U.S. national security apparatus, and while others who equaled his stature would come and go, Jackson stayed. He made careers and he broke them. It was Jackson who forced the United States Navy to promote Hyman Rickover from captain to admiral, and who thereafter arranged for the navy's retirement rules to be annually suspended for the father of America's nuclear fleet. And it was jackson who sent word to the Joint Chiefs of Staff in 1973 that any promotion in the air force for Lieutenant General Royal B. Allison would be blackballed by the Armed Services Committee. Allison had testified in favor of the first nuclear weapons agreement with the Soviet Union. Allison told Jackson, "Senator, you have ruined my career."

It was Jackson who brought James Schlesinger to Washington, and who shepherded him from the Bureau of the Budget to the Defense Department, and who later had him made secretary of energy. And it was Jackson who fought Jimmy Carter's nomination of Paul Warnke as director of the Arms Control and Disarmament Agency and, when he failed to stop the nomination, welcomed his resignation. Jackson worked quietly, but well.

Jackson was by no means a malicious man, and certainly not a conservative one. In 1953 he walked out of Senator Joseph McCarthy's Investigations Subcommittee of the Government Operations Committee, declaring that the powers given to the Red-baiter from Wisconsin put other members of the subcommittee in the position of having responsibility but no power. Senator McCarthy's assistant, Roy Cohn, said he was "going to get Jackson," who was "favorably inclined to the Communists." More than twenty years later, when Vice-President Nelson Rockefeller gossiped in what he thought was a private meeting that two of Senator Jackson's assistants were communist infiltrators, Jackson had Rockefeller come down to the Senate chamber and read out an apology. He did not smear and would not be smeared.

While Jackson was a powerful figure in Washington State and in Washington, D.C., he could not convert this into votes in between. In 1960 he had thought John Kennedy would name him as his running mate and was miserable when Kennedy picked Lyndon Johnson instead. His misery was not alleviated when Kennedy asked him to chair the Democratic Committee during the fall campaign, and after Jackson had announced his acceptance, made it clear his brother Robert Kennedy would actually make the decisions. A decade later, Jackson hired Ben J. Wattenberg as his speechwriter and entered the Democratic primary for the presidential nomination in 1972. Wattenberg had written a book called *The Real Majority,* which purported to show that most people wanted a Democrat who was hawkish on defense matters and liberal on spending matters, which was just Jackson's combination. The real majority did not materialize for Jackson, who fared very poorly in the primaries. Four years later, he again briefly dipped into the primaries, but this time they were won by a politician who said he was liberal on defense matters and conservative on spending matters—Jimmy Carter.

But if Jackson could not win nationally, he continued to pile up splendid majorities in the state of Washington. His success there was not only the result of his candid and direct manner and evident force of personality. His political stands were perfectly matched to his constituents' needs. He was strongly for labor legislation in a state with many unionized workers; he was strongly for civil rights in a state with many young white liberals and few blacks; he was a strong supporter of Great Society programs in a state in which many people depended on federal assistance; and he was strongly in favor of federal spending on projects like atomic power plants and dams, particularly if they could be built in the state of Washington.

These stands had given Jackson a very high rating from the Americans for Democratic Action and the AFL-CIO, which would have done him little good among Washington State businessmen, were it not that he was the single most persistent and intelligent hawk in the Senate. Jackson was so hawkish that Richard Nixon discouraged the Washington State Republicans from running a strong candidate against him, a gesture that cost Nixon very little since there was almost no hope of unseating the senator. Jesse Helms, keeper of the Senate Republican purse strings in the 1976 campaign, declared: "Hell, I'm not giving a cent to any opponent of Scoop's."

Jackson was sometimes called the senator from Boeing, though not in his hearing. The aerospace company was the largest employer in his state, and many of Jackson's favorite defense projects were also projects sought by Boeing. In 1961 he had launched a rigorous investigation, from his position as chairman of the permanent Investigations Subcommittee of the Government Operations Committee, into why General Dynamics of Fort Worth was building the TFX fighter-bomber (later called the F-111) and not Boeing of Seattle. A decade later, he had fought for government funding for a supersonic transport plane, the SST, to be built by Boeing. And in the late seventies, when America was renovating its nuclear arsenal, he had fought successfully for air-launched cruise missiles, which were to be built by Boeing. An important battle of his career, which was part of his fight against Henry Kissinger's nuclear weapons agreements with the Soviet Union, was the battle for a new heavy land missile for the U.S. He had advocated the missile since the sixties, had recommended the defense secretary who had in turn recommended the missile, and had prodded three successive administrations to take the necessary decisions to research, develop, and deploy the missile.

In 1979 the Senate Armed Services Committee had both the supplemental request for full-scale development in 1979 and the fiscal year 1980 authorization to consider. Departing from the usual pattern, it spent far more time disputing the supplemental request than the authorization for fiscal year 1980. The reason for this was Senator Jackson and his determined campaign for a 92" diameter missile, against Perry's drive for the 83". At this stage, MX politics and SALT politics were closely intertwined. Jackson had moved an amendment to the fiscal '79 supplemental, urging that "in further developing the missile for the MX program, no action shall be taken that would limit such missile to a throwweight less than the maximum permitted under strategic arms limitations agreements."

The fiscal year '79 supplemental, which came forward on 7 February, requested an additional $265 million to "accelerate" the MX program, and was offered on the assumption that the department would be ready to start full-scale development of both the missile and basing in mid-year. There was a related proposal to add $20 million to the Trident II program, so that the two could be synchronized, if need be. Perry wanted the programs synchronized if the President decided to build the 83" instead of 92" missile.

The supplemental clearly expressed the administration's decision to separate the base and missile decisions, a separation that might have been impossible, had McIntyre—the only strong opponent to the plan—not lost his seat in the Senate. Of the $265 million, $190 million was to "initiate full-scale development of a new ICBM to replace the Minuteman force in the later 1980s," and only $75 million was to "undertake investigations of MX basing alternatives."

The fight for the big missile committment was led by Jackson and Senator John Tower against committee chairman Stennis and McIntyre's successor on R and D, Senator John

Culver. The fighting over vertical silos and missile size took place behind closed doors in the crafting of the language of the bill to be reported out by committee. One aide recalled that "people were fighting over commas and periods." One side wanted maximum flexibility for the administration. The other side, Jackson's side, wanted Perry's 83" plan stopped. Stennis and Culver kept the language flexible, but the message had got through, and, by the time the Senate voted on 3 May 1977 to authorize full-scale development for MX, the administration had already inclined toward the bigger missile.

Within three months, the MX program had completely changed. At the beginning of 1979, even as late as April, both the air force and the office of the secretary of defense thought the missile should be housed in upright buried silos. The principal policy-maker, Bill Perry, thought it should be 83" in diameter, and that the larger version had dropped out. By May, the 83" version had dropped out, the silo had dropped out, and the favored idea was similar to the trench housing favored by the air force since 1975. By June, the big missile remained, and there was no agreement on a base for it at all. In those three months, a complex set of forces at the top of the Carter administration came into play, resulting in a decision unrelated to any of the decisions that had been made before.

In the first three weeks of May, there would be three meetings of a special top level policy review committee to examine the MX options. In those three meetings, which were chaired by Harold Brown, there was a total of six hours of discussion during which the missile plan was completely altered. Brown and Perry went into the first meeting on 4 May preferring an 83" diameter missile sheltered in multiple silos; they came out two weeks later, with some misgivings, proposing a 92" missile which would be carried by a transporter along an open trench. Before the end of 1979, the trench had been abandoned and replaced with roads along which the missile would "dash" on warning of Soviet attack (the "racetrack"); that plan had then been altered by dropping the dash capability, and the final plan was being revised in the light of a new series of objections.

When Bill Perry went over to the House Armed Services Committee at the beginning of February to testify on the full scale development request, he was quite convinced that the big missile, against which he had fought for a year, was out of the running. Asked what had happened to the 92" missile, he replied, "The 92" missile still exists on paper. We see no reason or basis for considering it one of the alternatives." He explained that "we see no particular advantage to having a larger volume and a larger weight in the missile. All of the options we are considering for deployment involve mobility, and all of the mobility problems become more complicated as the missile is increased. So we wanted the smallest missile we could get to achieve ten reentry vehicles." The only advantage of the 92" missile, he said, would be "further growth" in the number of warheads.

In a hearing a few days later before the Senate Armed Services Committee, Perry said there were three alternatives for the MX program. They were to proceed with the full-scale development of the vertical multiple protective system; to proceed with full-scale development of an air mobile; and to start full-scale development of the missile and continue research and development of the base—in other words, to separate the two decisions. Perry clearly favored the first alternative. He said: "There are only two concepts which will have received detailed programmatic consideration sufficient to arrive at full-scale development in April, one of these being the MAP system, now called the MPS system, and the other, the air mobile system. So we will have to either have the option of selecting one of those two systems in April, or, if for some reason we think neither of those is a satisfactory solution, the only alternative will be to continue R and D and look at the other alternatives." What actually happened was that yet another base system appeared in May, after the silo system had been rejected.

As late as March of 1979, Perry was insisting that the 83″ was the best missile. He said, 7 March: "I believe now that it is possible to maintain the option for commonality with the Trident II missile at no significant expense or no significant degradation of the performance of the MX missile. It only requires a decision to limit the diameter to 83″ and a decision to select the stages for MX, so we can take two of those three stages and make a Trident missile out of them." The Trident II, he had said in February, could achieve "hard target kill." The 83″ missile, he said "would be my recommendation."

Five options for America's nuclear arsenal over the next several decades were presented to the first meeting of the policy review committee on 4 May. The five included a plan for a land missile transported by truck on the nation's highways, a plan for a missile borne aloft by a airplane, and a plan to do nothing. These three were no longer serious options. They were included partly to enhance the attractiveness of the remaining two options, and partly to build the federal case in the environmental law suits which would certainly be brought against the plan for thousands of shelters in the western states. Under the federal law, the administration would have to demonstrate that it had considered all reasonable alternatives.

There were two serious options. One was to press vigorously ahead with the development of a highly accurate submarine launched missile called the Trident II or D-5. This was called option 5, or the "fully common" option. It would be deployed in the new Trident submarines and a small number would be deployed in fixed land silos, more to complicate Soviet targeting than to preserve the effectiveness of the land deterrent. At the same time the air force would deploy three thousand air launched cruise missiles in B-52 bombers until a new cruise missile carrying airplane was developed.

The second option, labelled option 2, was the MX missile option. Under option 2 the air force would deploy two hundred MX missiles in five thousand silos located in the western states. It would also deploy three thousand cruise missiles, and the navy would get the less accurate Trident I missile for its Trident submarines. The Trident II missile would not be accelerated.

Only the CIA's Admiral Turner supported the submarine missile option, but the silo MX also came under strong attack at the first Policy Review Committee meeting. While Brown listened, David Aaron and Frank Press argued that an MX missile placed in a silo was neither secure nor easily verifiable. It could not be quickly moved from one shelter to another, and the Soviet Union might be able to strew sensors over the missile field to detect the mass or other characteristics of the live missile. Since silos were now counted as missile launchers under SALT, it would be difficult to plausibly claim that these silos should not count as launchers.

Six days later Brown and General Jones returned with a completely different basing scheme, a variant on the trench idea that John Hepfer had first worked on five years before. They suggested the missile be deployed on rails in a twenty mile long open trench, upon which blast shelters would be constructed every few thousand feet. On warning of Soviet missile attack, the MX could travel quickly along the rails to a new location—it could "dash on warning." This scheme would take up ten thousand square miles of land in Utah, Nevada and Arizona.

The PRC could agree that this was at least a plausible scheme to take to the President and the National Security Council. It could not as easily agree, however, on the right size for the missile. Perry was so strongly in favor of the smaller diameter missile that he testified in favor of it before the Senate Armed Services Committee between meetings of the Policy Review Committee. Just before the third and final meeting of the PRC, Perry testified that either the 83″ or 92″ missile would be "a pretty effective military weapon, not only compared to anything we have developed in the past, but also compared to the [weapons of] the Soviet Union". He said it was an issue of perception rather than military capability because "even a smaller missile has a fantastic military capability, hard target kill, soft target kill both." He said it was "a factor of three or four greater than the Minuteman and it is very close to the capability of the large MX missile and is very close, somewhat larger, to the [deleted]." The deleted comparison is presumably to the heavy Soviet SS18, which Brown would later say he would not accept as a swap for MX.

Though it had the same military capability as the larger missile, the smaller missile could be transported more easily on land, and could be taken to sea or put in an airplane if no land shelter proved feasible. These were all powerful arguments, and the only military argument against them was that the larger missile could be equipped with a greater number of warheads if the SALT limit of ten was later abandoned. It would be able to carry the same number of warheads as the heavy Soviet SS18 could, were both not limited by SALT. But if SALT limits on warheads were abandoned, so also would SALT limits on total missile number be abandoned, and the United States could as easily deploy more missiles as add more warheads to those already deployed. These were compelling arguments, but Brzezinski as well as the Chairman of the Joint Chiefs, General Jones, was adamant that the United States should build the biggest. If there was to be only one more missile under the proposed SALT agreement, let it be the biggest possible—that would have the most salutary affect on the perceptions of other nations, and on the perceptions of the U.S. senate.

Hard as he fought Perry could not overcome the combined weight of opposition from the air force, Senator Jackson on the Hill, and Zbigniew Brzezinski in the White House. Brown had long supported him on the issue, but at the third PRC meeting their resistance broke, and they agreed on the recommendation for the biggest missile, to be deployed along a trench running between shelters. Brzezinski would later say he had "rammed through" a recommendation for the big missile. Like option 5, this option 2 was tentatively estimated to cost $78 billion in 1979 dollars.

On one critical issue there was little disagreement. The initial force size would be two hundred missiles, a figure selected for two reasons. The total number of warheads added to the inventory by the new missile would be two thousand, which was just equal to the present total of warheads in the Minuteman III and Minuteman II fields. It was also equal to the number of warheads required to destroy with reasonable certainty the number of hardened targets in the Soviet Union that it was thought would likely remain after a first strike at the United States. It was possible, therefore, that the United States could bargain away all its Minuteman missiles in a SALT round, and still have enough highly accurate warheads left to fulfill the requirements of the single integrated operating plan. That two thousand warheads were also sufficient to substantially destroy all Soviet land missiles in an American first strike was not widely remarked, but was nonetheless true.

The 4 and 5 June meetings of the National Security Council in the cabinet room of the White House were the formal conclusion to more than two years of dispute within the Carter administration on the MX. They would last a total of four hours, concluding with a dinner hosted by Carter on the evening of 5 June. By the time Carter convened his officials, all the reasonable alternatives to the MX had been excluded. The administration had already presented Congress with a request for funding for full scale development for a new land missile, and the Policy Review Committee had already found grounds to exclude the alternative of relying on submarine launched missiles. Officially, Carter was to decide on whether or not there should be a new land-based missile, what size it should be, and how it should be based. In reality, these three closely connected decisions had been all but made, and all that now remained was to patiently hear out the objections and to compile a record of rational decision making should it ever be required by the courts hearing environmental objections from the western states. They were, nonetheless, important meetings for the participants; in them the alternative future directions of the nuclear arms race were ceremonially presented, and the preferred direction adopted. That, at least, was the plan. So persistent were the difficulties in agreeing on a base that though these two meetings produced a firm presidential decision on the missile's size, they did not produce one on how it should be deployed.

According to Brzezinski, who laid out the arguments for the president, the essential choice was whether or not to retain a triad of weapons—three systems deployed in different ways so that the vulnerability of one would not lessen the deterrent value of the others. When the issue was put like that, the president was guided in the desired direction, because building a new land missile, which was actually a counterforce weapon, appeared to be strengthening deterrence. The alternative, Brzezinski said, was to accelerate the development of the Trident II submarine-launched ballistic missile, but any future Soviet advance in anti-submarine warfare could suddenly render these weapons vulnerable to attack. Deployment of two hundred missiles in an invulnerable base would allow the United States to trade away its Minuteman missiles in subsequent negotiations with the Soviet Union, and at the same time the construction of the missile would make the most of the American force allowed in the current SALT agreement.

Brown declared his preference for a land-based missile, and explained the plan to lay them out in trenches fitted with hardened shelters. This system would be both secure and verifiable, he argued, since the Soviets could observe the missiles periodically through windows opened in the shelters' roofs, yet the missile could travel so quickly on warning it would be useless to launch an attack against it even if its location was known.

Carter conducted the meeting by asking questions and seeking opinions rather than encouraging direct debate. If the Russians race us, how will we respond? he asked. What have we done about verification? On these issues there was still dissent among the officials who attended the meetings, and they expressed it freely. His budget director, James McIntyre, for example, remained opposed to a full scale development decision. He objected that there were too many uncertainties in the program for a prudent decision to fund full-scale development. It was not clear that the basing system would work, and, if it did not, choosing the 92" size precluded too many alternative bases. Nor was it clear that the Soviet Union could not overwhelm the system by building extra warheads, and he wondered what the cost of meeting that challenge would be.

Asked for his opinion, Press argued that the proposed basing system had weaknesses. It was hard to verify unless all shelters were opened at once. It would be hard to preserve location uncertainty unless dummies were put in the empty hardened points, in which case it would be hard to verify. He pointed out the weakness of the MX basing mode as it was proposed, and also pointed out the weaknesses of the other modes. He did not push a system.

Carter also queried the head of the Arms Control and Disarmament Agency, General George Seignious II. Seignious had been an unusual and controversial choice for the job he held, and his selection had been hotly criticized by liberals. The *New York Times* had called it a "disingenuous political maneuver that could only boomerang." General Seignious, with the unusual style which was to characterize his handling of the Arms Control Agency, said that the "editorial in the *Times*, published a day or two before Thanksgiving, was a very ungrateful thing to do to disturb the equanimity of a person who is conscientiously seeking to serve his country." A retired general, the president of a military-style college called The Citadel in Charleston, South Carolina, Seignious had been chosen by Carter to replace the dovish Warnke at the head of ACDA in October 1978 for the very same reason the administration was now keen to make a decision on MX—to mollify the hawks in Congress. Forty senators had voted against Warnke's confirmation—enough to scuttle SALT.

General Seignious was in favor of MX. He had been, actually, at least since the previous December, when he had told his very first press conference that more money would be needed to modernize the strategic triad. Pressed by Senator McGovern in his Senate confirmation hearings, Seignious had affected not to register the distinction between the basing mode and the question of the missiles' payload and accuracy, slipping off the point with the comment, either very disingenous or very ingenuous, no one ever knew with the general, that "surely no one is serious in the belief that we will attack the Soviet Union first."

Questioned about his membership of a conservative group which had as its major aim to "stop SALT II" General Seignious explained that "I joined for one explicit reason—and I had not read the program that they advertized in the newspaper. I joined because Admiral Moorer and General Lemnitzer were and are on the senior advisory committee to my college, The Citadel"—an explanation that was probably and woefully quite correct. As Senator Javits remarked, a director of ACDA could not join groups simply because his buddies asked him. Seignious was also a member of the American Enterprise Institute and other conservative groups, so his eager support for MX was not unexpected, nor perhaps very important. What was important was that General Seignious had taken the place of Paul Warnke, who said that MX was "absurd" and hoped to bargain it away in the next round at SALT.

Carter asked Seignious whether there was any difference between the arms control impact of an 83″ or a 92″ missile. Seignious said there was not. Carter then asked him whether MX would be destabilizing or stabilizing. He said that the most destabilizing fact was the vulnerability of land missiles, that MX would correct this, and that therefore it was stabilizing.

Six months after this meeting, Seignious was to retire on health grounds. He had in a little under a year approved and encouraged a more momentous change in America's nuclear arsenal than any of his predecessors. He left to his successors the job of handling its impact on the arms race.

Of all the participants at the National Security Council meeting, only the director of Central Intelligence, Stansfield Turner, spoke strongly against the fundamental idea proposed by Brzezinski: that America needed to have a new land missile to preserve the triad, and that the missile should be the biggest of the designs offered. Stan Turner attended the meeting as an adviser. He was a "statutory adviser" under the National Security Act, which put him a little in front of Press, but a long way behind Harold Brown and Cy Vance. Stan Turner had been comfortable in the adviser's role; one of his rules in redeeming the reputation and effectiveness of the CIA after its internal traumas and public humiliation was to insist that he was simply an adviser and nothing more. Others could make policy. Stan Turner just offered advice. But on this issue Turner was in a muddle. As CIA director, he had views about mobile basing, about the likelihood of the Soviet Union penetrating the deception, about the projections of Soviet accuracies and the exchange ratios that were given as arguments for a new missile in a new mode. His information on these issues, however, wasn't exclusive and wasn't very different from that held by Harold

Brown. But before being appointed director of Central Intelligence, Turner had been NATO's southern commander and an admiral in the U.S. Navy. He was an intellectual among sailors, a Rhodes scholar who had worked on the navy staff, and who had written several papers while commanding the naval war college at Newport, Rhode Island. Turner had spent his seagoing career in navy surface ships, but he strongly believed in the navy's strategic role, in its submarine fleet with their long-range nuclear missiles, and he realized that this meeting actually posed a choice between the air force and the navy. He had been in Jimmy Carter's class at Annapolis (though they had not known each other), and he thought there was a chance to make an end run.

His fundamental objection to the land proposal was that the Soviet Union needed only an additional forty-six hundred accurate land warheads to be able to overcome the forty-six hundred additional shelters proposed for MX. He believed that could easily be achieved, even under SALT II constraints, and that, without SALT II constraints, the Soviet Union could add warheads more cheaply and quickly than America could build shelters. In a race between warheads and shelters, the kind of race about which Perry had once been despondent, the Soviet Union had many advantages. The consequences of this, he said, were twofold. One was that the MX would spur competition, not suppress it, and that it would proliferate warheads on both sides. The second was that, by deploying MX, the U.S. would be greatly adding to the value it attached to MIRV limits on the Soviet Union. In other words, it was handing the Soviet Union a bargaining advantage. He supported, instead, a modified version of option 5, the extra Trident II missiles, cruise missiles, and added his own idea—which had once been Brzezinski's—of some small land missiles on trucks in, say, Alaska.

Of all the older men in the room, the most uncomfortable was Vice-President Walter Mondale. A Minnesota liberal of impeccable credentials, Mondale had sponsored or supported almost every piece of progressive legislation in his thirteen years in the Senate, from open housing to busing to children's welfare. He had been a consistent opponent of military spending and particularly of novel military technology. He had voted against anti-ballistic missiles, multiple independently targetable reentry vehicles (MIRVs), and even NASA's space shuttle. In his opening statement at the July 1969 hearings on the plight of migrant workers, he had said: "Three minutes after we launched our men to the moon from Cape Kennedy, I banged the gavel here in Washington to open the hearings on the miserable conditions of the blueberry pickers in eastern North Carolina. . . . Perhaps we belong to the moon, but we surely do there, in North Carolina . . . with all the resources the nation could mobilize, if it only wanted to do so." He had been a formidable senator, a strong ally of Hubert Humphrey and the most influential voice in the Minnesota Democratic Farmer Labor party. But those closest to Mondale detected a weakness, a willingness to go along and to compromise. When Mondale had been hospitalized for an operation it quickly became a standard joke that he was having a backbone inserted—a joke repeated by his fellow Minnesota senator, Eugene McCarthy, and the Minnesota reporter who would later become the vice-president's press secretary, Al Eisle. He supported the war in Vietnam right up to 1968, which was a long time for a liberal. He had not thought it expedient to accept George McGovern's offer of the vice-presidential nomination in 1972.

After six weeks of strenuous campaigns to test the chances for the 1976 presidential nomination, Mondale withdrew. "I do not have the overwhelming desire to be President which is essential for the kind of campaign that is required," he told reporters. "I admire those with the determination to do what is required to seek the presidency, but I have found that I am not among them." Nonetheless, Mondale had become the most powerful vice-president for generations. He had been, as he explained, "privy to all the facts and options being considered" by the president. He attended the weekly foreign policy and defense breakfasts with Vance, Brown, and Carter. He had coordinated a liberal Africa policy. In the early days of the administration, he had been able to place some of his own people in key jobs. The most influential of these appointments was that of his former foreign policy aide, David Aaron, to be staff director of the National Security Council—an appointment that his boss, Zbigniew Brzezinski, did not like, but felt he had to live with.

Mondale's big year had been the first—1977—and the administration had changed a great deal since then. In 1977 Mondale had supported a regionalist line in Africa which was strongly approved by the Africans and strongly fought by the powerful faction in the administration which believed that each Soviet move in Africa must be confronted with an American countermove, and that the Soviet's enemies must be the Americans' friends. He successfully pushed legislation on electoral reform, including public financing of congressional elections and instant voter registration. He supervised the White House task force working on a reorganization plan for national intelligence operations and toughened its proposals for curbing domestic abuses by the FBI and CIA.

In 1978 things had begun to change. The administration was pilloried over the Katangan raid into Zaire and Ethiopia's crushing defeat of Somalia. The administration was pressed to support the coalition government in Salisbury, Rhodesia, and toward the end of the year it conceded U.S. visas to Ian Smith and Bishop Muzorewa. Those who had been identified with the liberal line on Africa, like Mondale and Andrew Young, began to lose credit in the administration. The collapse of the shah in Iran focused attention on the CIA's intelligence capability, and through a peculiar turn of logic, those who had opposed domestic abuses by the CIA were now blamed for the organization's shortcomings. As international events and domestic unpopularity began to overwhelm the administration, the domestic liberals like Mondale faced a choice between fighting or moving with the tide and keeping intact some of their influence. Mondale moved, and found himself in the unlikely position, the week before, of reviewing with Brown the options that were to be put to this meeting, casting out the only ones that were consistent with the positions Mondale had taken in the Senate. Two months before, Mondale had said that "it is possible that, in the early to mid 1980s, the Soviets, with a surprise attack, could destroy most of our land-based missiles." Vulnerability, he said, was something "we are working very hard to avoid." In the National Security Council, Mondale backed the big missile.

When it came his time to be heard, there was no ambiguity in the position of General David C. Jones on the issues before this meeting. Now fifty-eight, Jones had been chairman of the Joint Chiefs of Staff for little over a year, the highest job in the uniformed services and the culmination of a thirty-seven-year career in the U.S. Air Force. Jones had joined army air during the Second World War, had seen active duty in Korea, and then Vietnam. Jones was a pilot, and all his service missions had been in fighters and conventional bombers. Now the most important part of the air force, the fastest route to the top, was not in the Tactical Air Command (TAC), which commanded fighters, but in the Strategic Air Command (SAC), which controlled the B52 bombers and the ground-based intercontinental missiles. What Jones thought about strategic warfare, and its needs, he had learnt while working as aide to Strategic Air Command chief, General Curtis E. LeMay from 1955 to 1957, years during which the SAC commander had fought hard to get a nuclear-powered bomber for strategic strikes, when he had sought bombs of such ferocious and extraordinary power that even the air force chiefs began to doubt his judgment, and when he had begun that swing to the Right, common enough at the top of the air force, which was to conclude with LeMay's campaign as vice-presidential nominee with the Southern racist George Wallace. Jones had profited by that experience, and it had helped lift him through the ranks of other TAC pilots and on to the top of an air force increasingly concerned with the mathematics of nuclear exchange ratios, damage expectancy, circular error probability, and the purely theoretic calculus of reliability, accuracy, yield, speed, and reaction time. Jones's successor as air Chief of Staff had a doctorate in physics. That was the way things were going, and Jones in his public utterances supported the air force focus on strategic weapons systems.

He had accepted the cancellation of the B-1 bomber (though with the greatest reluctance), a concession that helped his later nomination as chairman of the Joint Chiefs. He had resisted pressures to make an end run to Congress on the B-1. "I refused to become involved," he said. Because he had gone along with the B-1 cancellation, Jones had lost friends among the hawks on the Hill. Later that year, the most belligerent of the hawks, Scoop Jackson of Washington State, would ask Jones: "You may have made a lot of recommendations, General, but you were not successful. That is the test. You were not successful. How can we rely on you, sir?" and later he would say: "During your tenure as Chief of Staff of the Air Force and Chairman of the Joint Chiefs, you have not been able to achieve any of these new strategic systems." Jones knew he had problems where they mattered most, and he had no intention of vacillating on MX. He thought the United States should spend more on nuclear weapons in the future, even if the SALT treaty was signed, and he identified as the key issue the growing vulnerability of America's land-based nuclear tipped missiles. Jones had a long record of support for the advanced missile and a new basing mode—he had been Chief of Staff of the air force a year after the program was precipitated from the elements of other programs; he had energetically pushed for its funding and for air force control over the project. He now attended the meeting that would not only decide whether those efforts would be realized, but would also decide whether the air force would continue to be the principal agent for America's nuclear deterrent, or whether it would lose out to the navy.

Carter contemplated the arguments, and went with Brown, Jones, and Brzezinski—the agreed position. They would build the biggest missile. In the president's judgment, Perry would recall, "The geopolitical arguments outweighed the technical arguments." They would meet again by September to work out the basing mode, which they understood would be some form of horizontal, land multiple protective shelter scheme, which was both secure and verifiable. It was a decision, Carter concluded by saying, with which he "felt comfortable."

8
Revolt of the Hawks

AFTER more than two years of studies, after hours of meetings in the Pentagon, in the White House Policy Review Committee, and now in the full-dress National Security Council, the Carter administration had reached its decision. But, while it had decided many important questions on the new missile, it had still not found a place to put it, which had been the central problem since the vulnerability of existing land missiles and the need for a new land missile were simultaneously pushed onto the national agenda at the beginning of the seventies. At the NSC meetings, the president had made what his advisers thought were fundamental decisions. But the execution of those decisions depended on what some of his advisers considered a mere detail—finding an acceptable missile base.

Carter and his advisers had the choice, according to Dr. Brzezinski, of either keeping the triad of nuclear forces or putting the strongest component of their offensive forces to sea. They had decided to keep the triad by building a land missile that was not invulnerable but would cost the Soviet Union so many warheads that attack would not be worthwhile.

There were two reasons Carter had decided to keep the triad. The first, the one that appealed most to a president inculcated with the submarine navy's doctrine of deterrence, was that it insured against the other two legs of the triad suddenly being endangered, and therefore guaranteed the central principle of the nuclear strategy—that America should always have an invulnerable retaliatory force of sufficient size to deter a first strike. But now there was another reason to keep the land missiles and make them invulnerable. They were the most accurate leg of the triad, and the planned missile was more accurate than the most accurate of existing land missiles, the Minuteman III. Land missiles were the most easily commanded and controlled and co-ordinated offensive weapons, so that the new missile could be used in a mass, simultaneous attack on Soviet land missiles and submarine pens and bombers, to reduce the amount of damage that a Soviet nuclear strike could wreak in the United States. The MX was to be many times more lethal than the Minuteman III, and it was therefore well adapted for the job of limiting damage that was an essential prerequisite to the use of nuclear weapons in war. MX was always officially described as a weapon that could destroy Soviet missiles remaining after a first strike on the United States. Since the Soviet Union would be unlikely to oblige the United States by retaining these missiles, the MX could only serve its purpose of hitting Soviet silos if it struck first. MX is necessarily a first strike weapon.

They had decided to keep the triad, to build another land missile, and, in the course of deciding that, in the nature of weapons decisions, they had decided to postpone the new and more accurate missile for the submarines, the D-5. This was one implication not then acknowledged—that instead of rushing ahead with the D-5, which was intended to replace the Trident I missile then being deployed, it was on an indefinite schedule for completion sometime toward the end of the new decade. There were many problems with achieving precision accuracies with submarine-launched missiles, and they would not be addressed with the same urgency that would now be given to the land missiles. So, in rejecting the option of going to sea, which Stan Turner so vigorously propounded, the Carter people had decided to limit the sea deterrent within its present bounds.

They had decided on two hundred of the new missiles, and that the new missile would be 92" in diameter. The force size decision was important, because it meant that while the new missile would theoretically be able to destroy the entire Soviet force, it was too narrow a margin of warheads over targets to ever make the threat a believable one. As the air force would later reveal, however, it did not regard two hundred missiles as anything other than a preliminary figure.

The missile size decision was perhaps the most difficult and unfortunate of the decisions made in June. The big missile could not be put to sea if no land base proved workable because its diameter was too great for the Trident submarine firing posts. It could be put in the air only with the greatest difficulty (it was not "optimized" for air basing), and, when it came rolling off the production lines in 1986, whichever administration was unlucky enough to have to do it would have to find a base somewhere in the United States. As David Aaron later remarked, "the problem in retrospect was that once we made the missile size decision, the basing system was confined to two choices—multiple shelters or ballistic missile defense."

Perry had testified in March 1979 that "in the case of airborne missiles there is a desire to hold the weight down and their range is between one-hundred-ten-thousand and one-hundred-fifty-thousand pounds," compared to the one-hundred-ninety-thousand pound missile selected by the administration. As to deploying the big missile as a "true mobile" on trucks, the air force would disclose in March 1982 that the assembled missile was too heavy for ordinary roads and bridges, and that bridges would have to be strengthened even to move the one-hundred-ten-thousand pound first stage with its transporter.

The 92″ size made things easier for SALT, because it was as big a missile as could be built, and it satisfied those who, like Brzezinski and Senator Jackson, thought that if America was to have only one new land missile, it should be the biggest. But the size of the missile precluded many sensible options for basing, and it was too big for the kind of mobility on land that Al Latter had advocated so many years before. The Carter administration would decide to "dash" the missile from shelter to shelter, but its size worked against it, and the final plan excluded this capability. A big missile was hard to hide, hard to move. It was a detail, it was unnoticed at the time, but it was the biggest mistake in the whole history of the MX program. John Toomay, Al Latter, Bill Perry, Michael May, Frank Press, and Harold Brown had all preferred the smaller missile. At the final moments, Jackson and Brzezinski had persuaded Carter. Brzezinski later recalled that he was surprised he had had so little difficulty persuading Carter to accept the 92″.

They had decided all these things, but they had not decided on a place to put the most terrible weapon ever devised. That was left to Bill Perry and Harold Brown, who once again had to sort through the advantages and disadvantages of each basing scheme to find one that was both least vulnerable and most confidently verifiable. The unzipped trench had evolved from the collapse of the silo scheme and the resuscitation of the tunnel idea that General Hepfer had been working on since 1974. But it had problems with electromagnetic pulse effects, with the likelihood that one explosion would immobilize the missile carrier, and with ways to minimize these problems without making the numbers of missiles impossible to verify for the Soviet Union. The NSC meetings had left Brown and Perry with the general instruction to develop a base that was horizontal, so the missile could be moved, and that had multiple protective shelters, so it could be hidden. What kind, and where, was not known.

Perry and Zeiberg pondered this problem through June and into July, and for a Defense Systems Acquisitions Review Committee meeting on July 21 came up with the outlines of a combination of road-mobile basing with horizontal shelters. They developed their idea to include forty-six hundred shelters and two hundred missiles as the preliminary size, with the capability of rapid expansion to seven thousand shelters. It would be in Utah and Nevada, and the missile would be carried on a transporter-erector-launcher that could dash on warning of attack to another shelter. This was to address the problem of catastrophic intelligence failure that had been raised by David Aaron. This July meeting was followed by a Policy Review Committee meeting in the first week of August at the White House, chaired by Brown. What was now beginning to be called the racetrack mode was approved with little opposition but with considerable debate about the costs and the amount of land involved. Office of Management and Budget Director McIntyre refused to accept Brown's figure of $23 billion for the entire system, saying that it would cost closer to $40 billion. He also insisted that it would use at least ten thousand miles of roadway, which was far above the amount estimated by the air force. They could not agree, so an irritated Carter insisted they go away and come back to him with an agreed costing. They did, and came back with $33 billion. This figure, that was later said to have arisen from the most careful cost estimates produced by the most complex models on the most sophisticated computers, was actually a split-the-difference compromise between Harold Brown and James McIntyre. "The $33 billion figure was produced from air," General Hepfer recalled. "By that time we had gone through so many iterations we were no longer certain of costs."

With an agreed basing mode and an agreed cost, the racetrack scheme was presented to the president in a National Security Council meeting on 5 September 1979. It was approved with only formal opposition, and promptly announced. The September decision was to build two hundred missiles in a system of forty-six hundred shelters. Each missile was to be carried on board an imaginative vehicle called a transporter-erector-launcher (TEL) within a closed loop (the racetrack) that consisted of twenty-three shelters spaced about seven thousand feet apart on a road some ten to fifteen miles long. The number of loops in each complex was to range from three to eight, making for a total of forty MX complexes to be located in a single field in southern Utah and Nevada. The TEL would carry the missile and also a one-hundred-forty-thousand-pound shield to prevent satellite observation of the canister and its deployment in any particular shelter. Given a dash speed of ten to twenty miles per hour, the vehicle—with its weight of nearly half a million pounds—could move from one shelter to another in the loop within the expected warning time of a Soviet missile strike. That, so far as Harold Brown and Jimmy Carter were concerned, was the final decision, the final selection of a basing mode that had been sought by two administrations over six years. As it happened, the life of this basing mode was seven months, rather less than the average for the airborne, tunnel, and silo schemes that had preceded it.

Officially both the basing mode and the number of missiles to be deployed had been decided at the highest level of the administration. In reality neither issue had been settled. In October 1979 General Kelly Burke, then director of operational requirements for the air force, told a Senate subcommittee that "we have described an initial system of some two hundred missiles. There has been no recommendation on the actual force size, and that won't be made until the production decision in 1983." By that time another administration would be making strategic nuclear policy for the United States.

Among the abundant ironies that followed the Carter administration's decision to build the biggest possible MX missile in June 1979, two were particularly galling to the alliance of hawks and doves that had, for their separate reasons, favored the development of the missile. The first irony, the overwhelming one for the arms controllers in and out of the administration, was that deciding to build MX, which had been sold as a requirement for SALT ratification, did not buy SALT ratification at all. True, the Joint Chiefs told Jimmy Carter in the week after his MX decision that they would support the SALT agreement as negotiated. That was a plus. But the Soviet invasion of Afghanistan at the end of 1979 decisively tilted the scales against the agreement, which had little chance anyway, and the administration withdrew it from Senate consideration. The arms controllers found themselves with MX, but without SALT, a result pondered with chagrin by Paul Warnke in his discreetly sumptuous law office across Lafayette Park from the White House.

The second great irony was that as soon as it became clear that the residents of Utah and Nevada were not at all pleased with their selection as the hosts for the new missile system, the most vigorous proponents of new weapons systems in the Senate, the most hawkish of senators who had most vociferously warned of the impending window of vulnerability, became equally ardent opponents of the missile. There must be a missile, yes. But in their state? No! Conservative Utah Senator Jake Garn, for example, had portrayed himself as a ferocious hawk on defense issues, demanding in senate committees an early administration decision on a base for MX. When it came, Garn declared that the people of his state were "patriotic, determined, loyal," however, they "should not be asked to bear an unreasonable share of the burden of national defense." Very soon the argument became that the racetrack scheme was designed to meet SALT constraints, and since they opposed SALT, they could therefore oppose the racetrack.

The key figure in the congressional opposition to the plan to deploy the missile in Utah and Nevada, the man who would later, with justice, claim credit for scrapping that plan, was Senator Paul Laxalt of Nevada. No senator had banged the drum for more defense spending more vigorously than Paul Laxalt, no senator had warned more colorfully about the growing Soviet threat to American ground missiles, no senator had done more to repudiate the strategic arms limitations agreement reached by the Carter administration, and no senator would do more to make sure that, if the new missile was built, it would not be deployed in his home state. Over the course of two years, Paul Laxalt recast himself from a wrathful hawk to an ardent Nevada environmentalist, reflecting the political fact that the residents of Nevada were the kind of rural conservatives most likely to see the world in the simple and dramatic terms of national chauvinism, and least likely to tolerate, in their thinly populated hills and valleys, the modern contrivances of war and the multitude of strangers who would come to build them.

The tunnel system and all the variants of multiple silo and shelter schemes had in common that they were spread out over a large area. All the work done by the air force on the geology of the regions, on the dispositions of population and industry, concluded that if the system could not be built substantially in Utah and Nevada, it could not be built at all. Therefore, to prevent the scheme from being built in Utah and Nevada would come automatically to mean there could be no multiple protective shelter system at all, and the planners would inevitably be driven to deploy the missiles in planes or in submarines or in land reservations protected by some as yet undeveloped form of ballistic missile defense. The air force could see this political trajectory but it could not alter it, because the decision would be taken far above the political level that the air force could reach. The fate of the mx depended now not on the military industrial complex or on the formidable apparatus of air force persuasion. It depended on a long-standing political friendship between Paul Laxalt and a candidate for the Republican nomination for the presidency, Ronald Reagan.

The man who became president would later protest that Senator Laxalt had not influenced his decision on the multiple shelter scheme, but Senator Laxalt thought differently. A fellow Westerner, a man with Reagan's own relaxed attitude toward politics, Laxalt was the Republican candidate's closest friend in Washington. He had met Reagan when both were minor figures in Barry Goldwater's run for the presidency in 1964. He had been governor of Nevada when Reagan was governor of neighbouring California, he was one of the earliest to counsel Reagan to run for the Republican nomination, and he had managed his close but ultimately unsuccessful run against Gerald Ford in 1976. It was Laxalt who had watched from the Senate as the Carter administration deteriorated in 1978 and 1979, and who had judged that the times were propitious for another Reagan campaign for the Republican nomination. And it would be Laxalt who would manage that campaign too, and give the nominating speech in Detroit, and refuse, in the interests of unifying the party, the vice-presidential nomination it was his to accept. Later, when Ronald Reagan first came to Washington as president-elect, it would be Laxalt who greeted him at the airport. When the new president's advisers put together their lists of nominees, it would be Laxalt with whom they would check the names for top jobs, and it would be Laxalt who would rush to the George Washington University hospital on a day at the end of March in the first year of the Reagan administration, who would speak with the wounded president as he was being wheeled to the operating table with a bullet in his lung, and who would later report to the press that the president, the colleague with whom he had often gone trail-riding in the empty hills of Nevada, had told him, one Westerner to another: "Don't worry, I'll get out of this."

An informal man who sported cowboy boots under the cuffs of his dark, senatorial suit, a handsome, vigorous man with white hair and black eyebrows, who could play a strong game of tennis, Laxalt declared that he had decided to take life at a more leisurely pace after the turmoil of a divorce and the stress of the governor's office. His Washington office was not the usual hurried Capitol Hill office, his staff were not the usual high-powered and endlessly busy young people on the make. His was not a big state, its interests were simple and straightforward, and Laxalt was popular enough not to have to spend all his time preparing for the next election. He was a conservative, but he was not an intolerant conservative. His father had been a Basque shepherder in the hills of Nevada, his mother had run a boardinghouse in Reno to fill out the family income. He remembered his roots as he remembered his accomplishments, so that his colleagues found him mature and able, easy to deal with, and a good companion.

Laxalt did not fight on all issues. He picked ones that were important to him, and he fought tenaciously. He had fought the Carter administration on the Panama Canal treaties and came within a few votes of defeating the president. He had at first been uncertain about the MX project in Nevada, saying that he was sure the people of Nevada would take it if it was really necessary. But, as it became clear that the people of Nevada, where nearly three-quarters of the missiles would be based, would not warm to it under any circumstances, Laxalt became an implacable and lethal opponent.

For Laxalt, as for his Utah colleage Jake Garn, with whom he worked closely, the MX issue was a difficult one. They had both been strongly critical of the Carter administration for delaying a decision on the missile. But now that it was going ahead, they could not support it. Both were facing reelection in 1980 and needed to control an issue that could be useful to their opponents. What they needed, and what they soon found, was a plausible argument to oppose the missile on national security grounds, not on arms control grounds. They also needed something more substantial than an argument, and this they found, too. They needed the support of colleagues, and they needed to persuade Ronald Reagan that it was a bad idea to locate the MX in Utah and Nevada.

As Reagan's campaign manager, Laxalt had many opportunities to speak to the candidate, and he presented the issue to him in electoral terms. It was a pressing issue in two states, he told Reagan, and since there was nothing to gain by endorsing a scheme proposed by the Carter administration, the candidate should declare his unqualified support for the missile, express doubts about the proposed base, and promise to look at the whole matter again when he was president. Reagan took the advice and made a speech in these terms in Salt Lake City during the campaign.

Finding the hawk arguments to defend what otherwise would seem a dovish position took a little more thought. Laxalt was too junior in the Senate to command attention on the major committees, but he was a member of the one committee whose support was all but essential to the survival of the shell game. This was the Military Construction Subcommittee of the Senate Appropriations Committee. From this obscure position, Laxalt orchestrated a quiet but effective campaign to make opposition to the shell game a respectable position for military conservatives. As leader of the Republican minority on the subcommittee, he was able to arrange a series of hearings in 1980 and use them to construct a strategic and environmental objection to the shell game. Three of the paladins of the military Right, General Daniel Graham, Admiral Thomas Moorer, and Dr. William Van Cleave, testified—with tortuous logic—that the shell game would take too long to construct, that its complexity was a requirement imposed by SALT verification provisions and not by military necessity, and that better solutions could be found in the rapid deployment of a great many m issiles in ordinary silos, or in anti-ballistic missile defense.

Admiral Moorer repeated his recommendation that the missile be sent to sea on surface ships, a recommendation he had been making for several decades. In a thoroughly confusing piece of testimony, General Graham said that the MPS reflected an adherence to "bankrupt U.S. nuclear doctrines" like mutual assured destruction, and then bewilderingly added that "the deployment mode for the MX is designed to soak up the effects of the very Soviet weapons systems that should be the prime targets for MX in a counterforce role," thus underlining the insoluble contradiction of developing a first strike weapon purportedly for a second strike mission.

To these witnesses against the shell game, Laxalt was able to add doves like Herbert Scoville and Sidney Drell, creating a coalition of the Right and the Left against a system of deployment that had once been supported by both the Right and the Left.

Congressional opposition to the announced basing system rose right through 1979 and into 1980. It was led by Garn of Utah and Laxalt of Nevada, and it brought them into an unexpected alliance with the most liberal members of the House—Ron Dellums of California, and John Seiberling of Ohio, chairman of the Public Lands Subcommittee.

Even as President Carter and his advisers sat down to decide on the missile in June 1979, the protest against basing it in Utah and Nevada had already begun. The air force environmental impact statement for the silo-based missile system, prepared well before formal approval of the system to clear some of the hurdles that would lie before it, focused on Utah and Nevada as states that abundantly possessed what a multiple basing scheme needed most—large amounts of vacant land, far from the coasts and from the borders of Canada and Mexico, with the geological structure that allowed holes to be dug cheaply, and sufficient water to supply most of the huge construction workforce that any multiple basing scheme would involve.

Even then, even in May as Harold Brown worked through the alternatives presented by his advisers and narrowed them down to options two and five, the House adopted an amendment by a very worried and forward-looking representative, Virginia Smith of Nebraska, expressing the sense of Congress that MX should be deployed on the "least productive land that is suitable and available." If there was to be an MX, Representative Smith told her colleagues, it shouldn't be in Nebraska, it should be somewhere else. Land in Nebraska was too good for missiles.

Once Carter announced the racetrack scheme in September, and the ranchers of Utah and Nevada understood what it would mean for their range lands, there was still more action on Capitol Hill. Six days after his announcement, the House overwhelmingly defeated an amendment by Representative Ron Dellums to delete all funding for MX. Dellums would keep trying. On the same day, Congress just as convincingly defeated an amendment by James Santini, the conservative of Nevada, that would allow at most one quarter of the MX shelters to be deployed in any one state. Santini would also keep trying.

Over the following months, an unexpected coalition developed against MX. John Seiberling and Ron Dellums were well-known opponents of the Pentagon. So was Oregon Senator Mark Hatfield, who in October unsuccessfully tried to delete MX appropriations in the Senate Appropriations Committee. But others now joining the coalition were not only friendly toward the Pentagon, they were the most hawkish people on the Hill. In November, although the Senate defeated another attempt by Hatfield to stop MX, it passed—eighty-nine to nothing—an amendment to the defense appropriations bill by Senator Ted Stevens of Alaska. Inspired by the senators from Utah and Nevada, this amendment forbade the department to commit the country to only one basing mode—that is, it required the department to work on more than the racetrack system. By December, the Congress fight was on in earnest, fueled to high heat when Senator Proxmire inserted in the congressional record a law drafted by an air force office which would have short-circuited the legal obstacles to the MX project.

With hearings of the House Public Lands Subcommittee keeping up the pressure in their home states, the senators of Utah and Nevada moved early in February 1980. Senators Cannon, Garn, Hatch, and Laxalt, in a letter to President Carter, observed that "racetrack is clearly a product of an era of presumed United States-Soviet cooperation which, if it ever existed, is clearly no longer with us. As we see it, the time has now come to recognize that the changed security environment also provides us with a chance to build a new generation ICBM, and base it in a mode which would be cheaper, more effective, and come on line quicker than would be possible with racetrack." Here was the hawks' response. Just what this alternative might be remained unclear but, in their letter of 7 February, the senators of Utah and Nevada essentially laid down the set of arguments that would be used, eighteen months later, to cancel any multiple shelter base.

In May and June of 1980, its coherence and time rapidly being consumed by the president's battle against Edward Kennedy, the administration tried to regain the initiative for multiple basing. Advised by a new Defense Science Board study conducted by retired General Glenn Kent, Brown and Perry announced a new basing mode, one that made some cosmetic changes for reasons unconnected with the congressional opposition, but which were publicized as major changes intended to address the objections raised in Congress. It had long been apparent to air force planners that the dash capability of a half-million pound vehicle was more theoretic than actual. That was dropped, and, with it, a number of the more costly features of the September 1979 scheme. Brown announced that the racetrack would be replaced with the "loading dock." This meant that the closed loop of the racetrack could be replaced by straight roads, so there would be less construction, less expense, less ground covered, and, accordingly, less effect on the environment. The awesome contraption, the TEL, was replaced by a simpler transporter, and the erector-launcher mechanism was linked with the missile canister. In the new scheme, the transporter merely put the missile in its shelter, from which it could be fired after it was slid out and erected. The package resulted, it was said, in an estimated saving of $3 billion, but the missile could be moved only slowly and with difficulty.

The mollifying effect of this in Utah and Nevada was zero. In June 1980 Governor Matheson of Utah announced that he would not support deploying the missile in the proposed shelters in his state. The Western opposition strengthened as the construction and deployment effects of the system became more widely known. In hearings in 1979 and 1980, the air force had estimated that the construction force would peak at twenty-five thousand to forty thousand workers, plus their dependents, that the job would require nearly three million tons of cement, ten thousand miles of new roadway, a total deployment area of seven thousand square miles, and more than a tenth of the perennial yield rainfall of the area.

For the remainder of 1980, the Carter administration flailed against a series of domestic and international reverses: the doubling of oil prices in 1979 resulted in worldwide inflation and recession; American diplomats in Teheran were imprisoned by revolutionary guards; SALT II was dead and detente finished; and the MX basing system gradually sank. Out in the electorate, an increasingly confident Ronald Reagan said he had doubts about the horizontal shelter MPS scheme. By the time the air force released its draft environmental impact statement (the third) on MX just before Christmas 1980, Jimmy Carter was serving out the last weeks of his term, and the MX was once again in question.

9
Undeciding

Whereas last year I testified that MX is the number one priority for the Air Force, this year I think the B-1 is the number one priority for the Air Force —*General Lew Allen, 29 October 1981*

ON the afternoon of Friday, 2 October 1981, Ronald Reagan walked into the East Room of the White House to address his second press conference in three days. The spacious, high-ceilinged room, where wooden eagles brooded from their perches above the double doors, was crowded with reporters and photographers. They were awaiting what Defense Secretary Caspar Weinberger would call at various times the most important decision a president "has ever had to make—at least in our lifetime," "the most important weapons decision ever made by a President," and—his most cautious description—"the most important decision of this Administration." This momentous decision, the president soon told the waiting reporters, was a "comprehensive plan" to "halt the decline of our military strength" and "revitalize our strategic forces." Included in the $180 billion plan was the construction and deployment of two new bombers and the accelerated development of a submarine-launched ballistic

215

missile known as the D-5. Nor was that all. The president would also request money for new techniques of commanding and controlling the nuclear forces that could survive and operate over an extended period of warfare. He would also press ahead vigorously with the MX program. But one thing he would not do was to go ahead with the multiple shelter scheme approved by Jimmy Carter or with any other multiple shelter for the missiles. "We have concluded that these basing schemes would be just as vulnerable as the existing missile silos," the president told the press conference. Thus he canceled the scheme that had racked the Carter administration for four years, that had already cost several billion dollars, that had been the subject of fifty volumes of reports, of innumerable pages of public debate and testimony, and thousands and thousands of hours of time of the most skilled officials in Washington.

Like the airborne missile of 1973, the closed tunnel of 1976 and 1977, the vertical silo of 1978, like its various predecessors, the multiple shelter became just so much wasted paper. Instead, the administration proposed to deploy a small number of missiles in superhardened silos, and continue research and development on a permanent home for the orphan missile. But the missile would still be produced on time and to the specifications approved by the Ford and Carter administrations.

Since 1973, the air force had pressed on with the development of the missile, no matter what happened to the base. Its size and accuracy characteristics had never altered. In all the ups and downs of the MX story, all the setbacks and problems, this had never changed. The missile itself, the most important thing, was proceeding on schedule—in fact, it was well ahead of schedule. The new missile, vastly more lethal than the best present land missile in the American inventory, a better weapon than the best Soviet missile, would begin coming off the production line in 1986. All that had happened in the four years of the Carter administration and the first year of the Reagan administration was that the deployment plan went back to what it had been in 1976—first to be deployed in silos, while other alternatives were examined. The MX missile had not only survived but prospered under the successive administrations, and the missile's 92" diameter, confirmed by president Reagan on 2 October, precluded it from being deployed at sea and made it difficult to deploy in a plane. A place had to be found for it, and it would have to be on land.

Behind the president's surprise announcement of the cancellation of the MX basing system was nine months of vigorous dispute within the administration, dispute that pitted the air force and the Joint Chiefs against the secretary of defense, two powerful senators (John Tower and Paul Laxalt) against each other, and the president against the military establishment.

Secretary of Defense Caspar Weinberger, a good-humored, confident man with pixie ears and a drooping mouth, was sixty-three when he came to office and, unlike his predecessor, innocent of the theory, technology, and doctrinal disputes of nuclear warfare. Brown had been a physicist with long experience in the Defense Department, a man who could independently evaluate the consequences and meaning of the options proposed to him. The new secretary was first and foremost a politician, then a lawyer, and then an administrator. He had succeeded in all three fields, he was imaginative, and he could catch a headline. But the defense establishment was a club, and Weinberger wasn't in the club. His public statements were dramatic, but soft. He wanted a six hundred-ship navy, he wanted to beef up the Defense Department so it could fight two and a half wars at once, he wanted to expand the defense industrial base to ready America for a long conventional war, he wanted to strengthen conventional forces and to increase the nuclear forces "with equal priority." Cap Weinberger was not good on priorities, on the dull matters of attaining the possible. But

he did know his way around the American West and around
the Reagan administration, and he very soon emerged as one
cabinet secretary who almost always got what he wanted,
and could count on the loyalty of Reagan's palace guard of
Edwin Meese, James Baker, and Michael Deaver.

A longtime political ally and friend of the president, Caspar Weinberger took over the Defense Department with a
flourish, several weeks before either the inauguration of the
new president or his own confirmation as secretary. In mid-
December he summarily dismissed William van Cleave from
his job as transition chief for the Reagan people in the department, and with him his assistants, aides, and political
hopefuls. Cap Weinberger was certainly on the Right of the
Republican party, but not the Right that William van Cleave
and his allies, men like Senator Jesse Helms, represented.
Cap Weinberger was a former chairman of the Federal
Trade Commission in the Nixon administration, and he had
been promoted by the president to be deputy director and
then director of the Office of Management and Budget, the
most powerful fiscal post in any administration, before he
had rounded out his career in the Ford administration as
secretary of health, education and welfare. He had been in
the Nixon and Ford administrations with Kissinger, with
Schlesinger (who was at OMB when Weinberger was appointed), and with the man he now insisted, over the objections of the ideological Right in the Reagan camp, should be
his deputy in defense, Frank Carlucci, a career public ser-
vant who had served in the Carter administration as deputy
director of the CIA. The sacking of van Cleave and the appointment of Carlucci cost Weinberger the votes of Senator
Helms and Senator East when his nomination came before
the Senate, but they were votes he could do without. They
were not the basis of his political support. Weinberger's supporters were the Republican elders—George Shultz, under
whom he had served at OMB, and who had been his boss the
last five years at the Bechtel Corporation in San Francisco,

and presidential counsellor Ed Meese, like Weinberger a Bay area lawyer who demonstrated in the eighties that the radicalism of the sixties in California concealed a very solid substrata of native conservatism.

Weinberger was certainly confident and plausible, but a little too ready, in the early weeks of his new job, to air views that he would later regret about the MX problem. He had plenty of reservations about the multiple protective shelter system, he freely told a number of reporters, and he couldn't see why the missile couldn't be put on board ships. Why, there could be so many ships with missiles the Soviet Union could not attack all of them, and tests had already been conducted in the sixties in a project called "Hydra" which showed the missile could be fired from a float collar after it had been rolled overboard. Plausible, yes, but convincing— no. The navy certainly didn't want its attack ships turned into cargo carriers for nuclear missiles. It was hard enough that so many navy dollars went into strategic nuclear submarines. And those ships would be vulnerable—to satellite and ship observation, to attack by barrage and by submarine. It was also a relevant though not decisive consideration that the SALT II draft agreement forbade deployment of ICBM's on sea going vessels other than submarines. It was not a sensible way to handle the problem, and the secretary, like so many of his predecessors, soon found himself struggling in the widening and unfathomable complexities of basing the missile. One idea was firmly rejected by the secretary— the idea of putting them into existing silos or silos harder than the existing silos. "I would feel that simply putting it [MX] into the existing silos would not answer two or three of the concerns that I have," he told his nomination hearing in January, "namely, that these are well known and not hardened sufficiently, nor could they be, to be of sufficient strategic value to count as an improvement of our strategic forces."

Weinberger wanted Carlucci as his deputy more because

he had known and trusted him when both worked together in Nixon's OMB than because he was familiar with defense issues. Nonetheless Carlucci brought to his job strong views on nuclear strategy and weaponry. Carlucci was one of the most adept and fleetfooted of Washington's bureaucrats. With a Princeton AB and a year at Harvard's Business School, he had begun a career as a U.S. foreign service officer in Africa, working in the Congo during the civil war (1960) and in South America before getting a foothold in the Office of Economic Opportunity in the Nixon administration. The OEO in the Nixon administration may have been, for less experienced public servants, a political graveyard. For Carlucci, winding down the office was a chance to prove his political usefulness to the administration, and he was rewarded with the third-ranking job in the OMB in September 1971. He was useful there, too, and rewarded again in 1975 by the Ford administration with the ambassador's post in Portugal. That was a triumph for Carlucci who, at forty-five, returned to the State Department well ahead of many of the foreign service colleagues he had left behind in the first year of the Nixon administration in 1969. But Carlucci's real triumph was to return once again to Washington, this time as deputy director of intelligence and day-to-day administrator of the CIA under the most dovish of Democrats since 1945, Jimmy Carter.

Somewhere in this career, which was substantially in economic and political analysis rather than in nuclear strategy, Carlucci had formed strong opinions about the kind of weapons and strategy that America ought to deploy. He told his confirmation hearing that "I think we need to have the strategic capability to survive a Soviet first strike, and retaliate. I think we need to have a counterforce capability. Over and above that, I think we need to have a war-fighting capability." Five years before, Frank Carlucci's remarks would have caused a public controversy over nuclear strategy. In January 1981, at the dawn of the Reagan administration, the views did not even provoke an exploratory question from the Armed Services Committee of the U.S. Senate.

Carlucci also had strong views about MX, and they were not those of his former boss Stan Turner. "On the strategic side, I think our principal concerns are twofold," he said. "The first is Minuteman vulnerability. We are going to have to deal with that issue in an effective way. The second is the modernization of our aging bomber fleet." Later, he said: "I think any fixed land based system is going to be vulnerable. My own judgment is that we are going to have to go to mobile configurations of some sort. But certainly I would think that we could develop a system that would give us a greater assurance of survivability than the current Minuteman III."

Weinberger and Carlucci would be the department's political leaders. The intellectual leadership in nuclear policies would be provided by two other men who had been brought in at the beginning of the new administration. Swiss-born Fred Ikle was fifty-seven when Cap Weinberger picked him for undersecretary of defense for policy. It was not an unexpected appointment, nor an unimportant one. Ikle had been interested in nuclear weapons and nuclear strategy since the early fifties, and he brought to the undersecretary's office a greater intellectual sophistication in making nuclear war policy than many of his predecessors. His immediate predecessor, Robert Komer, had spent much of his time making plans for U.S. deployments in the Persian Gulf, leaving nuclear weapons policy to his subordinates and to Bill Perry. Ikle would bring to his office a completely different approach, and, within a few months, he had both initiated another study of U.S. targeting plans to result in a revision of the Single Integrated Operating Plan, and a revision of U.S. nuclear equipment plans, to increase America's ability to fight a nuclear war, not just deter the Soviets from initiating one. Under Ikle, the administration would proceed along lines already laid down by the Carter administration, but with less ambiguity and more speed. Ikle brought to the

Pentagon what Schlesinger had brought seven years before
—the thinking of RAND in the mid-fifties. Like Schlesinger,
Ikle was a RAND alumnus, and he saw as a central objective
the need to produce a nuclear stance that would allow nuclear forces to be actually used to gain a postwar advantage
for the United States, were the United States ever compelled
to use them.

Ikle had won his doctorate at the University of Chicago in
1950 and by 1954 he was at the RAND Corporation, where he
was to stay for another seven years. Like Schlesinger, Ikle
was a social not a physical scientist, and therefore distant
from the physics department at RAND. He was an innovator,
one of the first students of a central question of the nuclear
age, an entirely new field called the social effects of bombing.
It was central because theories of deterrence by threat of
strategic bombing depended to some extent on city bombing
being greatly feared. The analysis of the allied strategic
bombing survey in Japan and Germany after World War
Two demonstrated that strategic bombing was not at all
effective in destroying enemy morale, enemy facilities, or
enemy civilians. But the immensely long and complex survey was obsolete before it began. Instead of five hundred- or
six hundred-pound bombs, the atomic bombs and later hydrogen bombs would be measured in hundreds and thousands and finally millions of tons of TNT. For the air force,
Ikle thought about the social impact of bomb destruction. In
1953, at his first postgraduate job at the Bureau of Applied
Social Research at Columbia University, Ikle wrote a treatise for the USAF Human Resources Research Institute, entitled "The Social Effects of Bombing." It was, as the air force
commented, "of great value in determining the degree of
population resistance to air attack, and the most effective
method of utilizing air weapons upon urban targets." The
young Swiss immigrant with the fresh doctorate had found
a new field in which he was master. He was the scholar of
the city attack, the sociologist of nuclear targeting. Repub-

lished as "The Social Impact of Bomb Destruction," it was a careful, scholarly essay on holocaust.

Ikle's career prospered. From RAND he had gone to Harvard, and from Harvard to the Massachusetts Institute of Technology as a professor of political science. He returned to RAND in 1968 as head of the social science department until 1973, when he was appointed to the top job in the arms control community, the directorship of the Arms Control and Disarmament Agency.

In 1973 Ikle, who was not so much an originator in nuclear matters as an explicator of others' ideas, wrote about the shortcomings of deterrence in an article in *Foreign Affairs* magazine. This was published just as Schlesinger began to exert his influence in the Department of Defense, and some time after Dr. John Foster's targeting study had produced the elements of National Security Decision Memorandum 242. Ikle argued, as the RAND strategists had in the late fifties, that deterrence was not enough, that deterrence was a threat to do something which, if deterrence failed, it might be inadvisable to carry out. If it was clear that it would not be carried out, clear that America would not destroy the Soviet Union and invite its own destruction for the smallest Soviet nuclear provocation, then the threat was no longer even a deterrent and a new policy was needed. And not just a new policy, but new weapons and new facilities to make the new policy credible. This was the substance of his 1973 article, and of the RAND view that emerged in the fifties, and the view of Kissinger in the foreign policy messages of Richard Nixon.

Ikle's views had not changed to keep pace with the immense changes in nuclear weaponry on both sides. Active defenses—anti-missile missiles—had been ruled out in the first SALT accord, and MIRVing had so vastly increased the power of the offensive that a credible defense was much further away than ever. At the same time, the vulnerabilities of both sides had increased, making the necessary condi-

tion of a secure retaliatory force less certain. This was to
many people the central problem, but not to Ikle. To him, the
problem was what it had been in 1973—the problem of designing weapons and a targeting strategy that believably
equipped America to fight nuclear wars or to respond to
conventional attacks with nuclear weapons. This is what he
meant when he told the Senate Armed Services Committee
during his 25 March nomination hearing that "the use of
military force always has to serve a political purpose. . . .
This basic principle of military strategy is the most obvious
and yet, throughout military history, it has most often been
disregarded. In our system of values, we do not want to inflict
destruction for its own sake, but to halt aggression, to protect our country and our allies; and whenever we become
involved in armed conflict we must have a good idea, a solid
plan, of how we will bring this conflict to a satisfactory conclusion. Now, this principle of insisting on a political purpose
for the use of military force is particularly difficult to apply
when it comes to the use of nuclear weapons. I think for that
reason that in the last three or four administrations we have
had great difficulty in shaping and reshaping our nuclear
doctrine. We are still involved in the process, but we believe
that we are making headway, so that now we can be guided
by better nuclear strategic principles in selecting our strategic weapons systems."

Ikle was the nuclear theoretician of the Reagan administration. The engineer of the nuclear programs was Richard
DeLauer. Dick DeLauer was sixty-three when he succeeded
Bill Perry in the third-floor Pentagon office down the corri-
dor from the secretary's suite. Forty years a veteran of the
missile business, DeLauer had directed the first Titan missile program for TRW at Norton Air Force Base twenty years
before, and, as he had moved up the corporate ladder at the
Californian aerospace corporation, he had overseen the Minuteman I program and the Minuteman III MIRVing program.
Dick DeLauer began as a navy aeronautical engineer, and,

while he had become ultimately a member of the board of directors of TRW, he had never lost touch with the technical and engineering details of weapons. Like most of the TRW people, like most of the contractors in weapons, Dick DeLauer was as impatient with the requirements of arms control as he was loud in declaring his general support for the idea of arms control. Again like most of his colleagues, Dick DeLauer was all for "deterrence" so long as it meant the biggest, the most powerful, the most accurate, and the most invulnerable deterrent that Congress could be persuaded to buy. The idea of mutual deterrence, that the Soviet Union must also be confident in the invulnerability of its nuclear forces, was not one that appealed to Dick DeLauer. The idea was to complicate things for Soviet planners as much as you possibly could. That was the way the game was played, and DeLauer could scarcely repress his glee in playing it.

Dick DeLauer's position was not now the easiest one in the world, because the corporation in which he had made his career and which had appointed him a decade before to its board of directors was the contract supervisor for the MX project and depended for its unique place in the aerospace industry on the continued affection of the air force. DeLauer knew that the air force and TRW wanted the MX deployed in shelters in Utah and Nevada, and he had good reason to think that Secretary Weinberger did not. DeLauer himself was ambivalent. While working for TRW, he had closely followed the MX program at Norton. He had gone out there to the "black Saturdays" when Bill Perry had come out to assess the way the program was going, and he had been infuriated because, as he later recalled, "every time we turned around the President had a different goddamned objection based on SALT, or on verification." If DeLauer had an opinion on the matter at all, it was that the silo system proposed by Michael May and the Defense Science Board was the way to go, and that the objections to it on the grounds of verification were ridiculous. Fortunately, DeLauer didn't have to have a strong opinion on the matter because, by the time he settled down in the Pentagon, the secretary had already decided he wanted an independent committee to look at the problem of where to put the missile. DeLauer took the sensible position —reading the signs in the White House, in the secretary's office, and on the Hill—that other things were more important than the basing mode for MX. He was interested in revamping all the strategic nuclear forces, in pressing forward on all fronts at once. He had before him the results of a Defense Science Board summer study by his deputy, James Wade, on survivable communications. He soon had the results of another summer study by former air force secretary Thomas Reed, on the possibilities for ballistic missile defense. He was looking at the options for reviving the B-1 bomber, killed by the Carter administration in 1977, and pressing on with a new bomber that could not be so easily detected by radar. DeLauer had plenty to keep him busy.

The views of Carlucci, Ikle, and Delauer clearly suggested that the Reagan administration saw the strategic forces as weapons like others that should be improved and augmented for the conduct of nuclear wars—only in this way could deterrence be really effective and only in this way could America's postwar strength be maximized. It was not axiomatic in this administration that any nuclear exchange would quickly be total and catastrophic. Secretary of State Alexander Haig had called mutual assured destruction a "sterile, inhumane, immoral, and I think self-debasing strategy" during the 1979 SALT debates. In January 1980 George Bush, who was now vice-president, had told Robert Scheer of the *Los Angeles Times* that it was indeed possible to have a winner in a nuclear exchange. The vital part of the interview was this:

QUESTION: Don't we reach a point with these strategic weapons where we can wipe each other out so many times that it doesn't really matter whether we are ten per cent or two per cent lower or higher?

BUSH: Yes, if you believe there is no such thing as a winner in a nuclear exchange, that argument makes little sense. I don't believe that.

QUESTION: How do you win in a nuclear exchange?

BUSH: You have survivability of command and control, survivability of industrial potential, protection of a percentage of your citizens, and you have a capability that inflicts more damage on your opposition than it can inflict on you. That's the way you can have a winner, and the Soviets' planning is based on the ugly concept of a winner in a nuclear exchange.

This is the catechism of the nuclear war-fighting school: that after the exchange of ten or fifteen thousand hydrogen bombs, after the mutual destruction of all cities and their populations, industries, armies, means of transport and communications, dams and powerplants, one side or the other could be the "winner" in a sense which had military significance.

Cap Weinberger knew that the decision on a base for the new missile would be the most difficult he would have to make in his first year. The president was obviously unhappy with the political problems it caused in Utah and Nevada. The congressional delegations of both states were strongly opposed to the shelter scheme, and those congressional delegations were now finding their most effective voice in Senator Paul Laxalt, who was the president's closest friend on the Hill. But against all that weight of opposition, he found an unceasing and unanimous advocacy of the shelter system by the air force and by the Joint Chiefs of Staff. Sure, they agreed, it is difficult, but there is no alternative—we have looked at every possibility, and this is the only one that works. The air force was strongly supported by Senator John Tower of Texas and Senator Henry Jackson of Washington, two of the senators most widely respected on strategic issues.

With Laxalt's ready agreement and encouragement, Weinberger slipped around the solid wall of service advocacy and appointed a new panel to examine once again the alternatives for basing MX. For its chairman, he stepped outside the now crowded field of scientists and engineers who had worked in the past on the basing problem, and asked Dr. Charles Townes, professor of physics at Berkely, to head a new panel.

A Nobel prizewinner in laser and maser physics, Townes had met Weinberger during the Ford administration, when both worked on a science policy advisory committee. They had both lived in the San Francisco area, where Weinberger was a prominent Republican politician. Townes had worked on strategic issues in the early sixties, when he was directing research at the Pentagon's Institute for Defense Analyses in Washington. But Townes did not especially enjoy working on military problems, preferring instead the harder and purer work of theoretical physics, so he had become increasingly reluctant over the years to accept requests to work on strategic issues. Nonetheless, he felt the basing problem was one to which he could usefully contribute, and when the secretary called him in March he agreed to go to Washington and talk the assignment over.

In conversation with Weinberger and Carlucci, Townes insisted on a condition that would prove to be important for the reports of his panel. He said that he couldn't look at the problem of a place for MX alone. He needed to look at the balance of other strategic nuclear forces, and only then look at the ways in which the MX could be based. For the first time, Townes was implicitly raising the question of whether MX was really needed. He wanted to look at the question of vulnerability of all the elements of the triad at once.

Weinberger agreed to Townes's request for freedom to look at the issue as broadly as he wished, but asked for a report by the end of May—two months away. Townes demurred, suggesting the end of July. The secretary agreed, and, after discussing the membership of the panel, Townes set to arranging its first meeting as soon as he could.

The members of his panel, all chosen by Weinberger and Townes from a list of forty names, included some of the grandest names in the missile business. There was Simon Ramo, who had worked on the missile review panel with John von Neumann in 1954, and who had then gone on to build missiles in a corporation that later became known as TRW. The "R" stands for Ramo. Another member was retired General Bernard Schreiver, who had headed the first Minuteman program in the late fifties, and whose feats of organization were still legendary in the air force. Others included Michael May, who had chaired the Defense Science Board panel for Brown, General Brent Scowcroft, former defense official David Packard, and ten other industry heads, retired generals, and former Defense Department officials and academics.

Over the next three months, the Townes panel arranged its agenda and set to work to examine the general prospects for the triad. They excluded a detailed study of the choice for a new bomber, because that was already being done in the Defense Department, but they regarded themselves as free to look at sea and land weapons, and the command and control that would direct the forces in war. Dr. Townes reported first to the secretary in April to tell him the sentiment of the committee was very strongly against putting a new missile in surface ships, the idea that Weinberger had favored and thereafter ceased to advance. He did not again report to the secretary until early July, when he gave him a briefing on everything the formal report then being prepared would contain.

The Townes committee discussed the general strategic

ideas behind the pattern of American nuclear weapons deployment. They agreed it was necessary for America to deploy weapons capable of striking at hardened Soviet military targets, and that it was also important that America should have the ability to fight a prolonged nuclear war and emerge from it no worse off than its opponent. There was no important sentiment on the committee that nuclear war could be limited—most panel members agreed it probably could not be. Nor was there any conviction that American population or industry could be protected from nuclear attack. But they did accept the idea that nuclear war could be prolonged, and that the best way to deter nuclear war was to develop the capacity to fight a prolonged war. Prolonged does not mean that an exchange at weapons would be controlled, but that each side is likely to reserve weapons to disrupt the enemy's attempts to rebuild.

On the big question of where to put MX, the panel was able to reach some agreement and to present its insoluble disagreements as options for the secretary. They agreed, after a briefing on likely trends in Soviet warhead numbers and accuracy, that the multiple protective shelter scheme proposed by the Carter administration could be overwhelmed if the Soviet Union wished to build up warhead numbers swiftly, and if the shelter system was not defended by antiballistic missiles. This was one central conclusion upon which everyone could agree, though the conclusion was no more than had already been agreed upon by practically everyone who had looked at the basing alternatives over the last decade. In testimony defending the Carter administration plan, officials had already conceded that the forty-six hundred shelters could be overwhelmed if the Soviet Union added thousands of more accurate warheads. But they said that the United States could add more shelters, or it could deploy a ballistic missile defense that would be all the more effective for having to defend only one shelter, containing the missile among many that did not, a shelter that the defenders would be able to identify and the attackers would not. The possibility that the system could be overwhelmed had been admitted by Carter administration officials. It was nonetheless the weakest point in the logic that produced the multiple shelter plan, the vulnerability that had been so strongly criticized by Admiral Turner and then by Senator Laxalt and the MX opponents on the Hill. By focusing on this aspect, the Townes panelists were able to unravel the big problem with the plan, which was that it was much more expensive and politically difficult for the United States to keep adding shelters than for the Soviet Union to add new warheads.

Having established that the shelter scheme would depend on ballistic missile defense, and that such a defense did not yet exist, the panel went on to debate the likely effectiveness of this theoratical system. Charles Townes was inclined to think that a defense could be developed which brought down such a high proportion of incoming warheads that it would be worthwhile building it. Michael May was inclined to think that any ballistic missile defense could be overwhelmed by an increase in the number of attacking warheads. But they could both agree, as did the other panel members, that one strong recommendation should be more research into ballistic missile defense systems. This recommendation fitted in well with a study of ballistic missile defenses then being arranged for the Defense Science Board by former Air Force Secretary Thomas Reed, who had recommended the MX for full-scale development five years before.

The panel also looked at the major alternative to the land-based shelters, the alternative that had been pushed by Frank Press, and for which Bill Perry had attempted to preserve an option when he recommended the smaller rather than the larger missile. This alternative was a missile-carrying aircraft. It was presented in two forms to the Townes panel. One form was a cargo plane like the lumbering C5A, which could be loaded with missiles and deployed, like the B52, ready to take off from fields scattered through the United States. This idea was very strongly pushed by the secretary's office, but did not attract much support on the Townes panel. As May had concluded more than three years before in his Defense Science Board study, the missile-carrying cargo plane was vulnerable to the same kind of attack as the B52 bomber. In a sudden attack with missiles, most of the planes would be caught on the ground. It was important, if different weapons were vulnerable, that they should at least be vulnerable to different things and complicate the Soviet difficulty in striking them simultaneously. The panel showed more interest in another airborne scheme, which was a proposal for a plane that would be built to allow it not to cover great distances but simply to stay aloft for extended periods. This continuous airborne patrol idea was also recommended for research, though several panel members doubted that Americans were any more ready now to accept nuclear weapons continuously patrolling above their heads than they had been when the armed B52s were grounded. A more immediate technical issue was whether any such patrolling aircraft could not be continuously observed by Soviet satellites and targeted for barrage attack. The panel recommended this "continuous airborne alert" plan as the most promising deployment scheme.

The committee also gave serious consideration to an idea called deep silo reserve, or citadel. In this scheme, the new missiles would be buried so deep in rock formations that no nuclear explosions above or around them could fatally damage the missiles. But a difficulty was that it was not at all clear how the missiles could be retrieved from their deep underground shelters when it was time to use them. The deep silo option was recommended for further study, but as a supplement to some other basing scheme. Such deeply buried missiles would be useful, perhaps, in the aftermath of a nuclear exchange. They could not substitute for the quick, accurate kill demanded by the nuclear strategists.

These three ideas—ballistic missile defense, air patrol, and deep underground silos—were all recommended for further study. But what was to be done now? The Carter administration had been told that 90 per cent of American land missiles would be vulnerable to a Soviet attack in the mideighties, and that this was a reason to push ahead as soon as possible with the new missile and the new base. The Reagan administration and the Townes panel accepted the same numbers. If anything, they were more alarmed than their predecessors. For all the urgency, however, the panel could not agree at all on a solution for MX. A majority of the panel led by General Brent Scowcroft wanted to move ahead as quickly as possible with a diminished version of the Carter plan. He proposed deploying one hundred missiles in one hundred horizontal light shelters. If the Soviet Union would agree to deep cuts in missile numbers, if ballistic missile defense proved feasible, then the system need not be expanded. If the threat became more severe, then the administration would have the option of building more and more shelters. It was a foot in the door for the air force, but it was not a unanimous recommendation of the committee.

Another possibility suggested by some of the panelists was the deployment of MX missiles in existing missile silos. This had been the idea advanced by the air force in the mid-seventies, and it was revived and defended with the same arguments. The missiles would be just as vulnerable as the missiles they replaced, but, since they had ten warheads apiece to the maximum of three on the Minuteman III, more American warheads would survive a Soviet strike. That idea was firmly rejected.

This left the Townes panel in the unpleasant position of recommending further research on the missile base, with no decision for several years on which base would be best. In the meantime, should the missile be built? On this question, there was more dispute on the panel. Some members suggested the program be canceled, or that it be incorporated in the seagoing missile program. Others argued that it was now so close to producing results that it was well worthwhile continuing. The panel generally agreed to keep it going, arguing that in the final analysis the U.S. was better off with some modern land missiles, even if they were vulnerable. This was because, in order to achieve the accuracies necessary to attack silo-based missiles, the Soviet Union would have to use its land missiles. Since its land missiles took thirty minutes to reach their targets in the United States, and they would be observed by American satellites from the moment of blastoff, the Strategic Air Command would have enough warning time to get a reasonably high proportion of its B52 bombers on strip alert into the sky. If there were no land missiles to target, then the Soviet Union could strike the much softer planes on the ground with missiles launched from submarines off the U.S. coast. In that case, the warning would only be about fifteen minutes, and only half the number of planes would escape. Accepting this reasoning, the Townes panel said that land missiles should remain part of the U.S. force.

Since delaying the basing decision also delayed the deployment of two thousand new accurate warheads, the panel had to come up with some other way of equipping the U.S. with the ability to destroy Soviet missiles in their silos. The panel and the Reagan administration accepted, as the Carter administration had, a minimum SAC requirement for fifteen hundred to eighteen hundred accurate warheads to survive a Soviet strike. Their investigation led them right back to the second option that had been presented to Jimmy Carter and his National Security Council nearly two years before. This was option five, which relied heavily on a new submarine-launched missile designated the D5. Though the D5 would at best not be deployed until 1992 or 1993, it was likely that, by that time, technology would be good enough to drop the missile within lethal distance of the toughest Soviet silo.

The D-5 was designed for the Trident submarine and was the navy's term for the 83" diameter missile which Perry had wanted to adapt for land use. Since the panel agreed that the Trident was likely to remain invulnerable to attack right through to the end of the century, it was the obvious alternative once the multiple protective shelter was canceled. So the panel agreed that, pending a decision on how to deploy the new large land missile, the U.S. should press ahead as quickly as possible with the new submarine-launched missile.

The big problem with submarines was that of communicating with them quickly and reliably, without exposing the submarine to detection. Consideration of this problem was part of a general review of command and control which the panel conducted and which concluded with little dissent that improvements in command and control, not improvements in weapons, were the quickest and cheapest way of improving America's nuclear deterrent. In 1979 principal deputy secretary of defense, James Wade, had conducted a Defense Science Board summer study on the survivability of command and control in nuclear war, and there were also reports by the Office of Technology Assessment and the General Accounting Office on shortcomings in communications that would be necessary in war. Most of the communication was highly vulnerable to attack, like land lines, radars, and fixed transmission and reception stations. The only reliable forms of communication, the panel concluded, would be small and mobile, or based in satellites. Most of the programs to improve command and control had already been started in the Carter administration or the Ford administration. It was now simply a matter of spending a great deal more on them to bring them more swiftly into service. To Townes, the vulnerability of command and control was a more important problem than the vulnerability of land missiles, and his emphasis upon it presented a way in which the Reagan administration could meet western objections by dropping MPS, and at the same time claim to have increased America's nuclear might. As one of De Lauer's aides, James Wade, would later assert, improved command and control could be traded off against warhead numbers. Why this might be so, he did not explain.

Townes's report to Weinberger in early July suited Weinberger very well. True, it did not discover a way of basing the missile that solved strategic problems, but it did say the multiple protective shelter would not of itself solve the strategic problem either, which was exactly what Weinberger needed to fight off the air force. It unanimously recommended accelerated development of a more accurate submarine-launched missile and of survivable command and control, both of which could be portrayed as strong, assertive actions to rebuild America's defenses, even though what the secretary was actually doing was canceling a project that had been his predecessor's biggest contribution to strengthening those defenses. Since the recommendations provided for both stronger counterforce missiles and for enduring communications, they fitted in with the views of Carlucci, Ikle, DeLauer, and Wade, not to mention the vice-president and the secretary of state, that America should develop a believable war-fighting capacity. So there was a broad acceptance within the administration of the themes of the report. But beyond that, and beyond presenting a good reason to kill the multiple protective shelter, the report was not a great deal of help. How much the programs would cost, how many missiles and planes and submarines in total ought to be deployed, how quickly all could be made ready—these were all questions that remained open after Dr. Townes had concluded his study, and they would not be answered before political pressures forced the administration to announce its decision on MX. The fact that a majority of the committee had recommended the one hundred missiles in one hundred shelters scheme, which would have allowed for later expansion, was suppressed for another nine months.

From the time of Dr. Townes's briefing, the dispute over MX basing, which had been suppressed by the ongoing study, was renewed with vigor as the air force fought to keep the Carter plan, or something close enough to it to allow them to expand and modify it later.

The air force fight to keep an MPS system was led by Lieutenant General Kelly H. Burke, a gray haired, avuncular Southerner who had combined an interest in history with a career as a weather reconnaissance pilot, before he had found a fast ladder to success in the Strategic Air Command at the beginning of the seventies. As deputy chief of staff for plans at Offutt in 1978 Burke had closely watched the protracted debate over MX basing within the Carter administration. The following year he was moved to Washington to watch over the program, and at the end of 1979 the urbane, cordial general was appointed deputy chief of staff for research and development for the U.S. Air Force, a job which was as political as it was technical. Burke had seen the Republicans divide on the MX basing mode in 1980, and he watched with trepidation as the transition team headed by William van Cleave moved into the Defense Department at the beginning of 1981. Van Cleave had portrayed himself as an opponent of the MPS, but by the time he was ousted from his transition team job by Weinberger he was a convert, as were other members of the transition team in the air force and the defense departments. That effort was wasted, however, because Weinberger farmed the issue out to the Townes panel, and Kelly Burke found that neither he nor Lew Allen, the air force chief of staff, could get in to see the one man who might have helped, Ronald Reagan. They could work with Senator Tower, the Chairman of the Armed Services Committee. They could work with the now powerless van Cleave, but they could not get their view across where it mattered.

At the same time as Townes was reporting to Weinberger, Paul Laxalt was issuing a report against the multiple protection shelter. Now chairman of the Military Construction Subcommittee which held hearings in June on the basing problem, Laxalt reported that the MPS was vulnerable. The Soviets could deploy at least fourteen thousand warheads. A better solution was to place two hundred MXes in Minuteman silos and defend them with the small anti-ballistic missile allowed in the SALT treaty. Then either the Soviet Union would agree to deep cuts, or the U.S. would deploy a full ballistic missile defense. At the same time, he urged the administration to build the B-1 bomber, to enhance command, control, and communications, and to research a small single warhead missile, space-based lasers, and the apparatus for strategic war-fighting. Laxalt was promptly attacked by Senator John Tower, chairman of the Senate Armed Services Committee, who was now brought into the battle to attempt to save some form of ongoing multiple protective shelter basing for the missile.

By the end of July, Weinberger was making it known that he favored the airborne MX, with the missile transported on the C-5A. It was attacked by the secretary of state and the chairman of the Joint Chiefs at a National Security Planning Group meeting at the White House in July and referred to the Townes panel for examination and report.

At the beginning of August 1981, his tax and spending victories behind him, the president left Washington for California to spend the month vacationing at his ranch. It was during the ranch vacation that the president and his advisers would begin to put together the alternative to the shelter-based MX. On Tuesday, 17 August, the president helicoptered down to his penthouse suite at the Century Plaza Hotel in Los Angeles for a full-dress meeting of the National Security Council. It was attended by Secretary of State Alexander Haig, Ed Meese, Caspar Weinberger, National Security Assistant Richard Allen, chairman of the Joint Chiefs General Jones, U.N. Ambassador Jeane Kirkpatrick, Arms Control Director Eugene Rostow, and Presidential Counsel-

lor Jim Baker, and by the two principal protagonists at the
meeting, Charles Townes and air force Chief of Staff General
Lew Allen.

Charles Townes briefed the meeting on the conclusions of
his panel—that the MPS would not be survivable without
ballistic missile defense or Soviet restraint, and that two
options presented by his committee were for more research
on air mobiles and for more research on ballistic missile
defense. Meanwhile, he said, the U.S. should press ahead
with survivable communications and the D-5 submarine-
launched missile, as well as a new airplane and the cruise
missile program already funded by the Carter administration.

For Lew Allen, it was the first and only chance he was to
have to defend the multiple protective shelter system which
he had described as the air force's highest priority, and the
first and only chance he would have to express before the
president his grave reservations about any air-mobile missile.

A bomber pilot who had won his physics doctorate with a
thesis on high energy photonuclear reactions, Lew Allen had
spent his career working with nuclear weapons, space systems, and the technical information systems offered by space
technology. He had been assigned as a physicist to the Los
Alamos Scientific Laboratory in New Mexico where nuclear
warheads were designed and tested, he had been director of
space systems in the Pentagon, chief of the Air Force Systems Command at Andrews, and he had been director of the
top secret organisation for electronic spying, the National
Security Agency, and deputy to the director of Central Intelligence. Slight, bald, and undramatic, Lew Allen had filled
some of the most sensitive and secret jobs in the national
security apparatus of the United States. Only a few dozen
Americans had more classified data in their minds than Lew
Allen, but none of the experience, none of the data, none of
the secrets made the least difference in this forum where the

most important single issue of his tour as chief of staff of the
air force was being considered by the Reagan administration. He spoke vigorously and was heard with consideration,
but Lew Allen knew then, as he would ruefully admit after-
ward, that he had failed to convince the president.

Five days later, the coalition of air force leaders and the
Senate Armed Services Committee leadership tried once
again to persuade Reagan to refuse the air mobile and to
accept a limited multiple system. Senator John Tower and
his colleague Representative William Dickinson, minority
leader on the House Armed Services Committee, flew out
West to meet the president. They, too, expressed the gravest
reservations about the air-mobile idea, and proposed instead
what was now becoming the air force's last-ditch compromise. They argued that the president should build only one
thousand shelters, perhaps on an existing air force base or
military land, and deploy one hundred missiles among them.
This, they argued, would give better protection and more
surviving warheads in a shorter time than any other alternatives now being proposed. They came away feeling that
the president had been persuaded that the air-mobile plan
might be one for further research but not for immediate
action. They were not at all certain about how the president
viewed the alternative, which was becoming known as "one
hundred in one thousand."

The fifty-seven-year-old Tower had Reagan's kind of politics, but not Reagan's kind of personality. Tower was a
guarded, cautious man, so deeply distrustful of his political
opponents that he had, as chairman of the Senate Armed
Services Committee, ended a long tradition of having a single professional bipartisan staff by establishing separate par-
tisan staffs. Tower was short and a chain-smoker, and,
though his staff were fond of him, most people who met him
thought him a sour character. He had been an assistant
professor of government at a small Texas college in the
fifties, years during which he published little in his field and

devoted a great deal of time to the tiny Republican party in his overwhelmingly Democratic state. In 1961, in an unexpected change in voter loyalties that signified the end of the rule of the Texan conservative Democrats, Tower was elected senator in a special election. In the twenty years since, he had demonstrated a deep and abiding conservatism. "I think it's bad to have federal compulsion in this area," he said of Kennedy proposals to desegregate hotels and restaurants. He had also demonstrated a profound respect for the opinions of the military. A consistent supporter of American intervention in Vietnam, he had claimed to see signs of victory there long after others had seen the certainty of defeat. He complained that Defense Secretary Robert McNamara had cautioned "much too much restraint" in the conduct of American military operations in Vietnam and was glad to see that official leave for the presidency of the World Bank. Tower had vigorously supported the Joint Chiefs against McNamara in their demand for the deployment of a ballistic missile defense system. He deeply resented civilian second-guessing of what he regarded as military matters; he criticized Edward Kennedy for objecting to certain tactics being used in Vietnam, and he condemned a statement by Senator Fulbright on military education programs. "Only the military is competent to know what form and substance military training programs should take," he declared, "because civilians are not competent by training or experience to teach military tactics or strategy."

With his belief in the correctness of military advice, Tower wanted the shelters in Utah and Nevada. He was convinced that it was the only way to protect a new land missile, and that a new land missile was absolutely necessary to the defense of the United States. He was also convinced he could bring Ronald Reagan round to his way of thinking. As the months passed, Tower could see that the Utah and Nevada system was in much deeper trouble than he had suspected, and he took up the air force alternative, the foot-in-the-door option, of a hundred missiles in a thousand shelters, a plan that would have got the scheme going and left it for extensions later. It was this scheme that he explained to Ronald Reagan in Los Angeles on 22 August. The president listened amiably to all the arguments. He did not directly contradict the senator's view; he did not pose questions that suggested he would not agree with a multiple basing proposal; but, at the same time, Tower came away from his meeting with no committment. "I thought the decision would be for one hundred missiles in one thousand shelters," the senator would later recall. "I advocated it when I saw the president and we felt the proposition was not unfavorably received. There were indications the administration would go that way."

By late August 1981 the air mobile was clearly dead, and support was strengthening for the various modified versions of the MPS—one hundred in one thousand, which was the air force idea; one hundred in five hundred, which had been Brent Scowcroft's idea; and now a third version, which was the deployment of one hundred missiles in six hundred superstrong upright silos at the Nellis Air Force Base in Nevada. This plan was recommended by RAND researchers.

Up on the Hill, Paul Laxalt knew that the full MPS was dead—and, in fact, had been dead since 20 January, but he was very worried indeed about one hundred in a thousand. On 14 September he exercized a privilege that was always available to him but rarely used—he went down to see Reagan at the White House. Accompanied by Jake Garn, Laxalt saw Reagan, Meese, and Weinberger in the Oval Office. Both senators said they could not and would not accept one hundred missiles in one thousand shelters at the Nellis Air Force Base or anywhere else in Utah or Nevada. If two hundred missiles in forty-six hundred holes could be overwhelmed, they said, then one hundred in a thousand were twice as vulnerable. Another reason, less openly canvassed, was that one hundred in a thousand was patently the beginning of a much larger system, which could be expanded when time was more propitious.

By mid-September the administration had run through each of the options open to it and found each blocked by a powerful constituency. The air force would not have airborne missiles and nor would Senator Tower. Nor would they accept the smaller 83″ missile, the common missile. Utah and Nevada would not have the MPS in any form—one hundred in one thousand, one hundred in one hundred, one hundred in six hundred, or two hundred in four thousand six hundred. By the end of September, when it was no longer possible to avoid a decision, there was no decision to make. The only decision was how to put the best possible face on not being able to make a decision.

On Monday, 28 September, the president returned to the White House after a day of speechmaking in New Orleans and met in the second-floor sitting room of his private quarters with five of his closest assistants. It was a room newly redecorated in just the style of expensive warmth with which he was most comfortable. A crystal chandelier lit up the rich red-flowered pattern of two enormous sofas, overhung by a tall potted palm. In the center of one lounge was a matching red cushion crocheted with Ronald Reagan's initials in foot-high letters, and behind that a magnificent double-arched window through the thick panes of which the storied columns of the old executive office building opposite were reflected with distorted lines, as though seen through water. With him in informal conference on those red lounges was his triumvirate of his principal assistants, Edwin Meese III, James Baker, Michael Deaver, his National Security Assistant Richard Allen, and Defense Secretary Caspar Weinberger. With the exception of Baker and Allen, all were Californians, and not a single one of those now attending the final meeting to decide on strategic arsenal for the next several decades had worked on nuclear issues before they arrived in office nine months before. There was no pretence to a meeting of the National Security Council or the National Security Planning group. There was no lengthy presentation of options, no audiovisual presentation, no detailed calculation of the costs and benefits of alternative strategies. Nor need there have been, for the essential purpose of this meeting was to agree on a solution to a problem more political than strategic: how was the president to best present the cancelation of the MX basing system? After an hour's discussion of what would later be portrayed as the most important decision ever made by a president, he signed a prepared order for a National Security Directive canceling the work on multiple protective shelters and substituting for it a "strategic package" of large but uncertain dimensions.

The B-1, Stealth, Trident D-5 missiles, MX, survivable communications, air defense—they were all there, but, even after weeks of hearings, it wasn't clear how many there were in total, or what the program would cost, or even, in the case of communications, what exactly would be built. Secretary Weinberger said that one hundred missiles would be deployed, up to thirty-six deployed in superhardened silos. To get one hundred deployable missiles, the Pentagon said, would require the production of well over two hundred missiles since some would be needed for testing, some would develop faults, some would be needed as spares and replacements. But one hundred deployable missiles was just the number picked for the defense budget. Whether fifty or one hundred or two hundred or three hundred would actually be deployed had not actually been decided at all. That depended on several uncertainties that would not be clear until the mid-eighties. One important factor was a targeting study being conducted by Dr. Ikle and Dr. DeLauer which would look at the likely number of Soviet targets and the likely warheads available to the United States from all its nuclear weapons. That would be one factor. Another would be the basing modes finally adopted. The more missiles were expected to survive, the fewer would be deployed. And a final uncertainty was the nature of any arms control agreement with the Soviet Union, and the restraint it might place on the numbers of MIRVed missiles on both sides.

10

Movies, Pizzas, and Dollar Bills

DURING more than a decade of development, the military characteristics of the MX have not altered, yet the reasons offered for deploying it—and the manner in which it is proposed to be deployed—have changed frequently. The fact that the rationale for its existence could change so often while the missile stayed the same might suggest that there are a lot of different good reasons to deploy the missile, or it might suggest that there are only phony reasons, offered to justify an expensive and unnecessary addition to America's nuclear arsenal.

In 1976, worried that the scheme to base the MX in underground tunnels would never be perfected and never be politically acceptable, the Ford administration asked Congress to approve a scheme for putting MX in existing missile silos. As both the House and the Senate agreed at the time, it made no sense to put thenew missile in fixed silos, since they were just as vulnerable as before, and the target more lucrative. It might be true that the United States would have more warheads left over from a Soviet first strike if MX was in the holes and not Minuteman, but the difference in the number of surviving warheads would not be great and certainly not enough to compensate for the greater incentive for the Soviet Union to attack a ten-warhead missile than a three-warhead missile. The silo idea was thrown out, largely thanks to the leadership of Senator McIntyre, but seven years later, when Soviet missiles were said to be much more accurate and Soviet warheads more numerous, the Reagan administration was planning to do exactly what had been rejected by Congress at the end of the Ford administration. In the interval between silo plan I and silo plan II, the Carter administration had examined and rejected the underground tunnel scheme and the vertical shelter scheme, and it devised, adopted, and rejected several different versions of a horizontal surface base. Each and every basing scheme had been fulsomely defended by either air force or administration officials or both before Congress and the press, each had been explained in great detail and supported with enthusiasm, and each in its turn had then been deplored and laughed at before it vanished.

It was not only the base for the weapon that had changed so frequently in the decade of its development, but also the rationale for its existence. Like the successive basing schemes, the successive rationales were not so much refuted as forgotten and replaced. In 1973 and 1974 James Schlesinger had warned that the United States would go ahead with its new big land missile if the Soviet Union went ahead and put multiple independently targetable warheads on its land missiles. The rationale then was that the United States must be seen to be matching a future Soviet capacity to strike at American missiles, though why the United States needed to match this capability and what gain it achieved from doing so was never clearly explained. Later in the seventies, various other explanations were offered for the new missile. The air force said in one year that the Vladivostok accord had put a ceiling on Soviet weapons so the development of MX could be delayed. The subsequent year, officials testified that Vladivostok had put a ceiling on American weapons, and therefore each American weapon needed to be more accurate and powerful, and MX was urgently required. Sometimes MX was justified by what was said to be a growing list of hard targets in the Soviet Union. Sometimes it was justified by what was said to be the rapidly increasing accuracy of Soviet missiles. Sometimes it was said that what was needed was an invulnerable base, and sometimes it was said that what was needed was an accurate missile. By the end of the Ford administration, it was said that the missile could be deployed in fixed silos until the Soviet threat became more severe, and the air force disclosed plans to Congress to deploy three hundred missiles—enough to destroy twice the number of land missiles the Soviets then deployed. By the second year of the Carter administration, the rationale had completely altered once again. Only two hundred missiles would be deployed, and the emphasis was back on an invulnerable base that would stabilize the arms race. It was said that an MX force of that size would allow the United States to negotiate away its Minuteman missiles in return for Soviet reductions. Whatever the argument, the fact was that the allegedly dovish Carter administration, with the concurrence of virtually all its important members except CIA director Stansfield Turner and science adviser Frank Press, had gone ahead and approved the biggest addition to the American nuclear arsenal since the MIRVing program of the early seventies. And, at the same time as it approved this program, the Carter administration devised a series of directives on nuclear war which revised and updated the flexible response doctrines of the early seventies. For all his ambiguity and for all his public questioning of the doctrines of counterforce, Harold Brown in the mid-seventies followed very closely the no-cities strategy on which he had worked with Robert McNamara more than a decade before. Jimmy Carter, who once proposed to eliminate nuclear weapons, concluded by proposing to double their number.

In the history of the project, one of the outstanding patterns is the clear preference of the best informed of outside observers and even some air force specialists for the smaller diameter missile, the 83″. Bill Perry wanted a smaller missile, which was part of the original proposition of Al Latter. General Toomay's Tiger Team favored a smaller missile, and Michael May also thought a small missile was better for any kind of shelter scheme that involved moving the missile around. Right up until the final weeks before the National Security Council meetings of June 1979, Bill Perry and Harold Brown had pushed for the smaller missile against the weight of the air force and its friends on the Hill, led by Senator Jackson. The public argument was that the bigger missile would carry more than the ten warheads to which any missile was limited under SALT. But since there would be no restriction on the total numbers of missiles without SALT, the argument that the bigger missile would provide against the possibility of no SALT did not make sense. After all, it would not make much difference if the U.S. added warheads to existing missiles, or simply produced more missiles, and it could do either if there were no SALT limits. The real reason the 83″ missile was so vehemently opposed by the air force was that it would then be harder to resist the arguments for making a common missile with the navy, and harder to resist the inevitable decision of some subsequent administration to put the new air force missile to sea.

That the wrong missile eventually was selected by the president is chiefly the responsibility of Zbigniew Brzezinski, who claims to have "rammed through" the big missile decision during the National Security Council meetings of 4 and 5 June 1979. The national security assistant preferred the big diameter missile even though he had been, according to Harold Brown, in favor of a truck-transported mobile missile, which necessarily meant a light missile.

The Reagan administration presented its September 1981 strategic nuclear weapons program as a massive buildup, but there are plenty of reasons to wonder whether this is really so, and to wonder, too, about the strategic rationale behind what it is doing. There is a strong sense in the Reagan administration that, after several decades of circular thinking and argument on the subject of nuclear weapons, there is very little that can sensibly be said or done except repeat slogans that are more than ever remote from what is actually happening or what is actually planned. It may be that the administration has a new rationale and is keeping it secret, but keeping a strategic theory secret in the age of nuclear weapons is inconsistent with the one surviving principle—that any strategic theory must have as its goal that nuclear weapons should never be used, by either side. A secret theory does not deter.

The Reagan administration's buildup is actually pretty much the Carter program, with a few additions and deletions. Instead of two hundred MX deployed in horizontal multiple shelters, there will be an unknown number deployed in an unknown base at an unknown time. The general sense seems to be that it will be a lesser number. The air-launched cruise missile programs and the D-5 submarine-launched missiles programs are as they were in the Carter administration. Contrary to early reports, there will be no acceleration of the D5 submarine missile program, and the cruise missile program has actually fallen behind. The one great change the Reagan administration did make was to decide to build the B-1, canceled by the Carter administration, to fill in a few brief years before the new radar evading stealth bomber, which was also being developed by the Carter administration, is brought into production. As to the alleged emphasis on hardening and protecting command control and communications, this too was begun in the Carter administration, and the last budget request of the Carter administration for command and control improvements is difficult to distinguish from the "improved" program announced nine months later.

At the same time as the Reagan administration was

falsely claiming to have initiated a strategic weapons buildup, it was actually directing the major spending increases and the most profound strategic changes toward conventional weapons and forces. In hearings in 1981 several witnesses asserted, evidently as settled policy, that the criterion for defense planning is that the U.S. must be able to fight and beat a Soviet challenge with superior conventional forces. This criterion neatly justified the construction of three new supercarriers, a total of two hundred more naval ships, and improved tactical aviation and mobile strike forces. But as a strategic principle it was not only a reversal of U.S. policy since World War Two, but also quite opposite to the reiterated policy of the secretary of state, who insisted that the United States would not relinquish its right to the first use of nuclear weapons to overcome what was said to be its conventional inferiority in Europe. The prevailing notion that the Reagan administration was in reality far more interested in conventional than nuclear forces was strengthened in 1982 when it appointed service chiefs from conventional force backgrounds. A fighter pilot was appointed Chief of Staff of the air force, and a World War Two army veteran became chairman of the Joint Chiefs.

These contradictions within the Reagan administration point to a presidency that is in defense policy, as in economic policy, more often confused and incompetent than ideological and determined. In both economic and defense policy there is greater risk of error in taking the Reagan administration pronouncements as serious statements of purpose than in accepting the premise that the Reagan administration often works at cross purposes, and that the result is often incoherence in policy making.

The Reagan administration decision on MX was actually a decision to take a further decision at some future time. We do not know the strategic rationale for proceeding with MX under the Reagan administration. Nor do we know how many missiles it proposes to deploy. For the defense department budget it has used a figure of one hundred deployed missiles, which requires the production of more than two hundred missiles to allow for test firing, spares and so on. The actual number to be deployed depends on the results of force studies now being conducted, on negotiations with the Soviet Union, and on all sorts of shifts in political currents over the decade. Nor do we know how the MX will be based. Congress has resolutely opposed basing the missile in existing missile silos. The administration now proposes to base it either in aircraft or in multiple silos packed together in a ten-square-mile area. Neither idea has anything to recommend it except that its consideration will postpone for this administration the need to cancel what is becoming a prodigiously expensive failure. By September 1982 nearly $5 billion had been spent on the project, and the air force budget called for $4.5 billion more in 1983 and $5.3 billion in 1984.

In 1982 hearings, air force research and development chief General Kelly Burke said an airborne MX was the least likely alternative to be adopted since it had most of the disadvantages of the B52 bomber force and few redeeming features of its own. As Bill Perry has observed, the 92″ one-hundred-ninety-two-thousand pound missile is not well adapted to being transported in any aircraft. It weighs more than ten times as much as the very heavy nine megaton B53 nuclear bomb, or close to half the takeoff weight of a B52. A missile that, as General Burke observed, is so heavy it cannot be carried on ordinary interstate highways, is not the right missile to be transported on a continuous airborne patrol. Any aircraft big enough to carry the MX missile is big enough to carry more than sixty cruise missiles, which would be a much better cargo in any contingency other than a U.S.-launched first strike.

The second least likely alternative, according to General Burke, is "deep silo" basing, which means burying the missile so deeply in rock or cement that no explosion above it will cripple the missile. This is a revival of another old idea, which has been rejected in the past because a missile buried so deeply as to avoid detonations above is also so deep it cannot be retrieved when the detonations cease. As the Defense Department reported in 1980 to the Senate Armed Services committee, the deep silo basing system's "feasibility of egress to surface is questionable," it responds slowly to attack, it will take a long time to construct, its numbers cannot be verified by satellite, and it is unlikely that its command and control terminals will survive nuclear attack even if the missile itself does.

These two alternatives gone, we are left with only one by the Reagan administration: the deployment of the missile in single or multiple silos, protected by the army's ballistic missile defense system. This scheme, currently called "dense pack," is a renamed version of the "one hundred in a thousand" scheme pushed by the air force in 1981 when the Carter approved scheme was obviously failing. "Dense pack" purports to make use of the fact that incoming warheads can blow each other up or throw each other off course, but if "fratricide" can prevent an attack on MX, it can also protect the existing Minuteman fields, which means there is no need for a novel basing system. "Dense pack" essentially depends not on fratricide but on an anti-ballistic missile defense. General Burke regards this as the most likely alternative. James Wade, deputy to Dr. DeLauer, has long been in favor of ballistic missile defense. He told a House hearing in 1980 (in his inimitably difficult style) that "it was my judgment call that the possibility of an ABM system having a major play in the sense of defending and being part of the MX MPS system wasn't given the attention that it perhaps should have been given because of the fact that over the last four years the flavor was heavily oriented toward arms control and there was no interest in changing the SALT ABM treaty. If it made sense toward improving the survivability of our land based forces, I don't think BMD received the attention it should have."

Is ballistic missile defense a solution to the vulnerability of land missiles? The Townes panel thought not after looking at the classified evidence, and there are a number of reasons to think not after looking at the public testimony.

The first and most difficult of these problems is whether missiles can actually be defended with any reasonable certainty by other missiles. The current army version of ballistic missile defense (BMD) has three elements: a radar which tracks incoming missiles, a computer which distinguishes missiles from other objects, and a large number of small nuclear tipped missiles which are intended to intercept the incoming missiles six to twelve miles from their targets. The air force says that this system will work well with some form of multiple shelter base for the MX, because the intercept rockets need only attack Soviet missile directed against the shelter that contains the missile. But this is a specious argument; once the ballistic missile defense system is deployed, it (and not the MX) becomes the first target of the Soviet attack. Since the vulnerable part of the BMD is the radar and the computer, the essential task for army engineers is to develop a system that is fast enough to react to all incoming missiles, accurate enough to disable all of them, discriminating enough to distinguish between incoming warheads and all the chaff with which the incoming missiles will be loaded, and tough enough to withstand the shock of hundreds of hydrogen bomb explosions six to twelve miles away. The cost of such a system, could it be devised, would be considerable. Even to test such a system involves violating or canceling the ABM treaty with the Soviet Union, and without such a treaty both sides will, within a few years, have deployed missiles that have as their main target the missiles of the other side, as well as missiles to defend those missiles, yet each side still will be able to seek an advantage over the other by deploying missiles in sufficient numbers to overwhelm the other's defenses. The BMD can be overwhelmed, just as the MX in multiple shelters could be overwhelmed.

Even if we assume a ballistic missile defense works perfectly, however, there still would be no good reason to deploy it. If the United States can deploy an effective missile defense, then so can the Soviet Union. Within a decade, both sides would have deployed accurate MIRVed intercontinetal missiles protected by local missile defense. The intercontinental missiles would in both cases be targeted on the intercontinetal missiles of the other side, which we assume to be invulnerable to this kind of attack. The outcome of this game is that neither side is any better off, but both have spent billions rearranging their positions. If we alternatively assume that one side is able to perfect a ballistic missile defense and the other is not, then both sides are not only no better off—they are actually worse off. Both sides now have reason to fear the other will launch a first strike, either to use the missiles before they are lost, or in anticipation that the other side will wish to use its missiles before they are lost. This gets right to the heart of an issue that has never been properly examined in all the studies of basing modes for MX—whether it is actually in the interests of the United States to build and deploy highly accurate, multi-warheaded weapons intended to strike at Soviet missiles silos.

The arguments in favor of MX are usually of three kinds. The first is that a highly accurate land missile is needed for "flexible response" nuclear strategies—that is, that it is a "surgical" weapon which can be programmed to do just the job intended, and no more. This argument depends on two other ideas, which we shall examine in turn: that the effect of a nuclear attack can be predicted, and that a nuclear exchange, once initiated, can be limited to something less than the obliteration of major urban centers on both sides. A second set of arguments for MX usually rests on the idea that the Soviet Union has a lot of land missiles that will one day be highly accurate, so the United States should match this capability. And the final arguments for MX rest on the idea that, whatever the nature of the nuclear conflict, it will be less likely to occur, and America is more likely to emerge with advantage if it does occur, if America deploys an MX.

In the old Hutchinson salt mines near Kansas City, Metro-Goldwyn-Mayer is storing hundreds of movie film negatives and Pizza Hut is storing franchising records in crypts maintained by the Underground Vaults and Storage Company. Nearby, there's an underground headquarters for the Federal Reserve Bank of Kansas City, which can communicate via telex with the underground headquarters of the entire Federal Reserve system in Culpepper, Virginia. The Pizza Hut Company, Metro Goldwyn Mayer, and the Federal Reserve systems are hoping to ride out a nuclear attack in this deep mine, so that, when the conflict is over, America can still have movies and pizzas and dollar bills. But will a post-attack America want to see movies, eat fast food, and will the survivors trust paper money?

The answer is that there is no answer—we do not know what the effects of nuclear weapons will be if delivered in large numbers. Unless we can specify all the circumstances that in practice it would not be possible to specify, it is difficult to predict the effect of even a single large nuclear weapon. Although defense officials sometimes testify before Congress as though they had confident ideas about the effects of nuclear weapons, the Office of Technology Assessment in the U.S. Congress thinks otherwise. It reviewed all the secret work done in the Department of Defense, the intelligence community, and the Arms Control and Disarmament Agency between 1974 and 1978 on the effects of nuclear weapons, and concluded: "The complex issues concerning national recovery should nuclear war occur, or the post-war power and recovery capabilities of the belligerents, have as yet not even been properly formulated for analyses."

It is possible to calculate, using a variety of assumptions, what effect different levels and locations of bursts will have on people immediately after the explosion and the first few days following. These are the prompt blast and radiation effects. But even these effects vary within a wide magnitude, depending on the weather, on whether the population is at home or at work, whether the population is sheltered or not, whether it is night or day or summer or winter, whether the wind is blowing in one direction or another, whether the blasts occur near the ground or overhead, whether there are fireballs and subsequent effects from the blast. These variables most of which are unrelated to the factors that will bring about a nuclear exchange, actually account for a much wider range of variance in the number of people killed than do the number of weapons used or their size.

It is possible to say, for example, that a nuclear attack using twice the number of weapons will, all other things remaining equal, cause in certain population conditions one-third again as many prompt casualties. But if the wind is blowing toward a large city in the smaller attack, or if the bombs in the smaller attack burst near the ground and send up more radioactive particles, or if it is winter in the first attack and spring in the second, or if a thousand other uncertainties alter the circumstances of the attack, then half the number of weapons might kill twice as many people.

These variables, which change from day to day, week to week, make it impossible to plan with any certainty to kill a set number of people. It is possible to plan to destroy a set number of factories or missile silos or airfields, and be relatively confident of doing so if your side still has enough weapons. What you cannot predict is the number of collateral casualties—the number of people who will be killed as an incidental result of the attack on missile silos and bomber bases. This is a very important consideration when officials talk, as they increasingly do, about "surgical strikes" or "customized responses."

These uncertainties about the number of people that will be killed promptly by a certain kind of nuclear attack are only some of the unknowns. There are medium-term and long-term effects that are hard to calculate, but would probably be as great if not greater than the immediate effects. In the immediate aftermath of a nuclear explosion in a settled community, for example, there is no electricity, there are no hospitals, no doctors, no food supplies, no energy, no transport, little communication, and no knowledge of what will happen next. That also happened in the Second World War, but this time there may not be other cities intact to assist the damaged cities. When Hiroshima was struck by a small nuclear weapon, many thousands of people died immediately, many thousands thereafter, and so profound was the effect that the emperor asked for the war to be ended. Yet within two days, water had been restored to some parts of Hiroshima, and it was not long before some telephone and railways services were patched up. In a full-scale nuclear war, this would be impossible. Because it is impossible to compute the effects of not having health and city services operating after a war, it is not possible to compute the longer-term casualties.

Nor is it possible to compute the longer-term effects of radiation doses that are not sufficient to kill but do cause sickness and genetic damage. On this question, there is evidence that such effects are important, but there is no way of computing their magnitude.

Nor do we know what the effect of a war will be on a country's military capacity. What will its friends and enemies do if it is disarmed and helpless? Will its friends, newly important in what remains of the world, decide they want again a great America and a great Soviet Union? And finally there is the effect of war on the capacity to produce materials and food. Unless the remaining population can produce more than they consume, they will steadily deplete the remaining capital stocks. How long will it take to rebuild dams and factories, when the materials and technologies used in their construction are no longer appropriate or no longer available?

What this comes down to is that most estimates of the casualties of a nuclear war are estimates only of immediate casualties, because immediate casualties are easiest to predict, given census data and assumptions about the number of weapons used. The aftermath effects, the longer-term effects, which would be greater than the immediate effects, are not quantified or taken into account. And most of the estimates that are given refer only to biological survival, not to the survival of a standard of living, not to the survival of a political community and the political order as it had hitherto been organized, and not to the survival of a way of life.

What we do know about the effects of nuclear weapons is alarming enough. The most important immediate effect is the explosive blast, which is qualitatively similar to the blast from ordinary chemical explosions, but which has somewhat different effects because it is so much bigger. Most damage to cities comes from the explosive blast. The blast drives air away from the site of the explosion, producing sudden changes in air pressure that can crush objects, and high winds that move them suddenly or knock them down. In general, large buildings are destroyed by overpressure, while people and objects are destroyed by the wind. For the most part, blasts kill indirectly. People are blown out of buildings, they are hit by flying debris, houses collapse on their occupants.

Another lethal characteristic of nuclear weapons is radiation. There are two kinds of radiation. One is the direct radiation emitted at the time of the burst. The other is the radiation received from the particles made radioactive by the effects of the explosion, which are thrown up into the air and later come back to earth. This is known as "fallout." Direct radiation is intense, but its range is limited. For large nuclear weapons, the range of intense direct radiation is less than the range of the lethal blast, and it is therefore without effect. It will be absorbed by corpses. But in the case of smaller weapons, direct radiation may be the lethal effect with the greatest range. Direct radiation did substantial damage to the residents of Hiroshima and Nagasaki.

Since it is the fallout effect of radiation which kills distant survivors of the blast, one of the most important variables is the height at which weapons are exploded. If they are exploded on the ground, the fallout is much greater because the explosion kicks up dirt, dust, and rubble, and sends it into the sky.

A one-megaton burst exploded at the White House would generate a fatal radiation over 20 per cent of the area within the Washington Beltway, and the area within which radiation would pose a serious danger to health would extend in a westerly wind all the way to New Jersey's Cape May. But a ground burst is also the most effective way of destroying a hardened target like a missile silo. Thus an attack on Soviet missile silos would actually generate much more radioactive fallout than other kinds of attacks—for example, air bursts above military bases.

An Office of Technology and Assessment study in 1979 found that a full counterforce attack on all Soviet military targets, in which the United States deliberately tried to minimize Soviet fatalities by using small weapons air burst, in which the winds were favorable, and in which the Soviet authorities had warning, would kill far fewer people than an attack on Soviet missiles only, if the U.S. attacked the silos with one large ground-burst bomb apiece.

Announced American policy is to explode its nuclear weapons in the air. As a defense official, John Walsh, said to the Senate Armed Services Research and Development Subcommittee in March 1976: " . . . we don't plan fallout attacks. Our attacks are generally planned so that bursts go off in the area above the targets rather than at ground level." On the other hand, ground bursts are the only way of destroying Soviet missile silos, so Mr. Walsh may not have been offering a complete description of actual plans.

Almost all analyses of the effects of nuclear war are simple "two shot" sequences, in which the Soviet Union attacks America and the United States strikes back. They do not analyze the more likely situation which is that nuclear and conventional warfare will continue at a sporadic, lower level, continuously disrupting the evacuated and surviving populations. They do not consider the long-term effects of nuclear war or even some of the shorter-term effects. For what they are worth, however, the studies confirm that any kind of nuclear exchange will produce a large number of casualties, and that the number will vary widely as a result of circumstances that cannot easily be predicted. Executive Branch studies between 1974 and 1978 indicate that between two million and twenty million Americans would die within the first thirty days of an attack on ICBM silos alone. The uncertainties are the height of the burst, the design of the weapon, the direction and velocity of the wind, whether it is raining, the terrain, and the distance. The wind, for example, can effect the number of casualties by a factor of three, and often cannot be predicted.

Similarly, for an American attack on the Soviet Union, the number of casualties could depend more on the weather and the type of attack than on whether the attack is against all Soviet military targets or silos only. Depending on whether the United States uses smaller weapons detonated in the air or larger weapons detonated on the ground, casualties would range from 2.7 million to 13.5 million.

In a 1979 report of computer simulations, using all of the forces available to each side under SALT II, and assuming the Soviet Union strikes first, aiming only at military and industrial targets, the casualties increase hugely. This is because, although population is not directly targeted, industry happens to be located in or near cities. The Arms Control and Disarmament Agency simulation calculated that between twenty-five million and one hundred million people would be killed in each country, that industrial damage would amount to between 65 per cent and 90 per cent of total industry, that two hundred of the largest cities in each country would be destroyed, and that 80 per cent of all cities with twenty-five thousand people or more would be attacked by at least one weapon. It would be typical of a major nuclear exchange, the study reported, that a city like Moscow would receive sixty warheads within its city limits, and not a tree or a building would remain standing in the downtown area.

We do not know a lot about nuclear war, but our uncertainty is itself an important piece of information. If we cannot predict the effects of a nuclear weapon, if we cannot plan an attack, if there is really no such thing as a "surgical strike" or a "customized response," then we are right back to the idea that the only purpose of nuclear weapons is to deter their use by the other side, and all they deter is what they do best—the mass destruction of people. At the heart of the controversy over MX, over the most accurate, prompt nuclear weapon ever made, is the question of whether a nuclear war can be controlled. President Reagan told a questioner in 1981 that he could imagine a nuclear exchange limited to Europe, and his secretary of state, General Haig, confirmed that U.S. policy is to try to limit the war to the lowest level of violence—the lowest level, presumably, that is consistent with the United States attaining the objectives that caused it to go to war. But there are many reasons why it would be difficult to control a nuclear war.

To have any hope of controlling escalation, it is necessary to avoid destroying the other side's command and control. With no central command and control, it is more likely that individual nuclear weapons commanders will fire off their missiles in a general attack. It is declared American policy that escalation control requires the avoidance of the Enemies National Command/Control, but it is not necessarily U.S. policy to avoid it. This is because neither side believes the political and military headquarters *will* be avoided.

All day-to-day activities in the U.S. nuclear forces—the watch in the Offutt command post, the missile alerts, the

constant computation and recomputation of the optimal targeting plan—imply a kind of predictability and constant
control which would probably not exist in nuclear war. The
idea of limited exchanges of weapons, the first rung of the
Single Integrated Operating Plan ladder, is only possible if
both sides avoid the command, control, and communications
of the other side.

The U.S. must calculate that if it avoids the Soviet headquarters and communications lines, the Soviets may strike
at American headquarters and communications lines and
achieve an advantage. Some strategists, like the Brookings
Institution's John Steinbrunner, say that the command, control, and communications on both sides—the military headquarters, radio antennae, and so on—are the most vulnerable part of the weapons system on both sides, and
accordingly likely to be attacked first. Many official U.S.
strategists think the same way. Talking about a Soviet strike
on the United States, the then Under Secretary of Defense
Research and Engineering told a Senate committee in January 1979: "I would envisage if the Soviets would plan such
an attack they would indeed . . . go after our eyes or our
brains."

The eyes are the radars, and satellite terminals which
warn of a Soviet attack. As Dr. Perry explained in a hearing,
the warning systems are much more difficult to protect from
a nuclear attack than are missiles, so the only "warning" the
station could give is that the warning system is no longer
operating. If the Soviet Union was to carry through an attack from the warning stations to the White House, the
president would have about ten minutes from the report that
the warning system was malfunctioning to the incineration
of the White House. Is that time enough to consider the
options?

With the increasing accuracy of missiles, there is no large
fixed communications system, whether it is under the
ground or above the ground or circling the planet, that can-

not be destroyed by nuclear missiles or nuclear armed satellites. When the Senate Armed Services Committee was looking at a proposal for an extremely low-frequency transmitter for the submarines in 1977, it reported that "the survivability of our submarines and our signals to them are the decisive objects of this program. It is unfortunately not possible to devise a transmitter which could meet these objectives and which could also survive a concentrated attack from even a fraction of the Soviets' projected ICBM force . . . nor would a satellite-based transmitter, even if it could be validated at some indefinite future date, be survivable against a dedicated anti-satellite attack. Moreover, its ground-based communications link would be as vulnerable as an extremely low-frequency system."

What applies to communications systems designed to send messages to submarines applies equally to communications systems that keep contact between the political and military leadership in the United States and Europe. For this reason, the U.S. plan is actually to rely on circling airplanes to communicate with its land and sea forces, but these planes have their own limitations. They cannot communicate with ground stations if the terminals to do so no longer exist, they do not and cannot carry sufficient computing equipment to survey the state of the war, even if they could receive accurate data about it, and they can stay airborne only so long as their oil lasts—about seventy-two hours. Also, the planes are visible to satellites and can be barraged by ICBMS.

As "flexible response" has become more important, the communications and control needed to carry it through have become more and more difficult. Admiral Dan Murphy, who was undersecretary of policy in the Carter administration, told a Senate hearing in 1978 that " . . . in the old days, the command, control, and communications systems had to survive for a matter of minutes, and the strategy was to get warning and then push a button and have massive retaliation. You didn't have to worry about staying around to answer phones or to try to tune in radios or communicate with your forces; they had executed their mission. Now we must survive and operate [deleted] in order to implement our customized responses to any Soviet nuclear attack. This is a tremendous strain on our capability to command, control, and communicate."

If the command and control are vulnerable, can we be sure that field commanders won't take things into their own hands when a clash begins? John Steinbrunner began a debate about this in 1978, when he argued that since all the communications systems are vulnerable and are known to be vulnerable, there must be some ambiguity about which level of commanders can initiate the use of nuclear weapons in war. We are told in congressional hearings that field commanders in Europe cannot do so because they need to receive a code to activate their nuclear weapons. But what about the commander-in-chief of forces in Europe? Formally, only the president can make these decisions, but what if the president is dead, or out of communications? As Steinbrunner wrote: "We can be reasonably sure that, in order to prevent high risk of a disarming first strike, the American forces do have the capacity to conduct strategic war without the President. But in addition we can reasonably doubt whether the conditions under which this would be permitted to happen have been clearly and extensively defined."

Even if the United States could protect all or almost all of its nuclear weapons from attack, and even if it could protect as much of its communications apparatus as was necessary to conduct a prolonged war, it would still be only halfway toward meeting the conditions necessary for limited war. Since there are two players (at least), each must have the same survivable weapons and survivable communications. If the Soviet Union's forces or communications system is vulnerable, then it will not play by the rules suggested by the U.S. secretary of defense. If the U.S. were seriously convinced that nuclear war could be limited, it would take whatever steps it could to protect Soviet weapons and communications. Actually, the U.S., with progressive improvements in accuracy and warhead numbers, has done what it can to place Soviet nuclear forces at risk. What the Soviet Union has done by piling megaton on megaton in the cones of its rockets, the United States has done by the more graceful and also more effective method of increased accuracy and more warheads. In the face of increased American accuracy, the Soviets have hardened their missile silos, but have taken no other steps to protect their forces. Consequently, since the Soviets have more of their forces in fixed silos, they are vulnerable to American attack. As Robert McNamara remarked in the mid-sixties, the disposition of Soviet forces strongly suggests they do not believe nuclear war can be limited, and their military manuals point to the massive use of weapons—a mirror image of the war policy of the Strategic Air Command.

One frequently urged remedy for the vulnerability of Soviet nuclear forces is to put them to sea in submarines, but this is not necessarily a better option for the Soviet Union. The United States' surface navy is vastly better equipped than its Soviet counterpart, and its anti-submarine planes and ships more effective. The United States and its allies are able to track the movements of Soviet nuclear missile-carrying submarines from the time they leave Soviet waters until the time they return. Soviet submarines are noisier than American submarines and easier to locate. The fact that American missiles at sea are less vulnerable and therefore more "stabilizing" than land missiles does not mean that Soviet submarine-launched missiles are less vulnerable, or that the Soviet Union would not be under the same compulsion to use them before they are attacked as it is likely to be with its land missiles. Nor can the U.S. easily refrain from attacking them, because American ships are vulnerable to attack from other kinds of Soviet submarines which the navy will wish to quickly destroy in war.

The whole point of U.S. weapons is, of course, to counter the Soviet Union. Without the Soviet Union in the race, there would be no justification at all for anything but the smallest nuclear force, which would nonetheless be reckoned by the world a most powerful thing. Yet the American understanding of what actually motivates Soviet programs is very slight. The literature on the subject is a few Soviet manuals and the writings of a few scholars. It is nonetheless assumed, and it is perhaps the safest assumption, that the Soviet Union would like to be superior in nuclear weaponry to the United States if it could be, equal if possible, and certainly able to deter a nuclear attack on itself.

The debate over which country is preponderant in nuclear weapons seems endless, mainly because there are so many ways of measuring the concept. There are static measurements, which means measures of what the U.S. and Soviet Union actually have now. These are further subdivided into forces on alert and forces in total and, in a slightly different approach, into forces on fully generated alert and forces on normal alert. In each of these static subdivisions, there is a variety of ways of measuring the opposing forces, since each side has different kinds of weapons. They can be compared by the number of warheads, by the total explosive power of the total number of warheads, by the potential ability of the weapons to carry warheads, and by the number of warheads that can be delivered quickly with a little warning.

Taking the most pertinent of these distinctions, it can be said that the United States has very many more warheads now than does the Soviet Union, and particularly so when only alert forces are considered. This is because, although the Soviet Union has more submarines than the U.S., the U.S. actually has twice as many at sea at any one time, and each submarine carries one hundred sixty warheads or so. Leaving alert rates aside, the U.S. has more than nine thousand strategic nuclear warheads. The Soviet Union has about six thousand.

The Soviet Union, however, has heavier warheads, by and large, and thus has, in total, a greater megatonnage. But this is not very important because both have many more than they need to incinerate all likely soft targets like cities, and accuracy is of considerably greater importance in attacking hard targets. At present, American land missiles are somewhat more accurate than Soviet missiles.

The measure most frequently used to illustrate a Soviet superiority is hard target kill time-urgent weapons—that is, quick silo killers, which today means land missiles. The U.S. has somewhat over 1,053; the Soviet Union somewhat over 1,398. The Soviet Union weapons are heavier, which means that, as they are MIRVed, they can accept more warheads.

Of the five Soviet ICBM types, three are modern missiles which are being fitted with multiple independent warheads. While U.S. figures are not precise, it appears that the Soviet Union has at least double the number of accurate ICBM warheads as now deployed by the U.S., which gives it today a clear advantage in "hard target kill." But, because the U.S. has so many weapons at sea and in bombers, the result of an attack on U.S. missiles, bomber bases, and submarine pens and communications followed by a similar attack on the Soviet Union, would be to leave the United States with a clear advantage in warhead numbers. If both sides keep to SALT, this advantage continues.

Most arguments claiming a Soviet advantage are actually based on the fact that the Soviet Union has generally put its missiles on land, and the U.S. has deliberately divided up its somewhat greater number of warheads into planes and submarines. Since the mid-seventies, both sides have MIRVed their land missiles, so any one land missile, if each warhead has sufficient accuracy, can destroy more than one missile. It thus follows that, if the Soviet Union launches its missiles first, it will destroy more land missiles than it uses up. If this is all that is meant by "post-exchange assymetry," then it means very little. First, there is nothing that can be done about it, except hide your missiles, or simply build more and more, always faster than the Soviet Union can build its missiles. Second, even though the U.S. has somewhat fewer missiles, so long as it has more warheads than there are Soviet missiles, with various allowances for accuracy and reliability, then it can also destroy a higher proportion of the Soviet forces than it uses up, providing it strikes first. As David Aaron said in 1980: "Even in a first strike today, we can destroy 50 per cent more warheads than the Soviet Union can in a similar first strike against us." And thirdly, comparing only hard targets, and considering only what the U.S. would have left after a Soviet first strike against it, the U.S. would still be stronger than the Soviet Union after an exchange.

The U.S. strength, in spite of its smaller land missiles number, arises because its bombers, with their short-range attack missiles and later their cruise missiles, have a very good hard-target capability. In a 1978 study, using classified data, ACDA concluded that "the retaliatory capability of U.S. forces in 1978 exceeds the first strike capability of the Soviets against both hard and soft targets."

Different authorities offer different estimates of the gap that arises if it is assumed that the Soviet Union shoots first at U.S. land missiles in around 1985, but even the most dovish acknowledge that the Soviet Union would have a slight advantage in starting it, as compared to waiting for the U.S. to start it, and the U.S. would accordingly have a slight advantage in getting its missiles off before the Soviet Union launches its missiles. This is the great danger of the present assymetry: not that the Soviet Union would have any plausible preponderance in a crisis, but that both sides have a slight advantage in beginning the conflict. This is the reason MX in an invulnerable base had support from the doves as well as the hawks, but it does not solve the problem. The MX by itself has the capacity to destroy entirely the present Soviet ground missile force. For the U.S., one great problem will be if the Soviet Union adds missiles so quickly that the U.S. is forced to add shelters to meet the threat of bombardment. But a much greater threat is if the Soviet Union does nothing at all. Then both sides will be on a hair trigger.

Another approach to U.S./Soviet comparisons is to measure the amount each side spends on its forces. Again there are different ways of making these comparisons, which produce different results. The CIA usually does it on a dollar cost comparison, estimating the cost of the Soviet force if it were produced in the U.S. against the actual dollar cost of the U.S. forces. Since both forces are capital intensive, this is less prone to error than comparing forces where there is a high labor content. The CIA estimates that, in the 1971–80 period, Soviet forces cost three times as much as U.S. forces. If we exclude Soviet nuclear peripheral forces—that is, forces not aimed at the U.S.—then the estimated dollar cost of the Soviet forces was two and two-thirds the comparable U.S. outlays for the period. But a very large chunk of Soviet spending is for defense against U.S. bombers. Since the Soviet Union has very few bombers intended to deliver weapons on the U.S., and since anyway it is very little use for the U.S. to protect itself against bombers when it cannot protect itself against the far more numerous and lethal ICBMs, the U.S. spends practically nothing on defense against aerial attack. When one compares only U.S. and Soviet forces intended for intercontinental attack—that is ICBMs, submarines, and bombers—then the Soviet Union in 1980 was spending one-third as much again as the United States in 1980, and, while the Soviet total in dollars had been falling since 1974, the U.S. total had been rising since 1976.

Another difficulty in making these comparisons is that the U.S. and the Soviet Union have made their capital investment in strategic systems at different times. The U.S. spent a great deal in the early sixties, when the Soviet Union was spending very little. Toward the end of the sixties, U.S.

spending on the McNamara increases, which put it far ahead of the Soviet Union, was over, and the Soviets began spending mightily on their own programs. Through the seventies, the Soviet Union continued to outspend the U.S., though from the mid-seventies the trends changed, with the Soviet Union moving down and the U.S. moving up. As Bill Perry told a SASC hearing in May 1979: "Back in the early sixties, when we were building our strategic forces, we were spending about twice the rate of the Soviet Union, roughly U.S. $20 billion a year versus $10 billion in 1980. During the sixties, after we built up our forces, our spending of course dropped down to a level something below $10 billion a year, and has maintained that approximate rate up to the current time. On the other hand, the Soviet Union has built up to $20 billion and has maintained that rate for the last decade or so."

Ronald Reagan came to office with a promise to "immediately open negotiations on a Salt III treaty." Both his nominee as director of the Arms Control and Disarmanent Agency, Eugene Rostow, and his nominee as chief SALT negotiator, General Edward Rowny, assured the Senate Foreign Relations Committee consenting to their nominations that they would be ready to begin negotiations "within a few months" of their appointments. Not only were all these promises broken, but the negotiation position for any strategic arms talks that could occur became steadily more difficult to understand. The administration was opposed to both a "nuclear freeze" at present levels and to the existing SALT II draft accepted by the Soviet Union and signed by President Jimmy Carter. The administration claimed to want a deep cut in the arsenals of both sides, but it also insisted that the United States must "rebuild its defenses" before these cuts could occur. The contradiction in these positions was resolved with an expression of willingness to scrap older nuclear weapons when the new weapons, the B-1, the Trident

submarine, and the MX, were deployed. The basic administration position, reiterated by General Rowny in April 1982,
demanded a revision of the SALT II agreement so extensive
that no solution seemed likely so long as the United States
stuck to its position.

But even if negotiations were being conducted in good
faith and with urgency on both sides, no conceivable outcome can address the problem of the vulnerability of land
missiles. It is insoluble. If we accept that both the United
States and the Soviet Union now have or will soon have
warheads accurate enough to have a very high probability of
landing sufficiently close to a missile silo to disable the missile inside, and if we assume that these more accurate warheads and guidance systems are fitted into existing MIRVed
missiles (as is happening, on both sides), then no feasible
agreement can prevent the increase of each side's ability to
destroy the land-based missiles of the other side.

Both the Carter administration and the Reagan administration proposed "deep cuts" in either missile numbers or
warhead numbers on both sides to solve the problem of vulnerability, but this is plainly no solution. As long as one
missile with multiple warheads may destroy several of the
opponent's missiles, equal numbers of missiles or even
widely different numbers of missiles on either side, at any
level of magnitude, remain extremely vulnerable. If both
sides have just eight hundred land missiles each, and if only
half are MIRVed to the present limit of ten warheads per
missile, then each side has many more warheads than it
needs to destroy its opponent's land-based missiles—yet the
total number of missiles is much less than in the 1979 SALT
agreement, and the number of MIRVed missiles only half the
number allowed in that agreement. Only if one side has
vastly more missiles than the other is that side safe from a
first strike in which it would lose its land missiles—but it is
actually in more danger of a city attack than if it had no
missiles at all. This is because the other side, which is vulner-

able, now has an incentive to use its missiles before preemptive attack.

If there was any solution to this vulnerability, it was the the multiple protective shelter scheme combined with SALT restraints, which was essentially a way of matching multiple warheads for a single missile with multiple shelters for a single missile—bringing back into balance the strength of the offense with the defense against missiles, which had been upset by the introduction of MIRV. But the western states, the only possible sites for an MPS, would not accept the deployment scheme, nor would the Reagan administration. A multiple protective shelter scheme depended on SALT, which the Reagan administration rejected.

Even if the Carter deployment scheme had been approved, however, it could not have improved the security of the United States. It was intended to threaten the land-based missiles of the Soviet Union, and therefore it would have increased the incentive for the Soviet Union to strike first.

All of the developments that have imperiled the nuclear deterrents on both sides have taken place within the last decade—the MIRVing of missiles, the increasing accuracy of warheads, the acceptance of ideas of nuclear "flexibility" and war-fighting. These developments have had a profound impact on the uses and purposes of nuclear weapons, an impact we are only now beginning to understand. For the United States, which has for over a decade attempted to meet the problem by seeking a reduction in the Soviet threat or by inventing new ways to either protect missiles or increase the number of warheads required to destroy them, a decision will soon have to be made about the future of MX, but that decision cannot be taken without also deciding on the purpose of nuclear weapons. If we begin by recognizing, as Bernard Brodie did in 1946, that the only reason to possess nuclear weapons is to deter their use by the other side, since nuclear war will destroy both sides, we shall have begun well. The second important principle to recognize is that, no matter what the Soviet Union does, it does not increase American security to threaten Soviet missiles. It would certainly be better if neither side threatened the missiles of the other, but the only way that can now happen— the only way—is for both sides to scrap MIRV, which is probably not a serious possibility. Failing an agreement to scrap MIRVed land missiles, the second best solution is for the United States to recognise that threatening Soviet missiles does not solve the problem of the Soviet threat to American missiles. It only makes war more likely. Since there is no military purpose in deploying MX in either a protected or unprotected mode, and if we accept the fact that American security is not increased by threatening Soviet missiles, it is plain enough that the simple answer to the decades-old controversy over the missile is to scrap it.

Acknowledgments

THIS book could not have been written without the generous help of a great number of political and military officials, scientists, and politicians who have been involved in the decisions on the MX. I owe a special debt of gratitude for the advice and encouragment of one of the most perceptive analysts of nuclear weapons and strategy, Desmond Ball. Dr. Ball pointed me on my way when I began work in 1979, and was subsequently kind enough to offer some very helpful comments on a draft manuscript. While a number of people whom I interviewed in the course of writing this book wish to remain anonymous, I can thank the following for their time and patience:

David Aaron
Desmond Ball
Zbigniew Brzezinski
Lt. Gen. Kelly H. Burke
Anthony Cordesman
Richard DeLauer
Marilyn Elrod
Fritz Ermath
Leslie Gelb

Ted Greenwood
Morton Halperin
Major General Guy Hecker
Major General John Hepfer
David Johnson
Albert Latter
Senator Paul Laxalt
Peter Lennon
Senator Thomas McIntyre

Michael May
William Perry
Frank Press
Jack Ruina
General George Seignious
Ambassador Gerard Smith
Larry Smith
John Steinbrunner
Charles Stevenson

Major General John Toomay
Senator John Tower
Charles Townes
Victor Utgoff
James Wade
Ambassador Paul Warnke
Major General Jasper Welch
Seymour Zeiberg.

I also wish to thank Harold Brown for several letters outlining his role in the MX decisions.

For invaluable help I wish to thank the staffs of the Library of Congress, the International Communications Agency, the Department of Defense Public Affairs division (and particularly Jack Powers), the USAF Books and Magazines division, the public affairs staff of the Strategic Air Command, Offutt Air Force Base, the MX Project Office, Norton Air Force Base, the MX office, USAF, the Pentagon, and the documents staff of the Senate and House Armed Services Committees. Many friends encouraged me to persevere with this book, either by commenting on early chapters or cheering me up when I was most disheartened. Among those friends I particularly thank Monica Andres, Susan Anthony, Clive Cookson, Caroline Davidson, Andrew Feinstein, Ian and Lorine Marsh, John Morgan, Jody Reed, Jim Spigelman, Mike Steketee, and Brian Toohey. My agent, Robert Ducas, was a constant source of optimism, and my editor at Norton, Star Lawrence, of patient advice and guidance. Both Des Ball and Roy Werner, who read manuscript drafts and offered critical suggestions, performed magnificently in a difficult office of friendship. For a demanding and well-executed job of typing successive manuscripts I thank Gina Avvakoum.

Finally, I wish to thank Trevor Kennedy, managing editor, and Australia Consolidated Press for their confidence and support.

Index

shelters for, 145, 149–52, 167–69, 190–99, 203–5, 207–14, 230, 233, 236–40
silos, 114–21, 131–32, 149–52, 165–70, 175, 184–85, 187, 216–17, 219, 233–44, 245–46, 251–52
trenches, 96–97, 112, 115–21, 130–31, 133, 136, 143–47, 150–51, 175, 184–99

National Academy of Sciences, 140
National Security Council (NSC), 27–30, 32, 86–87, 128, 131, 155, 157, 187, 189–99, 200, 204–5, 234, 238–40, 248
National Security Planning Group, 238
National War College, 34
Navaho missile, 95
Nellis Air Force Base, 242
New York Times, 75, 153–54, 168, 191–92
Nike Zeus (missile), 124
Nixon, Richard M., 27–31, 33, 35, 61, 64, 108, 182, 223
Nixon administration, 27–36, 61–76, 93, 107
  ABM debate under, 107
  MX program under, 73–76
  SALT talks under, 62–67, 125
  "strategic sufficiency" criteria of, 62
  targeting strategies of, 67–73
"no-cities" strategy, implications for MX in, 44
North Dakota, University of, 85
Norton Air Force Base, 95–100, 112
Novak, Robert, 109–10
nuclear test ban treaty, 50–54
  Brown's support of, 51–54
  Latter's opposition to, 51–54
  McNamara's support of, 52

nuclear weapons:
  accuracy of, 106, 110–11, 115–16
  comparative measurements of, 266–70
  deterrence value of, 39–42
  effects on communications of, 261–64
  effects on population of, 222–23, 255–61
  flexibility of, 51, 93–94, 254
  increased yield of, 110
  relative characteristics of, 92
  strategy defined by, 54–56
  tactical vs. strategic, 42
  "time urgent hard target kill," 71, 267
  unique capabilities of, 36
  U.S. technological lead in, 99
  see also defense strategy; MIRVs; MX
Nuclear Weapons Employment Policy, 32, 68, 87, 90
Nunn, Sam, 165

Office of Economic Opportunity, 220
Office of Management and the Budget, 143, 158, 177, 204, 218, 220
Office of Science and Technology Policy, 142–43, 151
Office of Technology Assessment, 235, 255, 259
Offutt Air Force Base, 77–81
on-site inspection, 65–66
"Our Nuclear Future" (Latter-Teller), 51
Overseas Press Club, 73

Packard, David, 229–37
Pentagon, *see* Defense Department, U.S.
Pentagon Papers, 124, 157